A POPE FOR ALL SEASONS

A POPE for ALL SEASONS

TESTIMONIES INSPIRED BY SAINT JOHN PAUL II

Interviews by
MONIKA JABLONSKA

ANGELICO PRESS

First published in the USA
by Angelico Press 2023
Copyright © 2023 Monika Jablonska

All rights reserved:
No part of this book may be reproduced or transmitted,
in any form or by any means, without permission

For information, address:
Angelico Press, Ltd.
169 Monitor St.
Brooklyn, NY 11222
www.angelicopress.com

paper 978-1-62138-884-5
cloth 978-1-62138-885-2
ebook 978-1-62138-886-9

Book and cover design
by Michael Schrauzer
Cover photo © Vatican Media

This book is dedicated to Saint John Paul II
Marek, Maria, and John

CONTENTS

Acknowledgments   xii

Foreword   xv

CARDINAL STANISŁAW DZIWISZ   3
Former personal secretary and friend to Saint John Paul II

CARDINAL CAMILLO RUINI   12
Former Vicar General of the Diocese of Rome and a former consultor of the Congregation for Bishops

CARDINAL GERHARD LUDWIG MÜLLER   15
Former Prefect of the Congregation for the Doctrine of the Faith

CARDINAL ANGELO COMASTRI   20
Archpriest emeritus of St. Peter's Basilica, Vicar General emeritus of His Holiness for Vatican City State and President emeritus of the Fabric of Saint Peter's

CARDINAL PÉTER ERDŐ   25
Cardinal-Archbishop of Esztergom-Budapest and Primate of Hungary

MSGR. SŁAWOMIR ODER   29
Postulator for the beatification and canonization process of John Paul II

MSGR. PAWEŁ PTASZNIK   36
Former Head of the Polish Section of the Vatican's Secretariat of State

FR. ROBERT SKRZYPCZAK   43
Professor of theology and an expert on the Second Vatican Council

ARCHBISHOP TADEUSZ KONDRUSIEWICZ   53
Former Archbishop of Minsk – Mohilev, Belarus

MOTHER ADELA GALINDO   56
Founder of the Servants of the Pierced Hearts of Jesus and Mary

MAESTRO PLÁCIDO DOMINGO   70
Opera singer, conductor and administrator

HIS HOLINESS THE DALAI LAMA   73
The spiritual leader of Tibet

ARTURO MARI   74
For 27 years the photographer of Pope John Paul II

MELANIA TRUMP   78
Former First Lady of the United States of America

NORMAN DAVIES   79
Professor Emeritus of the University of London, author, lecturer, a Supernumerary Fellow of Wolfson College, Oxford

MAREK JAN CHODAKIEWICZ   89
Professor of history, the holder of the Kosciuszko Chair in Polish Studies, and director of the Center for Intermarium Studies, The Institute of World Politics, Washington, DC

GEORGE WEIGEL   96
Distinguished Senior Fellow of the Ethics and Public Policy Center, author, lecturer

JOHN RADZILOWSKI   99
Professor of history, director of the Polish Institute of Culture and Research, Orchard Lake Schools, Michigan

JAN ŻARYN   108
Professor of history, politician, author, and lecturer, director of the Institute for Heritage of National Thought, Warsaw, Poland

ZBIGNIEW STAWROWSKI   115
Professor, author, co-founder and director of the Józef Tischner Institute, Cracow, Poland

JOHN HITTINGER   120
Professor of philosophy and director of the Saint John Paul II Institute at the University of St. Thomas

RAFAŁ ŁATKA   126
Professor of history, author, director at the Institute of History of Poland 1945–1990 at the IPN

MARGARET MELADY   131
Former president of the American University in Rome, and former president of the Federal Association of the Order of Malta

LEE EDWARDS   138
Professor of political science and co-founder of the Victims of Communism Memorial Foundation

MICHAEL REAGAN   140
American political commentator, journalist, the son of President Reagan

GRZEGORZ GAŁĄZKA   149
Photographer who took the official image for the beatification and canonization of John Paul II

EDWIN MEESE III   152
Former United States Attorney General in the Reagan administration

PETER ROBINSON   157
Former speechwriter for Vice President George H. W. Bush and Ronald Reagan

NEWT GINGRICH   162
Former Speaker of the United States House of Representatives

PAUL KENGOR 168
Professor, author, lecturer, director of the Institute for Faith and Freedom

JOHN O'SULLIVAN 172
Former speechwriter for Margaret Thatcher, president and founder of the Danube Institute

RYSZARD LEGUTKO 176
Professor of philosophy, author, member of the European Parliament

EDWARD PENTIN 182
Rome correspondent and expert on the papacy and the Holy See

GIAN FRANCO SVIDERCOSCHI 186
Author, journalist, and Vatican expert

WŁODZIMIERZ RĘDZIOCH 194
Author, journalist, expert on the Pope and the Vatican, former Vice-President of L'Osservatore Romano

EUGENIUSZ MRÓZ 199
Friend, neighbor, and classmate of John Paul II

AMBASSADOR JANUSZ KOTAŃSKI 205
Former Ambassador of the Republic of Poland to the Holy See

AMBASSADOR ANNA MARIA ANDERS 215
Ambassador of the Republic of Poland to Italy and San Marino

AMBASSADOR ALBERTO PIEDRA 217
Former U.S. Ambassador to Guatemala in Reagan's Administration

ANIKÓ LÉVAI-ORBÁN 219
Author, entrepreneur, wife of the Prime Minister of Hungary

KRZYSZTOF ZANUSSI 221
Internationally recognized Polish film and theatre director, producer, and screenwriter

KAZIMIERZ BRAUN 228
Polish director, lecturer, author, expert in theatre, and scholar

MARTA BURGHARDT 239
Scholar at the Institute of Intercultural Dialogue in Cracow, author, lecturer, and expert in Wojtyła poems and dramas

STANISŁAW DZIEDZIC 245
Professor, Polish literary historian, author, lecturer, former director of the Department of Culture and National Heritage of the city of Cracow

FR. JOSÉ GRANADOS 250
Superior General of the Disciples of the Hearts of Jesus and Mary

PAOLO FUCILI 257
Journalist, author, lecturer, and expert on the Vatican and Pope

ACKNOWLEDGMENTS

I WOULD LIKE TO THANK MANY PEOPLE FOR their help with this project.

My special thank you to my husband, Marek. Working on this book may have made a saint of me, but it made a martyr of him. Thank you for supporting me from the beginning; being on call to read, comment, and advise on the manuscript whenever I asked; and encouraging me every day.

Thank you very much to all my interlocutors for their time, support, patience, and understanding.

I am so grateful to Angelico Press and the friendship of John and Kari. You are more than a publishing house to me, you are a home. Thank you for your beautiful work.

Thank you to those who helped me, supported me, encouraged me, prayed for me, and inspired me. Among those are: Ambassador Callista Gingrich; Lady Blanka Rosenstiel; Sister Ana Lanzas; Irena McLean; Mirka Lesner; Marta Burghardt; Włodzimierz Rędzioch; Angelika Korszyńska-Górny; Grzegorz Górny; Paolo Fucili; Wojciech Jerzy Muszyński; Sister Janet Siepker, FSE; Imre Molnar; Janusz Rosikoń and Grażyna Kasprzycka-Rosikoń; Grzegorz Gałązka; ks. Paweł Cebula; Anna Freska; Jennifer Feliciano; Michael Cialdella; Kasia Bosne; David Tobon; Tseten Samdup Chhoekyapa.

Thank you to all those who endorsed my book.

Thank you to my children, whose love, warmth, and innocence helped me overcome the challenges and navigate the most treacherous obstacles.

Thank you to my parents for always being my strength and my safe harbor.

Thank you to Saint John Paul II for your prayer, help, and support. I felt your presence and inspiration every day.

> I find myself before you without notes.
> I must find the notes within me,
> Because everything that I want and must tell you
> Is written in my heart
>
> *John Paul II*

FOREWORD

Uncle Karol Wojtyła

A POPE FOR ALL SEASONS IS A SERIES OF PRIVATE encounters with a saint. In over sixty interviews, writers, priests, politicians, scholars, and artists recount their own conversations and interactions with Pope John Paul II and consider his impact on their lives and how he forever changed the world that God put him in.

My wife, Monika Jablonska, interviewed people from all over the world. She spoke with them about John Paul II, touching upon arguably the topics most important to contemporary man: God, faith, the Church, humanity, ideologies, marriage and sexuality, communism. Monika herself sets the rhythm of each interview to capture the extraordinary heritage of Saint John Paul II.

Most of the interviewees are direct witnesses and sometimes even close personal friends of Karol Wojtyła. Some of the recollections are thus truly touching, like that of Cardinal Stanisław Dziwisz, the Polish Pope's personal secretary and assistant, or Msgr. Paweł Ptasznik, one of his closest collaborators at the Vatican. Of comparable importance is the account of Msgr. Sławomir Oder, who served first as a postulator for the beatification and canonization of John Paul II and then for the cause of the pope's parents.

The late Holy Father's personal photographer, Arturo Mari, shared a fascinating and intimate testimony about their relationship spanning nearly five decades. So did Plácido Domingo, who ruminated on his encounters with the late pope and described recording an album based on the latter's poetry.

Krzysztof Zanussi, an internationally acclaimed movie director and producer, recalls his direct encounters with the Polish Pontiff, which resulted in the films *From a Far-away Country: Pope John Paul II* and *Our God's Brother*. Of similar breadth are the recollections of top intellectuals, such as leading Plato scholar and European politician Professor Ryszard Legutko, as well as a surprising number of Americans, such as Ed Meese, Newt Gingrich, Michael Reagan, and Peter Robinson.

The unique stories of Monika's interlocutors have never been before shared in such depth or in one place. We rediscover John Paul II's life, work, travels, and friendships both before and during his pontificate.

Why *A Pope for All Seasons*? Karol Wojtyła had that *je ne sais quoi*, an attractive aura that made him, well, who he was: a saint, able to appeal to practically anyone he encountered under any circumstances and at any level, but especially the spiritual and the intellectual.

There are certain analogies between the Polish Pope and another man for all seasons, Englishman Thomas More (1478–1535), canonized half a millennium after his death. It was not just that both men lived frugally like monks, or that they cared about everyone around them but often forgot about themselves. It is chiefly that they were also both men of principle and formidable intellectuals in their own right, cultivating friendships with the leading minds of their epochs, as Thomas More did with Erasmus of Rotterdam.

Saint Thomas More was a lawyer, humanistic thinker, and Tudorian politician, who opposed the Protestant Revolution. More refused to countenance his sovereign's turn to Byzantine Caesaro-papism, when Henry VIII (1491–1547) proclaimed himself both the secular ruler of England and the spiritual head of the Church of England with no ties to the Throne of St. Peter. Subsequently, his erstwhile chancellor Thomas More refused to swear the Oath of Supremacy, for which he was charged with sedition and beheaded. "I die the King's good servant, and God's first" were reportedly his last words.

In 1935 Pope Pius XI canonized Thomas as a martyr, and in 2000 John Paul II declared him to be the patron of politicians and rulers, the quintessential "man for all seasons."

Yet John Paul II was himself "a man for all seasons." Just like his Renaissance forerunner, the Polish Pope obviously knew who he was—his own man, always at ease with himself, radiating the confidence and faith of one who is God's servant first throughout his earthly sojourn.

Karol Wojtyła was therefore able to project himself emotionally, intellectually, and spiritually in such a humanely attractive manner that he could become, in essence, practically everything and anything for nearly everyone. This concerned virtually all aspects of the man, including his deeply ingrained Polish nationalism, or patriotism, as they say in Europe when they want to avoid the opprobrium of the former term.

More was immersed not only in the Latin civilization of Western Christendom but also in his native culture of England. And as the author of the present book never tires of stressing in her earlier endeavor *Wind from Heaven: John Paul II—The Poet Who Became Pope* and elsewhere,

Foreword

one cannot even begin to understand Wojtyła without appreciating that formidable man's similarly formidable attachment to his native Polish land and its rich culture stemming from Christianity.

The Polish Pope grew out of Poland. He spoke her verities and poetry. His Marian devotion, with *Totus Tuus* as its anthem, was purely Polish. Wojtyła was Poland's true son. His success was to translate his Polish sensibilities and intellectual paradigms into the universal language of Catholicism as amplified by the Church Militant via the Seat of Peter, which he held for over a quarter of a century.

The universal dimension of Karol Wojtyła developed and emerged naturally, because of his religious and patriotic upbringing, rather than artificially, merely as a result of his training for the theater.

That is not to say that theater did not mean the world to him. However, it became a means to an end which, ultimately, was God, as Wojtyła preached most of his life.

One can say that acting came reflexively to the future pope because it allowed him to express his innermost beliefs via the God-given gifts of oratory, diction, vocalization, and body language that he enjoyed from childhood. His other attributes, heart and intellect in particular, contributed mightily to his saintly aura.

To grasp this, we shall do well to ponder a number of parallels between St. John Paul II and St. Thomas More. Here are some that I have not already mentioned.

The Polish Pope was convinced that the Holy Virgin guarded him. She never forsook him — and he never abandoned her, either in communist Poland or at the Holy See. Karol Wojtyła never allowed his love for the Catholic Faith to be weakened by the temporal temptations of the powers that urged apostasy or other forms of treason under Communism.

The same goes for St. Thomas More: Despite his love for his king, he never apostatized. He remained faithful to the throne of St. Peter, the rock on which Christ built his Church, and refused to give up Mary, the Mother of God, the Patroness of the Church, for the false glitter of temporary glory. He never wished for the Christian religion to become an all-male affair overnight by removing all female saints, including Mary. Instead, he chose martyrdom.

Both saints courted martyrdom for similar reasons. Consider this: After the Second World War, after the Iron Curtain had been erected, Karol Wojtyła was able to leave captive Poland, then under the Soviet occupation, to study in Rome. He was free, and he could have remained in the Free World. But he chose to return home upon completing his degree.

This was virtually insane, from a worldly perspective. Many in his position who returned paid with their freedom, and more than a few with their lives. But Wojtyła was a priest, God's servant first. It was his duty to be with his flock, to share its fate.

To put it plainly, the future pope elected to go back to his home country, where the Church was actively persecuted. The Communists continued the grim streak of clerical martyrdom started by the Nazis during the Second World War. Numerous nuns and priests were imprisoned; some of them were murdered for preaching the Word of Christ and the love of country and freedom.

Miraculously, Karol Wojtyła avoided that fate. He was able to serve his flock and the Church at large while navigating the shoals of communist totalitarianism. Throughout it all, he never broke down; he never compromised his faith. He did not become a turncoat or snitch. He did not betray himself, his friends, his superiors, or his flock.

And he remained true to Christ's commandment to love one's enemies. Once, in the late sixties, after he spotted a secret police car trailing him, he blessed the plainclothesmen publicly. He knew they meant him evil, but that did not matter. Love mattered.

Then, in 1978, upon his elevation to the papacy, which he considered his personal cross, he faced martyrdom persistently. There were several attempts on his life, most dangerously on May 13, 1981. He survived. He forgave the would-be assassin, and he prayed for him—like St. Thomas More, who kissed, embraced, and forgave his executioner right before he was beheaded.

John Paul II's earthly masters were, first, Cardinal Adam Sapieha (1867–1951) and then Cardinal Stefan Wyszyński (1901–1981). These churchmen exerted more spiritual and intellectual influence on Wojtyła than anyone besides his parents.

St. Thomas More enjoyed a similarly intense and enriching relationship with his mentors, Cardinal John Morton (1420–1500), Archbishop of Canterbury, and even more, perhaps, Saint John Fisher (1468–1535), who was also canonized as a martyr by Pope Pius XI and shares a feast day with More: June 22.

Thomas More was a loving family man. He loved his children so much that he would spank them gently, with feathers. He gave his first wife, Jane, advanced tutoring in literature and music. He taught his favorite daughter, Margaret, how to read and write, including in Greek and Latin.

Though he had no children of his own, Karol Wojtyła's ministry to the youth was legendary. In the 1950s, the college students whom the future pope mentored when he was a young priest and, later, the bishop of Kraków nicknamed him *Wujek* ("uncle"), a clear sign of trust and familial affection. Though often bestowed on close family friends in Poland, the nickname was not just a matter of custom but also a reflection of the warmth, intimacy, and holiness he radiated. A loving attitude towards all was his default. Some would say that it was so to a fault, that his cheerfulness and openness often made him too trusting. It prevented him from seeing evil in individuals, in particular the most skilled deceivers. As a philosopher, he could readily recognize and denounce evil ideologies like communism, but it was altogether different with evil individuals, who learned how to manipulate this good uncle. Or did they?

Either way, children both young and old sensed his cheerful kindness and wisdom and loved their *Wujek* accordingly: from the Jagiellonian University quads to World Youth Day. The object of their affection reciprocated in kind, just like St. Thomas More.

Father Karol was family indeed. In Poland, he took young people kayaking and hiking. There was always an outdoor Mass, prayer, and songs by the fire. One of John Paul II's favorite songs was called, *"Abba* — Father." Many who knew him felt he was like a father to them, or, more precisely, that he shared the love of their heavenly Father with them.

Karol Wojtyła cast a much wider net in his lifetime than did Thomas More, who, after all, was not a churchman. Fittingly, the Polish Pope's favorite hymn became Cesareo Gabarain's "The Fisherman of Souls," known in the United States as "Lord, you have come" and translated into Polish by Fr. Stanisław Szmidt, a Salesian monk, as "The Ark":

> *Lord, you have come to the seashore,*
> *neither searching for the rich nor the wise,*
> *desiring only that I should follow.*
>
> *O, Lord, with your eyes set upon me,*
> *gently smiling, you have spoken my name;*
> *all I longed for I have found by the water,*
> *at your side, I will seek other shores.*

> *Lord, see my goods, my possessions;*
> *in my boat you find no power, no wealth.*
> *Will you accept, then, my nets and labor?*
>
> *O, Lord, with your eyes set upon me,*
> *gently smiling, you have spoken my name;*
> *all I longed for I have found by the water,*
> *at your side, I will seek other shores.*

This book can be thought of as a collection of individual stanzas of the hymn that St. John Paul so enjoyed. Each interview is about an encounter with a saint, and so through him an encounter with God. In a sense, then, the unspoken first words that prompted every conversation in this volume may well have been, "O Lord, with your eyes set upon me, / gently smiling, you have spoken my name." *A Pope for All Seasons* says the rest.

Dr. Marek Jan Chodakiewicz
Washington, DC

A POPE
for
ALL SEASONS
TESTIMONIES INSPIRED BY
SAINT JOHN PAUL II

CARDINAL STANISŁAW DZIWISZ

Archbishop Emeritus of Kraków. He was personal secretary to John Paul II until the latter's death on April 2, 2005. In 1998 he was appointed titular Bishop of San Leone and Adjunct Prefect of the Pontifical Household. He was consecrated bishop by John Paul II on March 19, 1998. On September 29, 2003, he was raised to the dignity of Archbishop. On November 4, 2005, in Krakow, he began the diocesan process of inquiry into the heroic virtue of the Servant of God John Paul II (Karol Wojtyła). He was made a cardinal by Benedict XVI in the consistory of March 24, 2006, of the Title of Santa Maria del Popolo.

Your Eminence, you spent almost forty years with Pope John Paul II as his secretary. Which memory of Karol Wojtyła has stayed most vividly in your heart?

I consider each day I spent with the Holy Father as a great gift from heaven and an inscrutable dispensation of providence. Archbishop Wojtyła called me to serve, just as the Master once called the fishermen from Genesareth immediately, without any preparation. Likewise, without any preparation, I came the next morning and served as secretary to the Archbishop of Kraków for 12 years. Day after day I was able to observe his austere life, filled with prayer and work. I helped my bishop and cardinal in his many duties, and I accompanied him on all his trips. I also remained with Wojtyła in Rome when he was elected pope on October 22, 1978. And I stayed on with him until his death. I kept him company for twenty-seven years in the Vatican. The memory that has stayed most vividly in my heart and memory is related to the attempt on his life.

In your view, why was Karol Wojtyła elevated to the throne of St. Peter?

The Holy Spirit guided the choice of the college of cardinals. And at the human level? Although Cardinal Wojtyła lived on the eastern side of the Iron Curtain, which implied isolation, he was an extremely open person. He published a lot, in various languages. He traveled a lot, even though getting a passport and permission to travel abroad from the Communists was almost a miracle at that time. He was known among the cardinals for his participation in all sessions of the Second Vatican Council, and also for his membership in Roman congregations. Pope Paul VI highly valued the Archbishop of Kraków and had asked him to deliver a series of sermons at Vatican retreats. The Holy See was concerned about the Church in Poland, which did not fight with arms yet did not allow itself to be conquered by the communist regime. I must also add that Cardinal Wojtyła was an extremely sensitive and communicative person, knew many foreign languages, learned quickly, and yet, importantly, listened to what other people said. He was not indifferent to people's problems. This won him general sympathy and respect. He certainly had great charisma. He entrusted his entire life and the Church to the hands of Divine Providence and the maternal protection of Our Lady, so every challenge, no matter how difficult, was for him a natural submission to God's will.

Should we read the words of John Paul II at St. Peter's Square on October 22, 1978 — "Do not be afraid. Open, I say, open wide the doors for Christ" — in the context of Polish history, the heritage of faith, and the culture of his homeland?

I think we should understand them not only in the context of Poland. These words express the entire spirituality of Karol Wojtyła — John Paul II. These words were the motto of his life and the master key to his pontificate. They applied not only to Catholics, not only to Christians, but also to each modern man who is lost because he is distant from God.

Let's talk about the attempt on John Paul II's life on May 13, 1981. What would Poland's, and the world's, future have been if Our Lady's hand had not deflected the bullet?

This event took place forty years ago. In my memory, I can still see and hear what happened at St. Peter's Square on Wednesday, May 13, 1981, after 5:00 p.m. The weekly general audience was held. The Popemobile was making a second round of St. Peter's Square; the Holy Father greeted the faithful and blessed the children. No sooner had he handed back a two-year-old girl to her parents than two shots rang out. Hundreds of pigeons suddenly hurled themselves into the air, people screamed, and I glanced at a man trying to break loose from the crowd. I understood that the Holy Father had been shot. I was standing behind him; I couldn't see the expression on his face. I asked him, "Where?" He replied, "The stomach." "Does it hurt?" "Yes." The Holy Father collapsed into my arms. The car rushed through the Arch of the Bells, went down the Via delle Fondamenta, circled around the back of the apse of the basilica, and then hurtled down the so-called Grottone, the courtyard at the Belvedere, before finally reaching the Vatican health clinic. Renato Buzzonetti, the

Holy Father's personal physician, had been summoned to meet us there. The paramedics took the pope from my arms and stretched him out on the floor of the lobby. It was only then that we realized how much blood he was losing from the first bullet wound. The pope was lying in a pool of blood.

There was no time for first aid; every second was vital to his life. The first bullet, we would learn, had pierced his abdomen, perforated the colon, torn through the small intestine at several points, and then come out the other side before finally landing on the floor of the car. The second bullet grazed his right elbow and broke his left index finger before going on to wound two American female tourists. The Holy Father needed to have an operation as soon as possible. An ambulance immediately rushed him to the Gemelli polyclinic. What was going through my head was fear, an unimaginable fight against time; there was a feeling that the slightest wrong decision could have a catastrophic effect. At the same time, there was the sense of a powerful and invisible force that saved his life and removed all emerging and accumulating obstacles.

Although half-conscious, the pope was praying almost all the way. I heard him saying, "Jesus, Mother Mary." I was there. He lay prostrate with his eyes half-closed, barely able to move his lips. Suddenly, he looked at me and whispered, "I forgive the man who shot me." As soon as we got to the Gemelli, though, he lost consciousness. We arrived at the hospital very quickly; it was chaotic, and I screamed: "Go immediately to the operating room! Can't you see that he is dying?" And at that very moment, it finally dawned on me that, indeed, his life was in danger. I left the operating room before the operation commenced to stand outside. All I did was pray.

The worst moment occurred when Dr. Buzzonetti, white as a sheet, came up to me to ask me to give the Holy Father last rites. I did it immediately, but I was torn apart. The team of doctors who performed the surgery really did not believe at this point that the patient could be saved. His heartbeat and blood pressure barely registered. The first blood transfusion failed to take; thus, they had to do a second one. Luckily, they found some doctors who shared the pope's blood type, who donated their own blood for him. The procedure took five-and-a-half hours. Then it was over. Professor Francesco Crucitti was the surgeon in charge, and Dr. Giancarlo Castiglioni joined him after his return from Milan. Time stopped for me; I prayed, abandoning myself into the hands of God and calling upon Our

Lady; I felt peace and faith. The President of Italy, Sandro Pertini, came to the polyclinic and stayed with the Holy Father until the patient was wheeled out of the operating room. Pertini's concern was touching, most certainly not predicated upon political calculations. Cardinal Paolo Bertoli, the chamberlain, was also sitting outside the operating room, and he was ready to announce to the world, should that have come to pass, the death of John Paul II. Next they took the Holy Father to the intensive care unit, around 2:00 a.m. He came out of the anesthesia very early the next morning. He opened his eyes, looked at me, and asked if we had recited Compline. He thought it was still Wednesday, May 13.

The first days after the assassination attempt were terrible. The Holy Father prayed continually. And he suffered. He suffered a lot, but he accepted the pain with humility, as a grace, with gratitude to God that he could offer to shed blood for the Church and the world. I watched him day and night.

On Sunday, he recorded a short speech that was broadcast before the Angelus. Among other things, he said: "I am praying for the brother who wounded me and whom I have sincerely forgiven." At the same time, the Primate of Poland, Cardinal Stefan Wyszyński, was on his deathbed in Warsaw. I recall the last phone conversation of those two spiritual giants, both physically incapacitated. I stood next to the pope, who was weak, and I could hear the cardinal's feeble voice saying: "Holy Father, give me your blessing." The pontiff hesitated. Perhaps he sensed something; it seemed he wanted to push away the inevitable moment of the last goodbye. Finally, he said: "Yes, of course. My blessings and kisses to you."

Cardinal Wyszyński passed away on May 28. Twenty-one days after the assassination attempt, the Holy Father returned to the Vatican to galvanize the Apostolic See with fresh energy. However, he returned to the hospital after seventeen days. His strength was waning again; he had a high fever, and doctors finally diagnosed him with cytomegalovirus which was devastating his body. When the virus finally passed, they operated on his digestive tract. The date of surgery was postponed to August 5 — the feast of Our Lady of the Snows. On August 14, a day before the Feast of the Assumption, the Holy Father was released from the hospital for good. Two more months lapsed before John Paul II appeared again in St. Peter's Square. It had now been five months since the assassination attempt.

On May 13, 1917, the Virgin appeared at Fátima for the first time there. May 13 also marked the attempt on the life of John Paul II. At the Gemelli polyclinic, the Holy Father requested to see the Third Secret of Fatima. Did he comment on it?

Having regained his strength, but still at the hospital, the Holy Father started reflecting on what was, to say the least, an extraordinary congruence of dates. This was no coincidence. It was there, at the hospital, that the pope read the Fatima "secret." He received two envelopes — one with Sister Lucia's original Portuguese text, and the other with the Italian translation. In Sister Lucia's vision, he recognized his own destiny. He became convinced that his life had been saved — no, given back to him anew — thanks to Our Lady's intercession and protection. "A bishop dressed in white" is killed. The prophecy obviously did not come true because, as the Holy Father used to say, "One hand shot, and another guided the bullet." And today the bullet lies encased within the crown of Our Lady's statue in Fátima. The pontiff took the bullet there by himself; he prayed for a long time in front of the statue of his Protectress. They certainly had a lot to talk to each other about. At his Vatican terrace, he prayed most of the time in front of the statute of Our Lady of Fatima; he usually prayed the entire rosary there.

You once said: "Mother Teresa was a kind of mirror of John Paul II." Tell us about the relationship and bond between the two.

The Holy Father and Mother Teresa shared a bond of true friendship, reflecting their deep concerns for the Church. On numerous occasions Mother Teresa served as a kind of messenger to parts of the world affected by war where the Holy Father could not go, in Africa or the Balkans. They both showed a great deal of concern for life, from conception to natural death, and they completely identified themselves with this matter. The result of their shared concern for the poor was the house Dono di Maria for homeless women and also a cafeteria for men in need.

Mother Teresa always had access to the Holy Father, whenever she needed to talk to him about important things in the life of the Church and the world. The pope was deeply interested in Mother Theresa's activities on behalf of the poor, her care and love for them so they wouldn't die rejected. He expressed this during his visit to the hospices — so-called houses of death — of Mother Teresa in Calcutta. I witnessed meetings between Mother Teresa and John Paul II. These were the meetings of two people in love with God. They didn't talk much. They perfectly understood each other: it was a big friendship and communion.

Mother Teresa would often say that "holiness is simply doing God's will in your daily life." Jan Tyranowski — who was a central figure in the spiritual formation of Karol Wojtyła and helped him discover the Carmelite mystics St. John of the Cross and St. Teresa of Lisieux — said that "It is not hard to be a saint." In what did the sanctity of St. John Paul II consist?

The Carmelite saints were an inspiration in the daily life of the Holy Father. Jan Tyranowski introduced many young people to spirituality at Tyniecka Street in Kraków; Karol Wojtyła was one of them. His father also had a great influence on his inner life; he inculcated in him a devotion to the Holy Spirit. The future pope learned from him how to pray for the gifts of the Holy Spirit, which he continued to do until the last day of his life. The Wadowice community deepened the religious life of the young Karol, especially in devotion to the Mother of God, the Holy Mother of Kalwaria Zebrzydowska but also Our Lady of Mount Carmel from Wadowice. Wojtyła's vocation crystallized during the Second World War, when terror and evil nearly prevailed. He was a priest, bishop, and cardinal under communism. This was a very difficult period for the Church. These experiences strengthened his spirit; he entrusted everything to God's providence. He lived the Gospel. The sanctity of St. John Paul II was an unlimited trust in God and the fulfillment of his will; it was a complete trust in submission to Mary. "*Totus Tuus ego sum et omnia mea Tua sunt. Accipio Te in mea omnia. Praebe mihi Cor Tuum, Maria.*"

How much continuity was there between Karol Wojtyła of Wadowice and John Paul II in the Vatican?

John Paul II was closely associated with the city he was born in and with his community, in particular his high school, where he gained a passion for the theatre. He made friendships in childhood that lasted throughout his life. I must say that he was a true friend even to people who didn't deserve his faithfulness. In Wadowice, he respected and befriended adherents of Judaism. Wadowice was a community where Catholics and Jews lived together in harmony. During his visit to the Holy Land, he met with the Jewish community, including some people from Wadowice. In his heart, Wadowice forever remained the Holy Father's little homeland.

It should be said that the ecumenism of John Paul II is rooted in Wadowice. Likewise, his artistic passion began in Wadowice; it grew in Krakow, and accompanied him to the Vatican. He was very sensitive to the beauty of art, to music, to words, and to images. It is worth noting that he wrote his last poem in Castel Gandolfo. As Karol Wojtyła and as John Paul II, he loved nature, and he loved the mountains in particular. He was always the same person; he always remained himself. He embraced his roots, and he visited Wadowice as often as he could.

John Paul II was the most traveled pope in history. He continued the mission of St. Paul, the Apostle of the Nations. What was it about the pope's trip to the United States that particularly stayed in your memory?

The Holy Father considered his pontificate a service to God and mankind. He believed that as a shepherd, he should be with his people, encounter them — especially in their own countries. The Holy Father understood that it was easier for him to come to the faithful than for them to come to him. He kept a geographic atlas handy with countries and dioceses all over the world marked; when bishops came to him on *ad limina* visits, they didn't have to remind him where they came from, because the Holy Father knew by heart their names and which dioceses they represented.

After visiting Mexico in January 1979, and then his native Poland in June, the new pope decided to exercise his missionary influence primarily through apostolic journeys. He soon visited the United States, for the first of what became seven times. It was a meeting with young people in Denver that initiated the World Youth Days. This meeting, which could have been very risky for the pope, turned out to be a great success, at least according to the media around the world. It was understood that young people wanted to be with the pope, whom they took as a spiritual guide. Moreover, the Holy Father greatly appreciated the kindness of the entire nation, all the American people, including their leaders. In particular one should note his strong friendship with President Ronald Reagan. Both the pope and the president were anxious for world peace, yet they were also drawn together by their common interest in the theatre.

And then came Saturday, April 2, 2005. In your book Testimonial, *you recalled, "at a certain moment Sister Tobiana felt him looking at her. She put her ear up to his mouth. With a weak, almost inaudible voice, he said, 'Let me go home to the Lord.'"*

On that last day of his life, the Holy Father was fully conscious. He displayed full alertness and enormous peace. There was no drama, only great peace. And it was John Paul II himself who established this mood. He bade farewell to cardinals, officials of the Roman Curia, and also common people, various Vatican employees, and his housekeepers. We were all aware that he was about to go home to the Lord. At about 5:00 p.m. the physicians wanted to help him in some way, but the Holy Father gestured with his hand and whispered: "Allow me to go home to the Lord." He then uttered the words that had accompanied him throughout his life: *Totus Tuus*.

In the evening we celebrated Mass. It was the vigil Mass for Divine Mercy Sunday, a solemnity that was dear to the pope. Once more, we gave him last rites, and I was able to give him a few drops of the precious blood of Christ as Viaticum. We prayed very slowly and enunciated every word clearly so he could hear everything. So you see, in his very last moments, the Holy Father went back to being what he basically had always been: a man of prayer. He knew he was going to the Lord. After John Paul II had left us, we started to sing the *Te Deum*. We wanted to thank God for the gift he had given us, the gift of the person of the Holy Father, of Karol Wojtyła.

What do we need to build a civilization of love?

We need respect for other human beings, especially the poor and the suffering. We need to solve difficulties through dialogue, not through competition and force. We should believe that peace builds, but hatred and lack of understanding lead to armed conflicts, which ultimately always hurt people.

Prayer can truly change your life, for it turns your attention away from yourself and directs your mind and your heart towards the Lord. If we look only at ourselves, with our own limitations and sins, we quickly give way to sadness and discouragement. But if we keep our eyes fixed on the Lord, then our hearts are filled with hope, our minds are washed in the light of truth, and we come to know the fullness of the Gospel with all its promise and life.

John Paul II

CARDINAL CAMILLO RUINI

Cardinal Ruini's close association with Pope John Paul II dates back to the mid-1980s. In 1986 he was appointed secretary general of the Italian Bishops' Conference and then became its president in 1991. More significantly, in that same year the pope appointed him vicar-general of the Diocese of Rome. The two men made 192 foreign trips together.

How does Your Eminence remember the election of Cardinal Karol Wojtyła as the 264th pope of the Catholic Church, Bishop of Rome, and successor of Peter?

I remember that day well: I heard on television the announcement that the white smoke had billowed out from the chimney of the Sistine Chapel. Shortly after, Cardinal Felici announced the election of Cardinal Wojtyła, a name I did not know; he then added that the pontiff-elect was the Archbishop of Kraków. I understood that he was from Poland. When the new pope spoke from the balcony, I felt an immediate sympathy for him. From the beginning, I was happy with his election. I was 47 years old at that time and I was not even a bishop yet.

John Paul II was the first non-Italian pope in hundreds of years. How did the Italians welcome him?

It was undoubtedly a great surprise for the Italians. They were confused by the fact that the pope was not Italian, but a great majority of the people immediately felt connected with him through his charm, the strength of his faith, and the incisiveness of his message.

When did you meet John Paul II for the first time? What was your first impression of the Polish Pope?

I met him in the fall of 1984. I was Auxiliary Bishop of the diocese of Reggio Emilia-Guastalla. I had been chosen as one of the three vice presidents of the Preparatory Committee of the Ecclesial Conference of Loreto, which was scheduled for the following April. Therefore, I often came to Rome for the meetings of this committee. A friend of mine, Msgr. (now Cardinal) Giovanni Battista Re — the Assessor of the Secretariat of State — told me that the pope had invited me to dinner. I was very surprised but very happy. At dinner, the pope asked many questions about my preparation for the conference. I replied frankly, not hiding any difficulties or concerns. I immediately understood that the Holy Father was pleased by my honesty. After that I saw him several times before the conference. The pope made a great impression on me. I was impressed by his intelligence, his cordiality, and the faith and strength of mind he displayed.

John Paul II chose you to be papal vicar of the diocese of Rome. How did it happen?

I think the appointment materialized gradually. A year after the Loreto Convention, the pope wanted me to become secretary general of the Italian Bishops' Conference. For five years I played an important role there, while Cardinal Ugo Poletti was papal vicar for the diocese of Rome and President of the Italian Bishops' Conference. When the cardinal reached the age of retirement, John Paul II chose me as his successor in both roles. He communicated it to me personally a little bit in advance, and gave me some advice on how to carry out these tasks.

Which of John Paul II's encyclicals is particularly dear to you and why?

Dives in misericordia: this is an encyclical that expresses not only the thought but also the personal attitude and concrete behavior of John Paul II, as I had the opportunity to experience in the twenty years of my close service to him. Karol Wojtyła was truly "rich in mercy." He knew how to understand and forgive those who were against him, those who hindered him, and even those who tried to denigrate him. I was often surprised by his extraordinary ability to forgive, the fruit of his holiness.

Part of the Polish Pope's mission was his ability to listen to God and to other people...

John Paul II lived before God; he totally belonged to Him. The words *Totus tuus* that he addressed to Mary describe his relationship with God as well. His relationship with God explains his relationship with others. He paid attention to people, especially those who needed help, and he expressed his concern for them, in particular the poorest and those deprived of freedom.

What role did prayer play in John Paul II's life?

Prayer was the center and nourishment of his daily life. John Paul II spontaneously immersed himself in prayer whenever he had a free moment, even in unfavorable environments such as the cabin of a helicopter. He often spent several hours in prayer at night, or prostrated on the floor of his chapel. He considered prayer the most important task of the pope before God, for the good of the Church and humanity.

What do you miss the most about John Paul II?

I miss his visible presence, his guidance, and his example. But I know that he is present in the mystery of God's love and I entrust myself with full confidence to his intercession: I consider him my second patron, after St. Camillus de Lellis.

What is the message of John Paul II that should form the next generations in the Church and all humanity?

There are many words of this great pope that are valid for the future. I would like to recall at least two: one from the beginning of his pontificate: "Do not be afraid. Open, indeed open wide to Christ, the doors of your life"; and, next, the words of his first encyclical, *Redemptor hominis*: "Jesus Christ is the chief way for the Church. He himself is our way 'to the Father's house' and is the way to each man. On this way leading from Christ to man, on this way on which Christ unites himself with each man, nobody can halt the Church."

The global phenomenon of World Youth Day was initiated by St. John Paul II. What was the pope's message to youth?

To believe in Jesus Christ with all your mind. To love him with your whole heart, to build your life with him, to be his authentic witnesses, and to be brothers in Christ, regardless of any differences of nationality.

How would you respond to those who in recent times have questioned the holiness of John Paul II?

I think that anyone who questions his holiness is blinded by prejudice and doesn't know what he is saying. I especially feel sorry to hear the words of criticism from Catholics who raise doubts of this kind.

What do we need to build a civilization of love?

Above all, we need the grace of God and, by virtue of this grace, the capacity to love and act out of love, in our personal and public lives as Christians and citizens.

CARDINAL GERHARD LUDWIG MÜLLER

Prefect Emeritus of the Congregation for the Doctrine of the Faith. From 2012 to 2017 he was President of the Pontifical Biblical Commission and the International Theological Commission.

How did your journey with St. John Paul II start?

When John Paul II was unexpectedly elected pope on October 16, 1978, the people said with delight and pride: that's the Cardinal of Kraków who had earlier visited Bishop (later Cardinal) Hermann Volk in Mainz and as part of the German-Polish rapprochement and reconciliation received there an honorary doctorate from the Catholic theological Faculty of Johannes Gutenberg University in 1977. As a newly ordained priest, I was celebrating Holy Mass when a note was placed on the altar. On it was the name of the new pope, taken in honor of John Paul I, who had become pope that same year and was recalled to the Heavenly Father's house after a pontificate of only thirty-three days.

What did John Paul II mean for you? How did he affect your personal and professional life?

The first twenty-seven years of my priestly service fell during his pontificate. And so I experienced his work with full theological awareness as a chaplain, theology professor, and bishop. After the many depressing experiences of Vatican II, misconstrued by some, he was the inspiring source of a new Catholic self-confidence. We are — as *Gaudium et spes* said — the Church in the world today, but precisely as the Church of Christ, which is the sacrament of the world's salvation. The Successor of Peter unites the believers again and again in the confession of "Christ — the Son of the living God" (Mt 16:16). Because God created man in His image and likeness, man is the way of the Church in the modern world. In this, John Paul II is a role model in our commitment to the life and dignity of the unborn, the sick, the old, and the dying.

Was there any particular meeting or conversation with John Paul II that has left a special mark on you?

As a member of the International Theological Commission and advisor to three Synods of Bishops, I was regularly invited to his Masses in the Apostolic Palace and to discussions over lunch. I always admired his interest in each of his visitors and his excellent knowledge of the life of the Church and of theology in each country. When I made my inaugural visit as the new Bishop of Regensburg with him, he was delighted with the motto *Dominus Jesus* on my coat of arms. The declaration of the same name by the Congregation for the Doctrine of the Faith on the uniqueness of Christ as mediator of salvation begins with this original apostolic confession of Christ. For *he* is the Son of God, identical in nature to the Father, who came down from heaven for our salvation and accepted our humanity from his mother Mary; *he* is the one who redeemed us on the cross and opened the gate of heaven in his resurrection from the dead.

In what area of work did you collaborate with John Paul II?

I cooperated with the late pope in the International Theological Commission, where I was involved in the documents relating to the request for forgiveness in the Holy Year 2000 and the declaration on the diaconate.

What did the election of a pope from Poland mean for Germany?

Unlike Poland, Germany has been a denominationally divided, culturally antipodean, and politically torn country for 500 years. German Catholics, who could see themselves represented by Cardinal Ratzinger, were doubly delighted with the election of Karol Wojtyła. We admired him for enduring the atheistic persecution by the National Socialists and the Communists (from 1939 to 1989), but also as a bridge builder between the German and Polish nations. Because of this, and because of his commitment to universal human rights and the Christ-centered nature of his piety, John Paul II also impressed many devout Protestants. At his suggestion, during the apostolic visit to Mainz in 1980, we launched a study project on the lingering doctrinal controversies between Protestants and Catholics. A far-reaching understanding could then be reached, especially over the doctrine of justification, which sparked the separation of the churches in the West five hundred years ago. During the apostolic visit, I myself attended Holy Mass on a former airfield along with 200,000 people and the memory of it still uplifts me today.

What was the importance of the pontificate of John Paul II for the German Church?

One cannot speak of a German or Polish or American Church in a national sense. For Christ founded only the one Church that embraces all nations and languages and unites them in faith, hope, and love. There is only one Catholic Church throughout the world, but with the proclamation of the Gospel, the natural moral law, and social doctrine, it also has a positive effect on the peoples and states in which it is present. In Germany, the ecumenical situation is particularly tense. It is important in this secularized environment to be faithful to the Catholic confession and yet also to witness and exemplify common faith in the Triune God, the Incarnation, and the hope of eternal life.

How did the German people respond to the teachings of John Paul II?

It is known that the reactions to many of his uncompromising struggles against abortion and for the natural regulation of conception according to *Humanae vitae* were either critical or outright dismissive. But he was right on all these counts. To a large extent, from the contemporary perspective, sexuality is treated only as a commodity and man is a sex consumer and not a person who, in devotion and sacrifice, is lovingly united with the person of the other in the marital bond. John Paul II was right to support the latter vision.

Do you think that Karol Wojtyła as pope continued the spirit of the famous 1965 letter of the Polish episcopate to the German bishops: "We forgive you and beg for forgiveness"? Did he continue the process of reconciliation?

Who did more for the German-Polish reconciliation than he? Together with Cardinal Ratzinger, who later became Pope Benedict XVI, he is not only a role model, but also the enduring sign that a new beginning is possible when people are not blinded by the devil's hatred, but formed by the grace of Christ.

Which of John Paul II's encyclicals are the most authoritative papal statements with the most important teachings of the pontiff?

For me as a theologian—considering the need for a rational response to the modern criticism of Christianity—the intellectual highlights of John Paul II's pontificate are the encyclicals *Fides et ratio* (1998) and *Veritatis splendor* (1993). Both concern the foundation of morality in natural reason and revealed truth. The false dichotomy of theology and pastoral care in vogue today contradicts their common root in Christ, the incarnate Logos (the word and reason of God) and in Jesus, the good shepherd (the pastor), who gave his life up for his sheep.

On May 1, 2011, John Paul II was beatified by Pope Benedict XVI. What is the importance of beatification for you, the Church, and the world?

The canonization followed the request of the people of God, through whom God himself spoke to his Church. Canonization is not a monument that people erect for their heroes and that they overturn again when another political wind blows. Here the Holy Spirit manifested through the mouth of the Church the holiness of John Paul II, which was bestowed on him in a heroic degree of virtue — and authenticated by miracles at his intercession — on the basis of grace. He is a role model for every Christian. Future popes would be well advised if they commend themselves to his intercession and follow the example of his conception of Peter's ministry. What the pope is and how one judges his ministry is not decided by public opinion with its mundane and mediocratic criteria. It is decided by Christ himself, who gave Peter the main responsibility for ensuring that his Church depends on the "truth of the Gospel" (Gal 2:14).

Which of the teachings of St. John Paul II on the family are especially relevant today?

He did not present his own original teachings about marriage and the family, but only updated the teachings of Christ so that they could be better understood and implemented under the spiritual and cultural conditions of the world today. *Familaris Consortio* (1981) and his catecheses on human love in the divine plan of salvation, known as the "theology of the body" (1979–1984), are of great importance for the present and the future.

What do we need to build a civilization of love?

We must never forget that love cannot be just a program or even a general moral appeal. Love means active participation in the life of the Triune God, who is love in the relationship of the three divine persons and who fills our hearts with the Spirit of the Father and the Son. Only when we look at the self-humiliation (*kenosis*) of the Son of God in his birth as a human being and the shameful and brutal death on the cross do we begin to sense what a shattering and world-changing power the love of God is, how it grasps us, and commands to love *Him* above everything and to love our neighbor as much as ourselves. We live in a time of individual-despising projects of a new world order, the Great Reset, according to the spirit of radically godless "elites." They deceitfully propagate tolerance and pluralism at the expense of the truth of God and the unconditional dignity of man, which excludes abortion and euthanasia and the perversion of conjugal love between man and woman which the elites would substitute with any form of a sexual relationship. Woe to those who — as Esau once did — "sell" the birthright of the revealed truth and love of God for the convenience of political companionships (Gen 25:31), or even the Lord for Judas's "thirty pieces of silver." In our times that means donations of money from so-called philanthropists and the applause of the mainstream media to prompt us to "betray" and "surrender" faith to spiritual and moral relativism (Mk 14:10). It is not money, prestige, and power that save the world, only obedience to God's commandment: "Whoever loves God should also love his brother" (1 Jn 4:21). This is the legacy of St. John Paul the Great, whose intercession we want to recommend to ourselves, the Church, and the whole world: "For now, faith, hope and love remain, these three; but the greatest of them is love" (1 Cor 13:13).

CARDINAL ANGELO COMASTRI

Archpriest Emeritus of St. Peter's Basilica, Vicar General Emeritus of His Holiness for Vatican City State and President Emeritus of the Fabric of St. Peter

Your Eminence, when and how did your journey with John Paul II begin?

I met John Paul II for the first time in a private audience on March 11, 1991. I had been Bishop of Massa Marittima-Piombino for only five months. Therefore, I did not have a report ready to deliver to the pope on the activities of the diocese. The meeting was very friendly and conversation was completely free. At a certain moment, I allowed myself to say: "Can I ask you a discreet question?" The pope smiled and replied: "You can also ask an indiscreet question!" The question was: "Holy Father, how did you manage to return to St. Peter's Square after the terrible attack of May 13, 1981? I would have been very afraid!" The pope looked at me a little surprised and said: "And you think I was not afraid? Of course I was afraid, but remember that brave are not those who are not afraid. We all have some fears! The brave are those who despite their fears move forward with the mission Jesus has entrusted to them. So I did it and I continue doing it." I was so impressed by his answer, and I understood that John Paul II lived by abandoning himself to the hands of Jesus and trusting in the maternal protection of Mary.

You met John Paul II several times. What kind of person was he?

When Mother Teresa of Calcutta died on September 5, 1997, John Paul II said: "Mother Teresa was an open window, through which Jesus looked out and smiled at the world and gave trust and hope to many people." The same words can define John Paul II.

You were one of John Paul II's closest collaborators. Could you please tell me a little bit about your work with John Paul II and your working relationship with him?

John Paul II was like a father to me. I felt his fatherly love and I feel grateful for his trust in my poor person. Every time I met him, he shared with me the serenity, strength, and joy of believing in Jesus. John Paul II was a saint and I felt it!

Which of John Paul II's encyclicals, in your view, is most important, and why?

The encyclicals of John Paul II are like rays of light in the confusion and trauma of contemporary society. John Paul II had the courage to speak the truth even when it was uncomfortable, even when it was unpopular: he knew how to pay the price of fidelity to Jesus. What a wonderful example he left us! It is hard to choose between all the encyclicals, but the most relevant today are *Familiaris consortio* [*sic*; this was an apostolic exhortation] (November 22, 1988) and *Evangelium vitae* (March 25, 1995). In the first, John Paul II defends the family, because the family demonstrates a very clear plan of God expressed clearly in the body of man and woman. Therefore, whoever fights against the family fights against God and prepares a doomed future for humanity. And you already see something like that! The second encyclical defends the inviolability of human life from conception to death. In a "murderous" society like ours, John Paul II is a voice of civilization.

John Paul II was known for his great sense of humor. Would you like to share any anecdotes or jokes of the Holy Father?

I will limit myself to recalling a bold joke that he shared with me in the year 2000. There were some bad and unjust rumors about the Jubilee of 2000 and John Paul II commented: "How much gossip can be heard and how many criticisms are endured without any foundation. The Lord created man's bones so that he could easily stand on his feet, but he did not put any bones in his tongue! Maybe there should be some bones in the tongue, so a little arthritis would be enough to silence some people who are always ready to whisper gossip!"

Human suffering, unexpected suffering, the suffering that asks God "why?": this all forms the theme of the Book of Job. How do you see this theme in the teaching of John Paul II?

John Paul II was a man of faith, and he knew that we were redeemed by the sacrifice of the Cross: a sacrifice that Jesus filled with love. With love pushed to the extreme limit, Jesus opened within history the path of God's love that saves humanity. We must follow the same path: this is well understood by saints like him!

Some time ago, you said: "I am personally convinced that the most fruitful period of John Paul II's pontificate was that of his prolonged illness." Could you expand on these words.

During his illness, a French journalist commented: "Though John Paul II is now less efficient, he has never been more effective! His person sheds light." And, on the occasion of the attack in St. Peter's Square, the great journalist Indro Montanelli observed: "By forgiving his attacker, John Paul II showed us the meaning of the Gospel and the force that overcomes evil: goodness is always ready to manifest itself!"

Which of John Paul II's messages for young people should give guidance to future generations?

During World Youth Day in Canada in 2002, John Paul II gave young people this wise and powerful message: "Do not be like snails who leave behind a trail of drool: a drizzle is enough to erase it. You all leave behind you a trail of good: nobody can ever erase your good." Today, those words offer a criterion to evaluate many people who occupy public positions; in a few years their words will be erased because they are empty!

What do we need to build a civilization of love?

For a number of reasons, there is a need to return from the periphery of action to the source of action, which is contemplation. There has been, in our time, an explosion of external action at the expense of internal reflection. Charles de Foucauld already observed: "If there is no inner life, however great may be the zeal, the lofty intention, the hard work, no fruit will come forth." In the encyclical *Redemptoris missio*, John Paul II, with great clarity, wrote: "The temptation today is to reduce Christianity to merely human wisdom, a pseudo-science of well being. In our heavily secularized world, a 'gradual secularization of salvation' has taken place, so that people strive for the good of man, but man who is truncated, reduced to his merely horizontal dimension" (11). And, to overcome the temptation to secularize salvation, Pope John Paul II reminds us: "The call to mission derives, of its own nature, from the call to holiness: holiness must be called a fundamental presupposition and an irreplaceable condition for everyone in fulfilling the mission of salvation in the Church" (90). And he continues:

> The renewed impulse to the mission "*ad gentes*" demands holy missionaries. It is not enough to update pastoral techniques, organize and coordinate ecclesial resources, or delve more deeply into the biblical and theological foundations of faith. What is needed is the

encouragement of a new "ardor for holiness" among missionaries and throughout the Christian community, especially among those who work closely with missionaries.

It couldn't be clearer than that! St. John Henry Newman, to those who asked him what the most urgent thing for the Church was, without hesitation replied: "Holiness, first! Holiness, first of all!"

I say this, too, to the United States of America: today, in our world as it is, many other nations and peoples look to you as the principal model and pattern for their own advancement in democracy. But democracy needs wisdom. Democracy needs virtue, if it is not to turn against everything that it is meant to defend and encourage. Democracy stands or falls with the truths and values which it embodies and promotes.... Democracy serves what is true and right when it safeguards the dignity of every human person, when it respects inviolable and inalienable human rights, when it makes the common good the end and criterion regulating all public and social life. But these values themselves must have an objective content. Otherwise they correspond only to the power of the majority, or the wishes of the most vocal. If an attitude of skepticism were to succeed in calling into question even the fundamental principles of the moral law, the democratic system itself would be shaken in its foundations (cf. John Paul II, *Evangelium Vitae*). The United States possesses a safeguard, a great bulwark, against this happening. I speak of your founding documents: the Declaration of Independence, the Constitution, the Bill of Rights. These documents are grounded in and embody unchanging principles of the natural law whose permanent truth and validity can be known by reason, for it is the law written by God in human hearts (cf. Rom. 2:25).

John Paul II

CARDINAL PÉTER ERDŐ

Cardinal-Archbishop of Esztergom-Budapest and Primate of Hungary. In 1999, John Paul II named him titular Bishop of Puppi and Auxiliary of Székesfehérvár; he was consecrated a bishop on January 6, 2000. Two years later, he was appointed to his current positions. Cardinal Erdő was a founder and co-president of the Catholic-Orthodox European Forum. He has published a number of cultural and spiritual works. He has also received a number of awards and honors.

Your Eminence, under what circumstances did you first meet John Paul II? What was your initial impression of him?

I saw John Paul II for the first time right after he became pope. In the fall of 1978, I was at St. Peter's Square when the results of the papal election were announced and the pontiff was introduced to the City and the World. I was thus excitedly waiting to hear his first address. It was a very powerful one, a very encouraging harbinger, full of joy and hope. This was not a personal meeting, but a mass audience. I saw him and heard his voice while in the crowd. Later, Cardinal Lékai invited us — a group of priests — to a private meeting with the pope. The cardinal introduced each of us individually to the pontiff. I perceived that the Holy Father was very interested and attentive.

It can be said that John Paul II very much affected your life personally. Tell us about Karol Wojtyła as a man and as head of the Catholic Church.

Pope John Paul II was not simply a very good person but an extraordinary one. He had an aura that you could feel even without seeing him; you knew the pope was there once he entered the room. He commanded respect and inspired love. I deeply believe that he had special abilities and an uncanny intuition. After being appointed Archbishop, I went to thank him personally. I thought beforehand that I would mention to him issues that seemed important to Hungarians at the time. I hadn't even started talking when he brought up the topic himself. I don't think anyone prepared him for it. Through his person, we felt that Christ wanted to take care of us.

In 2003, two years before the pope's death, you received from his hands a cardinal's hat with the title of Presbyter S. Balbinae. What did this honor mean for you personally? What did it mean for the Catholic Church in Hungary?

The fact that the Holy Father had already appointed me Cardinal, after my earlier appointment as Archbishop of Esztergom-Budapest, meant that he knew the tradition of the community and the whole Hungarian people. The Basilica of St. Balbina is a very old church. It is also connected to Magyar Catholic history. The first Hungarian cardinal was buried there in the 13th century.

Tell us about Bolshevik Béla Kun's regime in Hungary following the First World War, and about Cardinal Mindszenty, leader of the Catholic Church in Hungary between 1945 and 1973, who personified uncompromising opposition to fascism and communism.

In 1918 Hungary lost the First World War as part of the Austro-Hungarian Empire. The republic was proclaimed in November 1918, but anarchy prevailed. The Western powers refused to recognize a left-liberal government in Hungary. They countenanced an annexation and a military occupation of much of our country. The nation fell into despair. In this situation, the left-liberals voluntarily handed over power to the communists, who introduced a reign of revolutionary terror and began to persecute the Church. In 1919, many priests gave up their lives for their vocation. It was then that, as a young chaplain, József Mindszenty was imprisoned for the first time by the Reds. In 1944, he was arrested again by the Nazis. In 1948, he was thrown in jail by the communists, and he regained his freedom only during the Hungarian Insurrection of 1956. Then Mindszenty claimed asylum at the American Embassy in Budapest, where he lived for over 14 years. He was a living example of courage.

Please reflect briefly on the relationship between the Hungarian Church and the communist regime in 1978.

In 1964, the Holy See and the People's Republic of Hungary made a partial agreement. This has been criticized by many but, in my opinion, it eventually produced some positive results over the years. After the election of the Polish Pope, John Paul did not replace Archbishop Agostino Casaroli, but, instead, promoted him, appointing him Cardinal Secretary of State. This meant that the process of relaxing relations between the Holy See and the Hungarian state continued.

How did Hungary react to the election of a pope from a Communist country?

Hungarian Catholics welcomed the election of Cardinal Karol Wojtyła as pope with enormous rejoicing. A fellow priest said, "It showed the courage of the Holy Spirit." Of course, the state authorities reacted to the news very cautiously. One sensed that they were afraid of the new pope.

John Paul II was the first pope in history to visit Hungary. He visited Hungary twice, in 1991 and 1996. As we know, Hungary is a secularized nation. What emotions did the Polish Pope evoke in your country?

St. John Paul II's first trip to Hungary brought a message of a systemic transformation and freedom. He encouraged and guided all our people, especially the Hungarian Church and its episcopate. Some liberal groups initially bristled upon his arrival, but these were not loud voices. It was during the papal Mass in Budapest that the news of a coup d'état came from Moscow. The pope and the massive crowd with him were confident that Soviet-style communism would not return.

John Paul II beatified a number of Hungarians, including Vilmos Apor (1997), Tódor Romzsa (2001), László Battyhány-Strattmann and Márk Aviánói (2003), and King Charles IV (2004). The Polish Pope also gave the Hungarians their saints: in 1989, Agnes of Bohemia (cousin of King Andrew II of Hungary); in 1995, the Holy Martyrs of Košice; in 1997, Hedwig of Anjou, Queen of Poland (daughter of King Louis I of Poland and Hungary); in 1999 Kinga (daughter of the King Béla IV of Hungary). What significance did these events have for Hungarians, Catholics and non-Catholics alike?

The Hungarian Church welcomed with great joy the beatification and canonization of those excellent people who were connected to our country and our people. Non-Catholics eschewed any serious objections, contributing to a national consensus of sorts on the topic.

On July 25, 2001, John Paul II sent—to Cardinal László Paskai, then the Primate of Hungary—an Apostolic Letter for the 1,000th anniversary of the Magyar Baptism. Please reflect briefly on this letter.

This letter celebrated the "Hungarian Millennium" beginning with the glorious event of the baptism of the Hungarians. In the splendor of the Esztergom Basilica, the very place where royal coronations took place, there gathered, deeply grateful, Hungary's President, the Prime Minister of the Republic, representatives of the Government and the Parliament, together with the magistrates of Esztergom, a multitude of the faithful, and many political leaders.

The apostolic letter discusses the ancient Crown of St. Stephen (István), which is the symbol of Hungarian national identity, of our history, and of the millennium-old culture of our country. The crown is venerated as a relic by the people. At the same time, it has a deep spiritual meaning, helping the present generation to build a future filled with significant values on the foundations of Christian institutions. St. Stephen saw the crown not only as an honor but also as a responsibility. The crown had to protect and develop his people in the spirit of human and divine culture. The Polish Pope also remembered the family of King Stephen, which was truly outstanding for its holiness. The house of Árpád has given the Church countless saints and blessed.

The pontiff called us to respect the value of family life and the importance of education. He warned us that a reductive conception of man inevitably causes serious harm to human development. St. Stephen is portrayed in art holding the sacred crown in his hands while dedicating the kingdom and his people to the "Great Lady of the Hungarians." The Hungarian people adhere so strongly to this act of dedication that Marian devotion has become a national characteristic. In his apostolic letter, the pope mentioned the Holy Mass celebrated in Budapest in the Heroes' Square, when he renewed the submission of Hungary to the "Great Lady of the Hungarians" together with the entire Hungarian people. At the end of his letter, the pope commended our country, as well as our ecclesiastical and civil leaders, to the protection of the Blessed Virgin Mary and asked for her guidance on the way to Christian virtue, solidarity, and peace.

How is the legacy of St. John Paul II cultivated in Hungary today?
There are many pictures and statues of Pope John Paul II in Hungary. We also dedicated a chapel in his honor in Budapest. Several Catholic institutions and schools also bear his name. His papal writings were published in Hungarian translation. We need the help of the Holy Spirit and the courage that St. John Paul II manifested.

MSGR. SŁAWOMIR ODER

Postulator in the cause for the beatification and canonization of John Paul II and in the cause for the beatification of his parents, Emilia and Karol Wojtyła. He is former Judicial Vicar of the Appellation Tribunal of the Vicariate of Rome; a former President of the Court of Appeals of the same Vicariate; a judge of the Bishop's Court of the Toruń Diocese in Poland; and a spiritual father to the priests of the Toruń Diocese.

> There is no room for routine in life;
> there is time to let God surprise you...

Monsignor, please tell us what left the deepest impression from your meetings with John Paul II.

I had several encounters with John Paul II. My first meeting with him took place the day he was elected Bishop of Rome and head of the Roman Catholic Church. It was a spiritual meeting. I was 18 years old at that time and I needed to decide about my future. Right after high school graduation, I planned to become a seminarian. Then Karol Wojtyła became pope. I remember all the great enthusiasm. However, I changed my mind and said to myself: "I will not enter the seminary." But why? I was afraid that this choice would be dictated by my emotions. Paradoxically, Wojtyła's election as Bishop of Rome affected my decision. However, God found a way to take my hand and lead me where He wanted: in this case, to the seminary.

My next meeting with John Paul II took place during his visit to a Roman seminary in November 1985. I was touched by it tremendously. I met the pope for the first time; it was the first time I was able to touch him. I kissed his hand for the first time. It was the first time I could talk to him in person.

The next meeting took place during the liturgy at St. Peter's Basilica at the end of the Bishop's Synod on December 8, 1985. But perhaps my greatest experience with him took place in the mid-90s. I was unexpectedly invited to the Vatican by Archbishop Dziwisz to discuss my job at the seminary; I was about to be transferred to the Curia. I remember well that that evening I stayed for dinner at the papal residence. What really struck me was the extraordinary simplicity of John Paul II and the poverty of his household. More than simplicity—poverty. The papal house was very modest. I remember that the Holy Father already had visible symptoms of Parkinson's disease and he had some eating problems. I was surprised by his incredible memory. He was talking about the seminary in Pelplin, Poland, where I had studied, as he had just visited it. He knew all the professors. He knew all the publications. I was completely surprised by the breadth and depth of his knowledge. I also discovered the simple kindness of the pope. Right after dinner, he walked me to the kitchen; it was his custom to go there after each meal to thank the sisters for having prepared it.

One other meeting was very special for me, a wordless one. It took place in 1992. He had just published *Pastores dabo vobis*, an apostolic exhortation on the formation of priests addressed to both clergy and the lay faithful. That year, the Holy Father washed my feet during the liturgy of Holy Thursday. It was a meeting without words, a unique experience. I remember the authenticity of this gesture of washing and kissing my feet. The spiritual experience of priesthood by the Holy Father, which I had an opportunity to witness here, will always remain a point of reference for me.

What did the papal apartment look like?

I did not see the entire papal apartment—I was only present in the waiting and dining rooms and the kitchen. I was struck by the simplicity of the place. There was no luxury there at all. There was no glamour. The furniture showed signs of use; it had belonged to Paul VI. During John Paul II's beatification process, witnesses spoke about the pope's detachment from material things. It was a sign of a certain freedom. For him, things were only useful as long as they served man. I remember a witness from Kraków who recalled that when Wojtyła obtained new items such as shoes or pants, he did not enjoy them for a long time. He often gave away such things when he met someone in need.

What was your reaction upon being appointed postulator for the beatification and canonization process of John Paul II?

It was an amazing situation. I first learned about the appointment informally. I was attending a meeting of Pope Benedict XVI with priests of the Roman dioceses. I remember precisely: it was May 13, the anniversary of the attempted assassination of John Paul II. I was supposed to fly to Poland that day. And then the pope pleasantly surprised us by announcing the start of the beatification process. I remember the great enthusiasm of all present as well as my own great joy.

I was in a hurry to get to the airport when Cardinal Ruini's secretary came up to me and announced that the cardinal wanted to talk to me. I was very unhappy with this because I had very little time to get to the airport. I even asked him if I could talk to the cardinal on Monday upon my return. However, he said: "The cardinal very much wants to talk to you and he asks to meet you now." I went to this meeting with the cardinal, who knew that I was in a great hurry. He asked me: "Did you hear what Pope Benedict said?" I replied, "I have heard it and I am very happy!" Cardinal Ruini continued: "And I am happy that you will be a postulator in this process and now you can leave." I was floored: that would become my life for several years thereafter. That was the story.

Do you see God's hand in this decision? Have you ever asked yourself, "why me?"
Certainly. The first thought that comes to mind when you face such a challenge in your life is: Why me? One of the icons that I brought with me to Poland from Rome is the copy of a painting by Caravaggio now in the Church of San Luigi del Francesi: *The Calling of St. Matthew*. It presents Christ entering a room where Matthew and others are counting money. Suddenly, Matthew turns around and says: "Are you talking to me?" This is the image that came to my mind at that time and which appears in my personal reflections very often: Why me? There are many questions in my life I cannot answer and situations I cannot explain. From the point of view of procedural economy and a certain logic, I would explain my appointment as postulator as follows: I came from the Polish milieu and I have never, during the pontificate of John Paul II or now, been associated with the Vatican community at large. I have worked for the diocese of Rome. I have served as a connection point between two worlds: the Polish and the Italian. My legal background probably in some way predisposed me to this postulator's mission—as did my previous experience leading the beatification process of Stefan Frelichowski, a priest and martyr of my home diocese in Poland. From this perspective and that of a postulator, my encounters with John Paul II meant a huge change in my life, as though the late pope preached a private retreat for me. Meeting a saintly priest has been an extraordinary gift for me.

Do you see being the postulator of cause of John Paul II as a sign of providence?

I felt the presence of the Holy Spirit, and support from heaven and providence. I do not even know if it can be said that the Holy Father was behind it. He was a very modest man and he did not seek public applause. During the process, I clearly felt that it was very inconvenient to the Enemy of the Church. I felt resistance and even difficulties in many situations. I felt such a dialectic between good and evil, sin and virtue, heaven and the denial of heaven. These were situations created by people, but also supernatural phenomena: I had a very serious car accident during the beatification of John Paul II, and a second one in Costa Rica before the canonization. I emerged unscathed from both.

Pope Benedict XVI told you: "Please work quickly, as fast as possible, but please work well." What was the greatest challenge for you during this process?

Certainly, I felt pressure from many different sides. Everyone asked: "when?" and "how long?" I was aware that this job should be carried out in the spirit of responsibility before people, but above all, before God. There were no shortcuts there. The trial had a historical importance. It was necessary to share with future generations our conviction that the sanctity of John Paul II was not an expression of some collective hysteria of the moment but rather was embedded in the history of a specific man who loved God and people.

Please explain the beatification and canonization process.

The process begins with a determination of "reputation for holiness." At least five years from the death of a candidate is necessary to verify this. In John Paul II's case, there was a very strong case, immediate and spontaneous, with people shouting *Santo Subito!* With the finding of reputation for holiness, the canonical process begins. There are two essential moments of this process: listening to the voice of the Church and listening to the voice of God. So we have the voice of God's people, the voice of the Church, and the voice of God. The voice of God's people is the one that screams *Santo Subito!* The Church's voice is the canonical process, and it is very complex. Testimonies are collected from living witnesses and documents are found in archives, libraries, and other places.

There are three committees involved in the process: the first appoints the bishop's delegate, who speaks to witnesses; the second examines all documents of a historical or archival character; and there is a third committee of censors and theologians who study all published writings of the candidate. The diocesan process commences with the publication of an edict in which the bishop announces the beatification process and invites witnesses to come forward. Some witnesses speak of holiness, but there are others who disagree with them. The first stage focuses on collecting evidence. If this process is concluded favorably, the case goes to the Congregation for the Causes of Saints. The postulator, on the basis of the collected materials — in cooperation with the relator of the case — must prove the holiness of the candidate. The collected documents are presented to the Plenary Congregation of Bishops and Cardinals. If their opinion is positive, then the entire process is approved by the Holy Father. This concludes the stage of human involvement. And then we wait for God's voice: there is the question of a miracle. Beatification takes place when the Church recognizes a miracle attributed to the intercession of a candidate for the altars. This is a beautiful and wise tradition of the Church. According to God's people a saint has died. We have tested the claim and examined the validity of this belief. And what does God say now? The Lord speaks in the sense that a miracle occurs. If all the elements are in order, then we have a proclamation by the Catholic Church. The second miracle comes after the beatification. One miracle is enough for beatification and one further miracle for canonization.

Which alleged miracles of John Paul II did the medical and theological committees find scientifically inexplicable?

There are two aspects: medical and theological. A claim of scientific inexplicability attributed to the intercession of a specific person is subject to analysis by many people. We have practitioners in the field of medicine, experts in theology, and researchers of the Congregation of Bishops and Cardinals. Finally, the Holy Father speaks on this subject. The medical aspect is subject to empirical examination, to determine whether it is possible to explain what happened scientifically. In the case of Sister Marie Simon Pierre, there was no way to explain her healing because Parkinson's cannot be cured.

What arguments were raised against the sanctity of John Paul II during the trial?

There were no arguments against the holiness of John Paul II. There were voices against starting this process at all as premature. Among those who were trying to oppose it, there were theologians, or more precisely liberation theologians, who were pointing to John Paul II's attitude toward priestly celibacy, women's ordination, and so on. There were also negative voices from the conservative circles. And there were further voices regarding the liberal attitude of John Paul II towards ecumenical dialogue or the interreligious meeting in Assisi. Once the trial was over, the media started talking about the abuses in the congregation of the Legionaries of Christ and the cases of pedophilia committed by priests. I would like to emphasize that all possible disputes were the subject of research during the trial and the conclusion we reached indicates unequivocally the lack of any evidence of any conscious and untoward malfeasance or neglect on the part of St. John Paul II in this matter. I am aware that some people are looking for a shadow of guilt in regards to John Paul II and therefore they question his sanctity. I want to be very clear. Neither I nor the commission involved in investigating the life of the late pope for sainthood — based on extensive research carried out in the Vatican archives and elsewhere — found any evidence that the pope consciously neglected or covered up the sexual abuse scandals.

Currently, you are involved in the beatification process of Wojtyła's parents.
It seems that I somehow became a part of the Wojtyła family. This is the initial stage; we are collecting testimonies. This part is done by the bishop's delegate. During my career as president of the ordinary tribunal of the Roman diocese, I had the opportunity to conduct many trials — not always as a postulator. Every single experience enriches my life. These processes seem like I am gaining friends in heaven, which for a man who remains a pilgrim on this earth is extremely valuable.

Interreligious and ecumenical dialogues were launched by Pope John XXIII and developed by John Paul II. However, Wojtyła has been severely criticized for promoting ecumenical dialogue.
John Paul II was one of the fathers of the Second Vatican Council. Ecumenical and interreligious dialogues were topics of the Council's reflection and a proposition for the future. John Paul II never gave up his mission of proclaiming the Truth Revealed; he never forgot that the primary mission of the Church is to bring the Gospel to everyone and to proclaim the name of Jesus as the only savior and redeemer of humanity. All efforts of the late pope were made in the spirit of respecting the dignity of every human being and building space for cooperation

between all people in a spirit of peace and mutual respect. They never aimed at relativizing the truth.

What must we do to build a civilization of love?

I will respond to this question as a man of faith. For me, God is the most important thing. God is a benchmark in our life. He both watches over reality and orders it. And based on this hierarchy of values, the priorities set by the Gospel, you can think about building a civilization of love. Next to God, we need honesty in our search for truth and then courage to live in that truth.

MSGR. PAWEŁ PTASZNIK

Former head of the Polish-Slavic Section in the Secretariat of State at the Vatican. He was John Paul II's main translator and secretary. Among other things, he translated the pope's will into Italian (from the original Polish). He also supervised the editing of various papal texts, which were invariably written in Polish. Msgr. Ptasznik has participated in various initiatives preserving the legacy of the Polish Pope. He also serves as a rector of St. Stanislaus Church in Rome, which ministers to Polish faithful and pilgrims.

Father Paweł Ptasznik and Karol Wojtyła have a lot in common, namely Kraków: the home of the first Polish university (founded in 1364), St. Albert Chmielowski and St. Faustina Kowalska, the Sanctuary of God's Mercy, and Wawel Cathedral. What role has Kraków played in your heart?

Kraków has always been close to my heart. My entire family lives there; I have friends there; and I return there very gladly. Kraków is a treasure of experiences related to my preparation for the priesthood as well as the mysterious tradition of history and the sacred. I remain immersed in the affairs of Kraków and its inhabitants, even if I live permanently in Rome.

When did you begin to work with John Paul II? How do you recall your time with him?

It was an enormous, undeserved gift that for almost ten years I could be close to St. John Paul II. The story starts in 1996. Before we started working together, I was invited to join him for dinner on January 1, 1996. This was an incredible experience. I was seated next to the Holy Father and given the opportunity to talk freely to him. He asked about my family and parish, where I came from. He knew in detail the history of the parish and even its current pastor. Then he asked me about my doctoral dissertation and we started chatting about theological topics. He was very interested in the role of the Holy Spirit in the sacraments. On the following day we started working together. When I think about John Paul II, I reminisce about the beautiful moments which I lived through with him: working together, talking, celebrating, traveling, and so forth.

What was the nature of your service with John Paul II?

Among my duties, I corresponded in Polish on his behalf with people who turned to him with a variety of issues. Of course, I would always clear my responses with him or with my superiors if the business at hand did not concern the pope himself. My work concerned official business, including responses to bishops and government representatives, but I also dealt with private matters. The most important part of my work was to write down, edit, and translate whatever the Holy Father dictated to me: speeches, homilies, documents. For a written text, one had to find references in the Bible and other sources that the pontiff quoted from memory. Then I would translate that into Italian. This gave me a chance to speak with the Holy Father in person practically on a daily basis. He was an eager listener and he shared his thoughts gladly. This was an enormous treasure for me.

Did the Holy Father ask you for to comment on the texts you were working on?
The Holy Father let me know that he needed a collaborator. He would ask me what I thought about a given topic; he asked for suggestions. Sometimes he would ask me to write them down so he could mull over them.

What language did the Holy Father use?
John Paul II nearly always wrote in Polish. Perhaps in private correspondence with people of other nationalities he would respond in their native tongues. He never hid that he was able to express himself most fully in the Polish language, and he cared about precision of expressions. Besides, his sensitivity in human affairs and spirituality was rooted in Polish culture and literature. He was a master of the word, and sometimes he would focus on the meaning of a single word to build an entire speech, sermon, or lecture. Frequently, this caused quite a bit of trouble with the translation because a Polish word would fail to find an equally rich synonym in other languages. Of course, the pope mostly drew from Holy Scripture, which he knew virtually by heart. He also would quote many fragments of the documents of Vatican II. Further, he was able precisely to indicate in which conciliar document, really in which exact place, the cited passage came from. He had an incredible memory.

Did John Paul II consult others in preparing his texts?
When writing important texts, exhortations or encyclicals or any other documents directed at the Church, he always asked for the opinion of the Congregation for the Doctrine of the Faith. However, the pope also would look for experts in a particular field and ask them to

consult with him. Further, when he prepared his speeches for foreign pilgrimages, he would ask native bishops from various countries to send him suggestions regarding contemporary events, issues, or problems in their communities. Further, when his lectures were aimed at a particular milieu (e.g., scholars, politicians, or non-Catholic leaders), he would consult with experts. John Paul II insisted on consulting with as many authorities as possible about everything that he was expected to sign.

What was John Paul II's attitude towards work?

John Paul II was a hard worker. He would prepare himself well ahead of any event he was expected to participate in. Every morning, except on Sundays and Tuesdays, he would dictate his texts, and then he gave audiences for politicians, bishops, or nuncios, and then he would meet with a variety of groups. In the afternoon he presided over the deliberations of individual Congregations and Councils of the Roman Curia. Also his meals tended to be working affairs. He read quite a lot.

Who was John Paul II for you?

John Paul II was an unsurpassable paradigm for me. He was like a father to me. This is not because of his official title but because of the naturalness with which he related to me. I endeavored to treat him with all due respect as a father, and he responded with paternal kindness, gracing me with a great dose of his trust. When we worked together, he truly treated me as a partner. He was also my teacher and spiritual guide. This was a peaceful school of faith, an evangelical outlook on the world and events, looking at man, at his dignity, and at his values. This was a school for me of serving man and, most of all, a school of prayer. I thank the Lord for my time with John Paul II.

Please reflect briefly on John Paul II's attitude towards youth.

In his letter to the young, *Dilecti amici*, the Holy Father wrote that they are the hope of the Church, and that is how he approached them. He always appreciated the value of youth, its joy and enthusiasm, curiosity about the world, openness toward the future, and search for the ways of life. The pope knew the problems and threats that young people encountered. He did not ignore them. He treated young people seriously and he did not dismiss existential questions they directed at him customarily. He put demands before them yet he also showed them various perspectives and awoke hope. The pontiff was authentic in his words and body language, which expressed cordial love and true interest in them, and the young instinctively felt that authenticity. And he was young at heart. His communion with young people, it seems, fueled him with youthful spirit. He confessed as much during a meeting with them at a Roman university: "You become who you hang out with."

Which works of the Holy Father would you recommend most?

Well, I would recommend first *Crossing the Threshold of Hope*; then *Be Not Afraid*; *Gift and Mystery*; *Rise, Let Us Be on Our Way*; and finally *Memory and Identity*. The spirit of John Paul II reveals itself. Next, I would suggest homilies and speeches, and only at the end his encyclicals and exhortations. For the young of great literary sensibility, I recommend the early output of Karol Wojtyła, where there is testimony to his sensitivity to the human condition and man's spiritual experience, richness of culture and art, and the beauty of the world. In his early literature one can discover with admiration the roots of the future Holy Father's insight into God, man, and the world.

You also edited several books by John Paul II. Which one is particularly close to your heart and why?

The Holy Father wrote his books usually during his vacations and therefore I was not involved in their creation. My task was strictly editorial: correcting the language, translating into Italian (except *The Roman Triptych*, which we hired professional translators to tackle), and supervising translations into other languages. I would present all corrections and suggestions to the Holy Father for his approval. Sometimes I would propose to move the divisions between chapters, an alternative title of a chapter, a different word order, or a more precise word. John Paul II either patiently accepted my suggestions or argued for the retention of the original version. Then it was my task to keep in touch with the publishers and to worry about the final product. My work on each title was an incredible adventure, an occasion for many conversations, and an opportunity to learn the thoughts of the pontiff. *Gift and Mystery* is perhaps closest to my heart. This was the first papal book I worked on. It was written in the context of the 50th anniversary of Karol Wojtyła's ordination. It became for me a sort of a guide to fulfilling my own priestly vocation. Another book that I gladly return to is *The Roman Triptych*. In general, all the literary works of Karol Wojtyła are very dear to me because of their spiritual depth, cultural rootedness, and poetic beauty.

How do you recall April 2, 2005?

John Paul II prepared us for the day of his death. On that day, around noon, I had the opportunity to bid farewell to the Holy Father. Archbishop Dziwisz called me and asked me to come. In the room, by the sick bed, there was already Cardinal Ratzinger. The pope was conscious. When I greeted him, he responded by looking at me and lowering his eyelids. We prayed together silently for a while. At the end of the meeting Archbishop Dziwisz asked the Holy Father to bless me. I knelt down by his bed, he put his hand on my head, and he made the sign of the cross, thus blessing me for the last time. I was aware of that, but I stayed calm.

In one of your interviews you remarked: "For me a more painful moment than the passing of the Holy Father was the time when Archbishop Dziwisz handed me the last will and testament of John Paul II and asked me to start translating it. This was truly painful." Please reflect briefly on this moment.

This was the moment when it penetrated my consciousness that the end was inevitably approaching. And that was painful. I cannot describe the emotions with which I read his words written in 1980:

> I would like once again to entrust myself entirely to the Lord's grace. He Himself will decide when and how I am to end my earthly life and my pastoral ministry. In life and in death [I am] *Totus Tuus* through Mary Immaculate. I hope, in already accepting my death now, that Christ will give me the grace I need for the final passover, that is, [my] Pasch. I also hope that He will make it benefit the important cause I seek to serve: the salvation of men and women, the preservation of the human family and, within in it, all the nations and peoples (among them, I also specifically address my earthly Homeland), useful for the people that He has specially entrusted to me, for the matter of the Church and for the glory of God Himself.

While translating these words, I thought about thousands of people in St. Peter's Square and throughout the world who were then united with the dying pope in one great prayer. Thus a request written in the last will and testament was fulfilling itself: his passing truly served the people and the Church; it complemented the essence of what he served for all his life. And then we had *Santo subito*, a process, testimony of miracles, beatification, and canonization . . . Incredible joy!

You collaborated with St. John Paul II, Benedict XVI, and Pope Francis. Please briefly reflect on these three different personalities.

I had a different type of a relationship with each pontiff. I was closest, of course, with John Paul II. As I have mentioned, our relationship was very personal and cordial. My contact with Pope Benedict XVI was less frequent but very cordial. He is a very kind, humble, and gentle man. In our conversations, we would refer back to his predecessor, his personality and teaching. But Benedict was also interested in the affairs of the Church in Poland, and frequently even my personal and family affairs. My interaction with Pope Francis was sporadic. I had a chance to talk to him privately a few times. This was nice. I value the current pontiff for his engagement; and I strived to serve him with as much devotion as I did his predecessors in the Holy See.

What do we need most today to build a civilization of love?

When we hear the term "civilization," we usually associate it with the development of society. However, when talking about building a "civilization of love," John Paul II focused on the human person and his immediate circles, starting with the family. The foundation of a civilization is the realization of the dignity of each person, which grounds his rights and duties: the right to life and the duty to respect the life of others; the right to freedom and the duty to respect the freedom of others; the right to one's own conscience and faith and the duty to respect the conscience and faith of others... We need to retain in our relationships this kind of conscious realization and the responsibility stemming from it. And the awakening and deepening of this consciousness, one's religious convictions notwithstanding, realizes itself through the fostering of a broadly understood culture. John Paul II often repeated that man lived truly a human life, became more of a human, thanks to culture. It seems that today this spiritual dimension of culture has been increasingly neglected and even lost in pop culture, which does not shirk from degrading the dignity of man for commercial and political reasons and even for mere pleasure.

If, to continue, we are talking about the civilization of love, we must observe that nowadays it is often confused with "tolerance." Tolerance is not love. It is indifference towards another person as long as his presence and actions do not impinge on one's own territory. Then tolerance turns into aggression. Tolerance leads not to love, which requires one to give up one's own good for the sake of another. John Paul II used to repeat, and now Pope Francis does, that in the social dimension the way to the civilization of love, and thus the civilization of life, truth, and peace, is fraternity. That entails not indifference, but a concern, full of care, for another person. Of course Christians have at their disposal yet another, perhaps even the most basic, motivation to build the civilization of love: the calling by God to build a better world in the name of fraternity, grounded in the truth that we all have the same dignity because we are created in the image and likeness of God and redeemed with the blood of Christ. It seems then that, most of all, we need a culture grounded in values, and fostering the brotherhood of men, in faith, which gives witness.

FR. ROBERT SKRZYPCZAK

Professor at the Catholic Academy in Warsaw; lecturer at the Center for the Thought of John Paul II in Warsaw; member of the Advisory Council at the Roman Dmowski and Ignacy Jan Paderewski Institute for the Legacy of Polish National Thought; lecturer and author of books and articles.

Father, you were close to the Holy Father. Once you wrote: "I shook the hand of John Paul II and we exchanged a few sentences in Polish. His eyes uniquely radiated an enormous amount of kindness, humor, and acceptance. John Paul II bestowed upon me a lesson in prayer." Tell us more about what John Paul II was like up close and personal.

When I was a transitional deacon, I was invited to a priestly ordination in St. Peter's Basilica as a representative of a European seminary. I had an opportunity to see how John Paul II celebrated the liturgy and how he prayed. The liturgy lasted two and a half hours. The pope was 76 years old. There were cameras, television crews, diplomatic corps, and politicians. John Paul II did not seem to notice them at all. He was constantly focused on God. I realized that I was standing a few feet away from one of the greatest mystics of the 20th century.

What did the Second Vatican Council mean for the Church?

So far, there have been 21 councils in the history of the Catholic Church. There were eight councils of united Christianity, until the spilt between the Roman Catholics and Eastern Orthodox. The last one, held from 1962 to 1965, is called the Second Vatican Council.

Councils are usually named after the place where they are held. A council is a great event for Christianity. It is a meeting of bishops from all over the world. Not of every single bishop — it would be too difficult logistically. The point is to make sure that the Church universal is represented by the leaders of various local churches.

The Second Vatican Council was convened by Pope John XXIII. It gathered over 2,000 Catholic bishops and hierarchs, including 64 Polish bishops. Karol Wojtyła, as a young auxiliary bishop of the Archdiocese of Kraków, was one of the representatives of the Polish episcopate. He was one of ten bishops who had the opportunity to participate in every session of the Council. Along with Cardinal Stefan Wyszyński and others, Karol Wojtyła became one of the chief protagonists of the Second Vatican Council. He was the last Council Father to ascend the throne of St. Peter.

How did the council shape Karol Wojtyła?

When I was working on my monograph about Karol Wojtyła at the Second Vatican Council, which entailed searching the Vatican archives for all discussions, proposals, drafts, and other mementos of the Council, I asked myself two questions: how did Karol Wojtyła influence the Council? And how did the Council influence Karol Wojtyła?

Replying to the first question: I managed to discover 25 interventions made by Karol Wojtyła during the Council. Over 2,000 people participated in the Council, and there were about 7,000 speeches and written interventions; there were, on average, just over two speeches per participant.

Karol Wojtyła was thus one of the more active participants. He delivered eight speeches in the conciliar hall and submitted sixteen written interventions. He further influenced the creation of various conciliar documents, most prominently the constitution *Gaudium et spes*. I was able to find an interview he gave to Victorio Posenti in which he confessed, just a few months before his election to the papacy, that he always traveled with two documents: the Holy Bible and *Gaudium et spes*, to which he felt a special attachment.

Wojtyła also had a great influence on the treatment of religious freedom. Man was one of the central subjects of the Council. In a questionnaire that preceded the Council, Karol Wojtyła wrote that it was a perfect moment for the Church to present itself to modern man. He said one had to use "a personalistic key." Man as a person must be at the center of the Council's deliberations. A man is endowed with dignity, an undeniable worth that cannot be taken away from him. The personality gifted to man should be treated by him as a challenge. Wojtyła would later use all his conciliar utterances as a source for his papal ministry. He always saw good in man. As a Christian, bishop, and theologian, he looked at everything through the prism of faith, and for him every person was potentially saved by Christ. Through the encounter with Christ, a man can develop his capabilities and his creativity, the capacity to love and forgive, to make his life a work of art.

How did Karol Wojtyła shape the Second Vatican Council?

I studied how others perceived Karol Wojtyła at the Council. I found Yves Congar's journals. He wrote about Wojtyła as "an impressive figure and amazing personality." Wojtyła made an incredible impression as a well-integrated man, a man of many values. I found another diary by the French theologian Henri de Lubac. In 1965 he stated: "We wish our Pope Paul VI many years in health, but one day we will have to face the loss of this pope and have to think about his successor." Karol Wojtyła was the only candidate for de Lubac, but he believed there was no chance of his election. Why? Because no one, in 1965, thought that one could choose a non-Italian pope, let alone from behind the Iron Curtain. As George Weigel wrote in his biography of John Paul II, until Karol Wojtyła was elected to the See of Peter, the concept of a Polish intellectual did not exist in many countries. Wojtyła showed us that Poland was a European nation with 1,000 years of Christian tradition, with many good monarchs who made their kingdom a bulwark of Christianity, and that we Poles had great spiritual and intellectual resources.

Before the Second Vatican Council, Cardinal Stefan Wyszyński had already been well known in Rome.

Cardinal Wyszyński was a great martyr of communism. He was a great presence. He was a man who went against the grain, a steadfast man. On October 13, 1962, at the first conciliar assembly, Cardinal Wyszyński was greeted with an ovation in the hall of St. Peter. Wyszyński was a symbol of the Polish Church and a symbol of the martyrs' Church. Wyszyński arrived at the Council already as a hero, while the Council itself became an arena where Karol Wojtyła introduced himself as a major figure. Wojtyła was already a representative of another Church, that of a well-educated generation, of people interested in the world, a personalist generation which understood the needs of human beings. He was a man familiar and comfortable with the universal Church. For Wojtyła, the Council was the work of the Holy Spirit. Nevertheless, he neither foresaw nor grasped all its impact. The main axis of the renewal of the Church predicted by Wojtyła was that the Council would focus on the roots, the foundation of the Church. What would give strength to the Church, he believed, was a re-discovery of the Resurrection and of the force and power of God's Word, and of the Church as a community of the saved.

Councils require much time to promulgate their messages and thus fulfill their intent. On the one hand, the Council carries within it something radically out of date. On the other, there is an incredible potential in it that still has not been fulfilled.

What were Karol Wojtyła's most significant contributions to the Council and its interpretation?

Certainly, John Paul II wanted to show what it meant to be a Christian or a post-conciliar Catholic. He was convinced that God spoke through events and spoke through the Council. In the 1950s, after returning from Rome, where he was sent for his doctoral studies, Wojtyła focused on the topic of marriage and family: human love, femininity, masculinity, and sexuality; how to build a marriage; motherhood and fatherhood. He organized three international conferences between 1975 and 1978. The first one was focused on the post-abortion syndrome; the second on the contraceptive mentality; and the third on premarital chastity.

Please also note that Wojtyła did not appear on the lists of papal candidates in 1978. Suddenly, he jumps out of nowhere like a rabbit out of a hat. The world froze because nobody knew Wojtyła. Suddenly he was elected pope and seemed to be perfectly prepared for the role. He immediately focused on topics such as human anthropology, the missionary nature of the Church, the new evangelization, marriage, and family. John Paul II is the only pope in the history of the Church who devoted so many speeches and catechesis to the theology of the body and sexuality. And why did Wojtyła focus on human love and sexuality? The world was witnessing birth control pills, abortion, divorce, a new understanding of partnerships and relationships, and so forth. Today, there is a dearth of love, an inability to build relationships, and a terrible loneliness which is the result of hedonism and individualism. What is that all about?

How did Karol Wojtyła know in the 1950s and 1960s where the main battle for separating people from God would take place? Today we are at the point of a clash of civilizations. Cardinal Wojtyła warned us about that as early as 1977. While visiting America then, he said that there would be an inevitable confrontation between the Gospel and the anti-Gospel, between the Church and the anti-church. It is amazing that Catholics did not take this to heart. How did he know this? We all would expect that the battle of separating man from God, which is atheism, should take place on the stage of politics, but Wojtyła warned us that the atheization would play itself out on the stage of human sexuality too. And why human sexuality? Because there is an inscribed sign of God in human sexuality, a proof of man's origin from God.

The Lord God created man in his own image and likeness, says the Book of Genesis: male and female he created them. An attempt to erase the difference between a man and a woman, to liberate oneself from one's biological sex and gift oneself with an artificial sexual identification, is a sin. People lose themselves in freedom because they do not know who they are. How did John Paul II know so long ago that the attempts to destroy this sign that man belongs to God, this fundamental relationship with man's Author, would take place on the stage of sexuality? This is the starting point for building a human identity. And the Christian vision of man says that man is not only who he is, but that he is also the one who reaches out and builds relationships with other people. Personhood implies the existence of a relationship. John Paul II reminded us that human happiness is not about giving yourself everything. Wojtyła says that you will be more happy, you will strengthen your humanity, when you make your life a gift for another human being.

At the Council, Wojtyła distinguished two types of atheism: atheism imposed by the state or system, which leads people to martyrdom, and an atheism that arises internally, where man is free. In the second case, paradoxically, the atheist lives in a free world but does not feel free. He is called to love but cannot achieve it. He possesses everything, but loneliness is killing him. The greatest epidemic of the 21st century is not the Coronavirus but loneliness. A man who lives in atheism is a man who has deprived himself, or been deprived, of the fundamental relationship on which all existence is based, the relationship to his Creator. Loneliness makes men yearn to belong. They try to treat their loneliness with collectivism, which is why intelligent and cultured Germans or Austrians gave themselves over to the Führer and why so many experienced communism. The educated elites of eastern Europe followed communism blindly.

Once André Frossard wrote: "From the perspective of history it seems almost obvious that we would not have had a Polish Pope in 1978 if Bishop Karol Wojtyła had not previously obtained a passport [from the Communist regime] to Rome and participated in Vatican II. Without the participation in the Council, let us say openly, he would have been a little-known figure, with no great chance of being elected to the See of Peter. It was the Council that elevated this man, whom the word of the Holy Spirit seduced and shaped, to the papal office."

Wojtyła became known thanks to the Second Vatican Council. The Council also shaped him. He studied and absorbed the Church. Observers said that Wojtyła was either speaking or writing things down during the deliberations. *Person and Act*, written in 1969, presenting the personalistic vision of man, was his philosophical or, rather, ethical commentary on the Council. He absorbed the universality of the Church within himself. If not for the Council, he would probably have remained a bishop in Poland. The Council gave him a chance to enjoy something that belongs to the Church only, universality. The Church reveals itself with a million faces, a thousand words, different ways of thinking. And the Holy Spirit makes one body out of it. This is the Church.

Was Providence at work in giving Wojtyła the privilege of leading the Catholic Church for almost twenty-seven years during the difficult post-conciliar period?

Consider the world before the conclave of 1978. This was the time of world terrorism, liberation theology, communism, etc. Later, there came the dramatic death of two popes in a row. From many a cry rose up: we want a holy pope! We want a charismatic pope! I think that call was heard. Wojtyła's purpose was to point us towards God. He was a saint. He was a mystic. In my conversation with Cardinal Burke about John Paul II and his travels to the U.S., the cardinal said that Americans loved John Paul II. I asked him directly: what did they see in John Paul II that they did not see in other popes? He responded: Americans saw him as a shepherd, while they saw other popes as politicians.

Will a contemporary Catholic, under the influence of John Paul II, be able to benefit from the Second Vatican Council?

I do not want to sound pessimistic, but it will be difficult for us to find a pope who can attract so many young people to World Youth Day, inspire new vocations, or canonize 482 saints. Let's also not forget how many sick and suffering people he has helped: during his lifetime and after his death. My pessimism comes from the observation of today's world and this new generation that tries to erase what we have received. There are many entities and forces in the world that do everything to stop people from thinking about John Paul II. He is attacked as if he had been responsible for pedophilia, often by the very people who are propagators of intergenerational love, which is to say pedophilia. They say that Wojtyła did not notice that one priest was a monster who presented himself as a holy man. I mean here Maciel Degollado, the founder of the Legionaries of Christ. I remember when Cardinal Dziwisz said: "I witnessed myself that this man was kneeling in front of John Paul II; he was bursting out in tears and explaining that they try to discredit him. And John Paul II believed. He always gave people the benefit of the doubt." Then there were the cases of Theodore McCarrick and Hans Groer, both charged with pedophilia. Both were promoted by the Polish Pope. But again, let's analyze it: there were two horrible nominations out of 260 cardinals nominated. Which head of a corporation would not want a manager who made a mistake only twice?

Once you beautifully said: "Society is aging; Europe is losing its memory as if in dementia; our identity has worn out and weakened in many places. John Paul II left to his successors and to all of us a Church which, despite everything, remains alive and young." Does this "young and alive Church" of John Paul II have a chance to survive in today's world of chaos?

This young Church is now an old church. If there is a generation of John Paul II, that generation is growing old. A new generation has arrived that didn't know John Paul II. They don't have the taste of what World Youth Day meant. They didn't have the opportunity to meet a man of this type: you see him and your thoughts go straight to God. After meeting someone like Wojtyła, you would like to go on a mission to the end of the world, or do something for humanity. This is what Wojtyła brought out of us.

People live in a state of religious pathos which focuses on secondary things. There is a religious attitude towards animals, a religious outlook on environmentalism or women's rights. People are increasingly frustrated; they cannot free themselves from fear, loneliness, and failure. I think that John Paul II undertook a certain form of seeding. He left behind for us an arsenal. A beautiful book has recently come out: *God Dwells in Holland*. The Netherlands used to be a nation of many saints and many missionaries, but now its churches have been closing. Today, there is an attempt to remove saints from the pedestal. They can't be there. Stars and celebrities are placed on the pedestal.

You once said in an interview: "At the same time, there came a great de-Wojtyłazation; there has been a great cleaning up after John Paul II." What did you mean by that?

There are many examples: the destruction of monuments to John Paul II, ascribing all social evil to John Paul II. I also see a duality in the Church among the faithful. For example, the Italian bishops issued a letter apologizing to the faithful for John Paul II's teaching on marriage and sexuality. In other words, we apologize for John Paul II. We apologize for him being demanding. We apologize for him preaching the Gospel. We apologize for him having conveyed to us the mystery of life with Christ. Two French theologians published an article in the influential French newspaper *Le Monde* saying that John Paul II should be decanonized.

I would like to clarify one thing here: John Paul II was not a politician, as some people say. The greatest achievement of his pontificate was not the defeat of communism but the restoration of faith in God's action in man — holiness. We started to believe again that God's love had a plan for our life, that one could describe life in terms of a vocation.

I remember an interview with Jasio Gawronski, an Italian of Polish origin, in which John Paul II said: "I have never claimed for myself such a role or such merits. Why? Because I saw that communism would collapse sooner or later. I sensed that it was proposing something false to people; it had a false history and a false vision of man." Primate Wyszyński, after being released from prison, knew how to help Catholics in an atheistic country: you need to strengthen their baptismal identity. Dan Rideli Baca beautifully wrote that the crisis of Western civilization, which is predicated on a certain degradation of the human person, can be overcome by restoring to man an undeniable human value, i.e., by personalizing him.

A vivid example of personalization is the establishment of the Solidarity movement in Poland, or World Youth Day. Through such things, many people came to believe that life made sense once again. I think that one day we will learn to go back to Karol Wojtyła, who cannot be known or understood without Christ.

What do we need to build a civilization of love?

John Paul II wrote us a beautiful prophetic letter, *Novo millennio ineunte* — "at the beginning of the new millennium." In this document, he asked himself: how are these generations going to deal with the new difficulties? He replied that the Church has no magic formula for human life, no merely philosophical or ethical advice, and no therapeutic program of any kind. Its only message is Christ. For us, the truth has the face of Christ. For us, therapy has the face of Christ. If we are able to preach Christ to the people and show them the beauty of Christian life, I will say, following Fr. Józef Tischner, that there is no way that it will fail to work.

I would like to point out that my choice of Polish language and letters was determined by a clear inclination toward literature... This opened up completely new horizons for me; it introduced me to the mystery of language itself.... As I came to appreciate the power of the word in my literary and linguistic studies, I inevitably drew closer to the mystery of the Word — that Word of which we speak every day in the Angelus: "And the Word became flesh and dwelt among us" (Jn 1:14).

John Paul II

ARCHBISHOP TADEUSZ KONDRUSIEWICZ

Belarusian prelate of the Catholic Church who served as Archbishop of Minsk-Mohilev from 2007 to 2021. In 1989, Pope John Paul II appointed and consecrated him Apostolic Administrator of Minsk, Belarus, and Titular Bishop of Hippo Diarrhytus.

Under what circumstances did Your Excellency meet John Paul II?

In 1986, while visiting Rome, during a general audience at St. Peter's Square on Wednesday, I was introduced to Pope John Paul II. I saw how people were drawn to him, how they listened to his every word, and how vividly they reacted to his gestures. I was pleasantly surprised at how carefully he listened to his interlocutor.

Tell us about your collaboration with the Holy Father.

The cooperation, a very close one, started after my episcopal consecration by John Paul II at the Basilica of St. Peter in Rome on October 20, 1989. I became the first bishop in Belarus after half a century. Everything was new for me, but the situation of the Church, in Belarus and throughout the former Soviet Union, was not new for John Paul II. In 1991, the pope sent me to Russia. I became the first Catholic bishop in Moscow. During my stay in Rome, he wanted to talk to me to get to know the situation better, to advise me and support me. He shared my successes and difficulties alike. When I spoke about the latter, he would always say, "Remember Mary's Fatima prophecy that her Immaculate Heart will triumph and Russia will convert." It lightened my heart.

What was your greatest surprise about John Paul II?

His was open to all people and to different religions, especially to the Orthodox Church. He was looking for unity. He supported the development of the social doctrine of the Church and its implementation. And, of course, he was the voice of conscience in the modern world. He courageously took up the most acute problems of the modern world in order to solve them.

In a world that allegedly rejected God and was divided by the ideologies of capitalism and Marxism, the election of the Polish Pope on October 16,

1978, must have been a great comfort to the Catholics in Belarus. What did the choice of a Pole as the successor of St. Peter mean for Belarusians?

I remember that day very well. At that time, I was a second-year seminarian in Kaunas, Lithuania. There was a great deal of unbelievable excitement and agitation, because the successor of St. Peter hailed from a communist country. The clerics and simple people agreed that he would know how to break the atheistic resistance. And they were not disappointed. A similar situation prevailed in Belarus: with the election of Pope Wojtyła, the star of hope started shining.

How was John Paul II's call — "Do not be afraid. Open the door to Christ"— understood by the faithful behind the Iron Curtain?

The faithful of the former USSR, including Belarus, welcomed the election of John Paul II with great enthusiasm. They asked one another when, if ever, the door of the Soviet Union would be opened to Christ, and was that even possible. This call of John Paul II gave them renewed hope that religious freedom would arrive, and it really transpired during his pontificate.

What was the pope's goal in striving for the unity of Western and Eastern Christians?

John Paul II understood very well the words Christ uttered during the Last Supper: "that they may all be one," and took them deeply to heart. The division of Christians is a bleeding wound on the Mystical Body of Christ and it must be healed. Further, unity is our strength. Christians should be united to face the challenges of the modern secular world together. The question now is not simply "To be or not to be?" but "To be or not to be for Christianity?"

Once you said: "John Paul II, of course, was at the center. When it seemed that everyone had thrown up their hands because the Soviet Union was so strong, he kept faith. He believed Our Lady of Fatima that Russia would convert."

As Christ says: "Faith moves mountains." Faith manifests itself through prayer. In times of persecution, there were no churches, priests, religious literature, etc., but prayer. Prayer needs action. And the major protagonist in this battlefield for the freedom and unity of Christians, especially with the Russian Orthodox Church, was John Paul II. He told me of his pain over the existing divisions and misunderstandings. He did his best. He told me how dear the icon of Our Lady of Kazan was to him. He kept it on the wall of his study for ten years before bequeathing it to Patriarch Alexi II of Moscow.

Once John Paul II said that "forgiveness is not weakness, but strength, because by it you overcome yourself."

By forgiving another, we truly reconcile with him, but at the same time we also overcome ourselves, our anger and our dissatisfaction. It is not easy. But the words of Christ on the Cross: "Father, forgive them, for they know not what they do," should lift us up. By forgiving, we cast off the burden of evil and set out on the path of peace. And the peacemakers will be blessed, says Christ.

Do you remember your last meeting with John Paul II?

I remember that meeting very well. It took place on March 8, 2005 — exactly one month before his funeral. I was in Rome and received the message that the Holy Father wanted to see me at the Gemelli Hospital. I was told to wait a while because he was saying Vespers. I entered the room and saw him sitting in a rather high chair. He recognized me immediately, smiled, and asked in a rather hoarse voice: "What's going on in Moscow?" It was all him: John Paul the Great — the Shepherd of the Universal Church. I was a bishop in Moscow at the time and he asked me about the Russian capital. We talked a bit about the situation of the Church in Russia. I left the hospital after receiving a blessing for myself and for the Church in Russia.

What do you miss the most about John Paul II?

His call to live by the truth that sets you free. The modern world ascends to the summits of prosperity, but at the same time it descends to the lowlands of morality, for modern man lives his own truth instead of the revealed truth.

What do we need to build a civilization of love?

We need the love of God and of our neighbor. Instead of lies there should be truth; instead of evil, good; instead of hate, love; instead of condemnation, forgiveness; instead of divisions, unity.

MOTHER ADELA GALINDO

Foundress of the Servants of the Pierced Hearts of Jesus and Mary, in the Archdiocese of Miami

What do you remember from your first meeting with St. John Paul II?

My heart met St. John Paul II on the day of his election, October 16, 1978. It was a deep experience of communion with his heart, beyond human understanding, but marked my life and my future in a singular way. I met him in person on September 11, 1987, during his pastoral visit to Miami. The Holy Mass was to take place in Tamiami Park, in the heart of the city. At that time, I was the leader of our parish youth group and of a formation group for young women. I had already made vows and was living in community with the first three young women with whom our Religious Institute began.

The night before the Mass, we, together with about 100 young people from our prayer groups, spent the whole night doing a prayer vigil with great expectation for the Holy Mass that was to take place the following morning. People began arriving at the park, which was divided into sections by chain link fences. We were in our section, singing, praying the rosary, reading writings of St. John Paul II, discussing his life as a young man and many other aspects of his life and witness. We were doing this until the time for Mass approached. Suddenly, St. John Paul II arrived in the Popemobile and began to go around the different sections. When he passed in front of us, our eyes met and in a matter of seconds I experienced the same communion of hearts that I had experienced nine years before when on the day he was elected I exclaimed, without fully understanding, that I found in him the heart I had been looking for.

Holy Mass began with a million and a half people shouting, "John Paul II, we love you!" It was such a manifestation of love and gratitude for this great man who was our pope. When the first reading began, suddenly the whole sky became very dark and rain began to pour very heavily upon us all. We could see that the dark clouds were covering only the park, and beyond it was as clear as a sunny Miami day. I could feel in my heart that a spiritual battle was taking place. The rain continued to grow stronger and then thunderstorms began.

We could see the national security and archdiocesan officials gathering to speak. My heart began pounding fast; I was afraid the Mass was going to be canceled. The rain and thunderstorms continued. Within a few minutes, we heard an announcement from the archbishop of Miami that for security concerns they were requesting that everyone leave, since we were in an open space with dangerous thunderstorms, and that the Mass had been canceled. I could not believe it. It could not be possible! I remember holding the chain link fence with both of my hands and praying in such a profound desolation as I saw the crowds running and leaving. I remember sensing that this desolation was the one that a mother feels when her children have abandoned her. I knew, somehow, that this was not only a personal experience, but that the Lord was allowing me to feel what the heart and womb of the Church, our Mother, feels when so many of her children abandon her and her Magisterium.

At that moment, I made a choice while I saw the multitudes leaving. My choice was to stay, because I knew that John Paul II was somewhere in a trailer or portable chapel not visible to the public, finishing the Holy Mass. I told the young people with us to feel free to go or stay but that I was staying. They all chose to stay, so I told them to run together to the front of the park, where the priests had been sitting, and to sing out loud for the Holy Father to know that some of us had not left him alone. We ran through the mud and finally reached the section just across from the altar, which was raised by probably twenty-five steps. I saw some FBI agents who wanted us to leave because, they said, the pope was not there. I responded by asking, if he was not there, what they were accomplishing by standing there. They tried to make us leave several times and every time I responded that I could feel the Holy Father's heart close by and that he would never interrupt a Mass but was probably finishing it in a portable trailer. Interestingly, the rain and thunderstorms stopped as soon as the multitudes left.

We sang with all the strength of our hearts for about thirty minutes, when suddenly I could see someone who had come out and was close to the altar. I recognized the Holy Father's Master of Ceremonies. He began to walk down the steps and came directly to me. My heart was beyond exultation. He kindly told me: "The Holy Father is going to come and greet you personally out of gratitude." There were a hundred of us young people, and maybe around thirty adults who had seen us stay.

Fifteen minutes later, the Holy Father, my beloved John Paul II, came out. I could see, even from where we were, the man dressed in white, with his hands crossed over his chest, with a smile that spoke so deeply to my heart. He came down from by the altar and approached us. When he was close to us, he turned to me, looked into my eyes as if we knew each other personally, and began to speak words that have remained engraved in my whole being until today. He said: "Thank you for your faithfulness, for staying with the pope in the middle of the storm, for not being afraid of the dangers that threatened you. You chose to be faithful, close to my heart." I replied through my tears: "Holy Father, I will always be faithful to you; I will always stay close to your heart; I will always be strong to face the challenges so as to be a good daughter of the Church, and of you." He looked with a deep humility and gratitude and said: "Because you have been faithful, because you did not leave and chose to stay, because you embraced any dangers the storm brought with it, I will bless you especially and I will give you an apostolic blessing for your present and for your future." We fell on our knees, and he blessed us. I kissed his hands and he held my face with his two hands and said again: "Thank you for your faithfulness."

He turned around and left, while we continued to sing until we saw the helicopter leave the area. His words were for me a confirmation of the spiritual communion I had experienced when he came out to the balcony on the day of his election. They also became a path for my life: *I will always be close to his heart, his teachings, and his legacy.* This is a reality for me as a foundress, and even more so after he departed for the Father's House.

What or rather who inspired you to found the Servants of the Pierced Hearts of Jesus and Mary?

The original grace for what would one day become our Religious Institute was given to me on July 11, 1984, just a few months after the consecration of the whole world to the Immaculate Heart by St. John Paul II. I mention this detail because somehow everything in our foundation is intertwined with actions, gestures, or teachings of our beloved saint. Being Marian by conception, as I describe myself, the *Totus Tuus* pope became for me, after Our Lady, a brilliant star to guide my path. On that July 11, I received an immense grace that we called in our history "the exchange of hearts with Our Lady." It took place at a Marian shrine, at the end of a youth mission. From that moment, I knew Our Lady was preparing me for a mission that had never even crossed my mind: "to live the mission of a pelican." The pelican was an image that, from the beginning of 1984, was manifested to me in prayer very regularly. The meaning of the pelican is the call to allow my heart to be pierced for others to have life.

In 1985, after reading the Apostolic Letter *Dilecti amici* and seeing how much John Paul II trusted in the response of the youth to do great works for God and Our Lady, I felt a strong sense of responsibility to be faithful to the promise I had made to Our Lady when I was a child: "I will always say yes to you, whatever you ask of me." Wanting to always be the smallest daughter of Our Lady and having experienced a deep communion with the heart of John Paul, I felt called to give my life entirely through making private vows and dedicating my life to fulfilling his plans of love and evangelizing many hearts in many places. Since I was a child, I wanted everyone to love Our Lady because I was convinced she was the sure path to Jesus. To Jesus through Mary! I never imagined that from that simple and small "Fiat," a short time later, some young women would want to follow the choice I had made. At that moment the Church requested that we begin living in community *ad experimentum*.

In 1990, our Marian charism of religious life received the first canonical approval as a Public Association of the faithful, in view of becoming a Religious Institute of Diocesan Right in the future. This final approval took place on March 25, 2000, during the Jubilee Year of the Incarnation, when St. John Paul II had said that during that year the pierced heart of Christ would be opened wide to pour forth many graces in the Church and he would distribute them through the heart of his Mother. We were direct recipients of this grace on March 25, the Solemnity of the Incarnation. Everything we are is Marian, everything in our history is Marian; everything is so marked by the presence of St. John Paul II while he was among us on earth, and in an even greater way, after going to the house of the Father.

Why did you choose St. John Paul II as a patron of your Institute?

In reality, I did not choose St. John Paul II as a patron of our Institute; rather, I would say, Our Lady chose to spiritually form our hearts to become one in mind, spirit, purpose, and mission. I have witnessed throughout my life to the spiritual and paternal care and guidance of St. John Paul II. He is the spiritual father not only of our religious family—sisters, brothers and priests—but of all our spiritual family which consists of deacons, lay members, families, university students, youth, missionary branches, and Marian missions in many parts of the world.

From the very beginning of our foundation, we were consumed by the ardor to evangelize in all ways possible. The call of St. John Paul II to be witnesses and missionaries of the New Evangelization, with a new ardor, new methods, new expressions under the banner of Our Lady, was so deeply engraved in our own apostolic identity and mission. In some mysterious ways, humanly speaking, I always sensed that Our Lady had given birth to this new religious institute to be in total communion with the heart of St. John Paul II and to have a mutual spiritual communion that would sustain and confirm the mission of each of us (maintaining the great distance between his mission and mine). All our apostolic endeavors inspired by the Lord and our Blessed Mother were, without us knowing at the time, a response to what St. John Paul II would request of the Church in his encyclicals, apostolic letters, addresses, etc. All his Magisterium would become the confirmation of our charism, identity, and mission, already written before he would teach it. He was the Petrine principle confirming this Marian charism, and we were the Marian principle responding with promptitude to the Petrine principle and incarnating his luminous and powerful Magisterium. This charism was born and gradually discovered itself to be a response, a singular response, to the heart of St. John Paul II.

Why did you decide to follow John Paul II and dedicate your life to keeping his mission alive?

On October 16, 1978, Karol Wojtyła was elevated to the pontificate, a great gift of the merciful heart of Christ and of the maternal heart of the Blessed Mother: a great, unimaginable gift for the life of the Church at the end of the Second Millennium. A man, a pope, who, with his oblative love and with his piercing gaze into the mysteries of the love of God and the mysteries of the human heart, would mark the path of the Church of the Third Millennium. On that day, my spiritual father was also born. I can remember, even though I was very young, that moment when he came out on the balcony — and I saw his face. By the grace of God, I was able to contemplate the profound inner freedom of his heart — and to exclaim these words: "I have found the heart that I have been looking for." Perhaps in that exclamation, I did not have a complete awareness of what my soul understood, but I knew that in St. John Paul II there was a luminous path which I had to follow, a gift that my Mother, Our Lady, was giving me! My path and my Marian heart had found in his heart their deepest identity, their fullest realization, the greatest confirmation of what Our Lady had taught me in the school of her maternal heart. I could follow this luminous star with freedom, with feminine interior strength and wisdom, and without fear in a world full of challenges that he had not only faced and confronted, but to which he had given us the answers by the choices he had made defending at all costs the dignity of the human person. All this was deeply engraved in my heart from early youth, and for the first time I found a human person that I could admire in his totality. His life was the most coherent testimony to his words.

Even though at that time it was difficult to find his writings, I did everything possible to obtain every word, addresses, document, audience that he gave. His Magisterium was a treasure for my heart, a gift that was so easy for me to understand and gaze deeply at. Therefore, I was convinced that this gift was also my task. I had to dedicate myself to teach and form all the dimensions of human life and the fundamental questions of the human heart, based on his Magisterium and legacy contemplated through the Marian charism that I had received. I fulfilled and continue to fulfill this mission through conferences, talks, radio programs, writings, social media, congresses, TV programs, interviews, pilgrimages, and all means available to make his legacy known and keep it alive in the heart of the Church.

Throughout his pontificate, as I constantly listened and studied every teaching he gave us, I understood that I had received the call to spread and promote the legacy of St. John Paul II as a fundamental task of my life. His legacy is a necessary and luminous path for the Church of the Third Millennium. This vocation would be particularly sealed in my heart and would also be a crucial task for me after his passing. So many deep experiences have marked this path for my life and mission, so many confirmations that Our Lord and Our Lady have requested this of me: I had to form many hearts to be witnesses to love, so as to go out into the deep of our difficult times, without fear, proclaiming that love is the essence and the vocation of the human heart and the only way of building a new civilization, a world that can be a home for the human person.

What's the legacy of St. John Paul II?

There are no words to describe the profound gratitude that we should feel toward God the Father for elevating, in the heart of the

Church and of the world and before our eyes, this great witness of love, truth, life and hope. Even after his death he continues doing what he did during his earthly life: being a witness. He was, is, and continues to be, in the heart of the Church and of the world, a great witness. The Lord and Our Lady raised up this luminous witness in one of the darkest periods of history to leave a legacy that can illumine the path and the history of the Church and humanity of the third millennium. As difficult as it is to choose some of the dimensions of his life that communicate in a clear manner his mission to be a witness, there are a few that I can mention.

To be a faithful witness, an ardent witness that love can do all things, that love is possible and that love is our greatest dignity, vocation, and mission. That love is not a utopia, but rather it is capable of building a new civilization when each heart makes choices of love with responsibility. He said, "Love explained everything to me, love solved everything for me; that is why I admired love wherever it is found"; this has been one of the mottoes of my life. Love is authentic only when it is responsible. What a teaching!

To be a witness that darkness and evil do not have the last word, that evil has a limit: the potency of Divine Mercy that pardons all, heals all, restores all, elevates all, and recreates all things. It brings out from all that is evil an infinitely greater good. Love always triumphs!

To be a witness to the gift of the maternal heart of the Virgin Mary; he was a son of Our Lady giving total freedom to her maternal mediation in his life. He was a great witness of the potency of belonging totally to Our Lady's heart, which is the most perfect and efficacious home and school for forming the human heart in the ways of heroic love, life-giving purity, and holiness. His *Totus Tuus* — "I am all yours and all that I have is yours" — created a revolution of love for our Blessed Mother that allowed her to touch millions of hearts and also to intervene in so many historic events.

To be a witness to the dignity and greatness of the human person, that man is capable of God, capable of loving as He has loved us. He is a witness that the human person was created for true freedom, a freedom that resides in the gift of being able to choose what is good, to make choices of the highest degree of love, choices that transform his personal history, the history of humanity, and the history of the world. Every choice of love has a profound effect that goes beyond the individual and has the power to change the course of history.

To be a witness to the salvific power of human suffering. John Paul II, formed in the school of the Cross since he was a child, was a witness that suffering, in all its forms, only reaches its most profound meaning and its highest fecundity if united to the Cross of our Redeemer. He knew the pain of the loss of his loved ones, his friends, his mentors, his brother seminarians... He knew the effects of lack of freedom, of the trampling of human dignity, of persecution, of war, of injustice, of loneliness, of infirmity, the tragedy of the destruction of human life and its dignity by totalitarian systems. He deeply understood that a society without God, a world without God, will always turn against the human person. John Paul knew the cruciform shape of human suffering: he learned the wisdom of the science of the Cross, teaching us its profound meaning and redemptive value.

To be a witness that love is the most precious gift and most arduous task of the human person. That love, which is always a gift, should be cultivated, guarded, communicated, and elevated with the mature response of the heart. John Paul was a valiant and untiring witness to the family and its mission in the life of the Church and the world. He taught us that the family is the place where the human person learns to love, experiences love, and is formed to love; that the family is the home and school of the human heart, the place where the civilization of love begins and is built. As he taught us: the family "is the way of man" and, therefore, is "the way of the Church."

To be a witness to the sacredness of life. He taught us to "embrace" each child and to discover in its face the tenderness of God. He taught us to defend life with courage in every Areopagus of the world; to make ourselves present in our historical moment and to be the voice of those who do not have one, to be the voice of the unborn; to be the voice of forgotten and abandoned elderly; to be the voice of those who suffer violence from others, to defend life in all stages.

To be an untiring witness of the New Evangelization that is so urgently needed in our world and in our times. He was a witness to the Gospel before men, before the Church, and before the world — unto the ends of the earth. With an acute gaze, with a missionary ardor, and under the star of the New Evangelization, he disposed himself with generosity to go to all peoples, to row all the oceans that presented themselves before his eyes, and to row them even though their waves were very high and the storms struck the bark of Peter. John Paul rowed out into the deep and he called us — the Church of the Third Millennium — to do the same.

What did John Paul II mean to you personally?

In the Song of Songs 8:6, the Lord gives us a very piercing word: "Set me as a seal upon your heart, as a seal upon your arm; for love is strong as death"; yes, indeed, love is even stronger than death, love is a seal upon the human heart, love conquers the uncertainties and fears of the human person. What a message so powerfully lived and transmitted by St. John Paul II, and which I have always lived by.

At his final illness, the world united in prayer with tears of sorrow; the heart of humanity accompanied in prayer and rendered its most beautiful tribute of love to the great witness to the love of Christ in our times. What a mysterious power love has! This is precisely what I believe to be the greatest legacy that St. John Paul II has left us, has left me.

Yes, he will be known in history as St. John Paul II the Great, but in my heart the title "the great" remains too small; it falls short of the greatness of his heart, of his life, of his person, and of his Magisterium. Among all the luminous treasures he gave us, the greatest has been, is, and will be to have been a true *witness to love and truth*.

His parting caused in my heart profound sorrow because, from the beginning of his pontificate, and in a particular way since the beginning of my vocation and the foundation of the congregation, his spiritual paternity had been fully connected to my soul. This paternity has been a beautiful gift of mercy that I received from the heart of Christ; a gift for my life, for the life of all the sisters, brothers, and priests, and for the spiritual family of the Pierced Hearts.

I can, with great certainty and utmost gratitude to the Lord, say that John Paul II has been the person here on earth who most influenced my heart, my person, my thinking, my sentiments, my way of gazing at life, of valuing the human person — and of understanding everything, even sufferings, as necessary for the fecundity of the Church and of the mission the Lord has entrusted to me. St. John Paul has been, and I know he will continue to be, the lighthouse, who after the Blessed Mother is the most luminous star that has illumined the narrow and arduous path of my life, vocation, and mission. He is the person that throughout my life I have most deeply admired and whose example I desired to follow. Because of my mission as a foundress and as an international speaker, and because of my constant presence in social media, I have encountered millions of people in the Church and in other sectors of society. I can say in all honesty that only St. John Paul II has truly touched my life because of all he was and did, and what he continues to be. As the Custodian of his pilgrim relic in North America, I have seen him acting just as he did when he made his apostolic visits throughout the world. I am a witness that he continues to fulfill the promise he made to us in his last trip to Mexico, for the beatification of St. Juan Diego: "I go but I do not go, I go but I stay.... Because even though I go, my heart will remain." I am so grateful that even though he went to the house of the Father, he has spiritually stayed with us, with me.

What are your thoughts on John Paul II and youth?

At his Mass of Installation on October 22, 1978, he came down from the sanctuary to approach the youth, and he gave them three statements that revealed his heart and his love for them: "I believe in you"; "I trust in you"; "the Church needs you."

From that moment the young people understood that St. John Paul II had a deep love for them, which had been manifested since he was a young parish priest in charge of the youth group. Young people were disoriented by the many forces and winds blowing in our society presenting them with ways of false happiness. The voice of the world was loudly speaking to their hearts, and St. John Paul II knew he had to raise the voice of Christ for them to find the true happiness that can only be found in him and in his Gospel. The storms of confusion were hitting their minds and hearts, and his closeness meant that in him they would find a good shepherd to lead them through the desert of our time, towards green pastures of true rest and peace, and pure waters of the truth that is the foundation of freedom.

The youth were seeking answers to the many questions raised in their hearts. St. John Paul II taught them that the only One who has all the answers for the restlessness of the human heart is Jesus himself. He created World Youth Day to gather the youth of the world and allow them to see that they were not alone, that they had a big family of brothers and sisters journeying the same path. But also, he wanted to be with them and let them present their questions, their dreams, their fears, and their desires, and with great paternal joy and serenity, to answer each of them, giving them a clear path to follow and not be lost in the way.

St. John Paul II knew the power and the strength of young hearts. So much depended on them. They were builders, not spectators. He wanted them to understand the importance of their stage in life — a time of fundamental choices, a time to discover their purpose and vocation in life, a time to define their place in history — and he exhorted them not to listen to the voices of the world but to be the sentinels and apostles of a new civilization. He believed that the future of humanity rested in the hands of the youth, in the choices of the youth, in the strength of the youth and their powerful witness to a culture of love and life.

Why was Pope John Paul II's canonization such a significant moment for the Church and the world?

The Lord says in the Gospel of Matthew (5:14–16): "You are the light of the world. A city set on a mountain cannot be hidden. Nor do they light a lamp and then put it under a bushel basket; it is set on a lampstand, where it gives light to all in the house. Just so, your light must shine before others, that they may see your good deeds and glorify your heavenly Father." This passage of the Gospel shows how much the Lord needs us to be a light in the world, and sometimes with more luminosity in dark periods. St. John Paul II was definitely in every stage of his life a witness to others in the coherence of his choices with the Gospel of Christ. This caused so many of his friends, even those who were not Catholic, to admire him and to trust in him, in the solidity of his character and in his unconditional selflessness. From his youth he was a clear light for many, especially in times of great tribulation, who were always seeking an answer from Karol, for the reason of human actions, human suffering, and the moral way of responding to the challenges they faced. He had answers, which he explained in a simple and respectful manner, because he had already been dealing and struggling in prayer with the same fundamental questions. From living so many painful human experiences, seeing the evil that men's choices were capable of and knowing that the human person had always the inner freedom to choose what is good and most noble, what is moral and ethical, he was convinced that it was truly necessary for the human heart to deal with fundamental questions and to reach fundamental answers that would really elevate the fullness of their human potentialities. He illumined his dark times, reminding those around him of this truth. He continues to do so, into our present historic times and for all humanity.

Through his canonization the light of his person, his heart, his wisdom, his witness, and his Magisterium were placed on a lampstand for the world to see or to remember. This legacy must continue to be a shining light for the hearts and minds of the men and women of the 21st century. As he once said in the *Letter to Families*, our age is marked by a crisis of truth that distorted all concepts, creating a false understand of the definition of every word. This has profound consequences for our choices, destabilizing the foundation of society. St. John Paul II believed that only when our concepts are correct would a new civilization be able to be built.

His canonization was a moment to remind us how much we need his legacy to survive as a healthy human society and to not fall into the traps of false concepts created by totalitarian systems, inhumane structures that manipulate language and concepts to sound in favor of the human person while in reality it is trampled, and by immoral and atheistic agendas to create a world without God. He told us very clearly that a world without God would turn against men. This was for him not a theory but a lived experience.

What do you anticipate will be most remembered about Pope John Paul II?
It is hard to name one or just a few things for which he will be remembered. Everything about him continues to be remembered by millions of people who still exclaim: "John Paul II, we love you." In my mission taking the pilgrim relic of his liquid blood throughout North America, I can tell you that people not only have not forgotten him but they miss him and are willing to spend fourteen hours in the heat standing in line just to venerate his relic for a few seconds, to present their intentions, to see some part of him and to feel his presence and closeness.

All of them have so many stories to share, so many testimonies of healing, reconciliations in their families, interventions of John Paul II in difficult situations in their lives. All of them trust in his powerful intercession. They remember something special that occurred to them when he came to their country in an apostolic visit. I myself have witnessed so many different types of miracles during the ministry with his relic.

He continues to act in the same way he did when he was among us, receiving each person and dealing with their specific needs. It is hard to explain this succinctly, but I can tell you that not only do people remember him but he remembers everyone he saw, he spoke with, he dealt with and touched, or who served him during those visits. This for me is a very moving witness that he continues to gaze at each of us with the same paternal love he showed on earth. Now it is even more visible and universal, since he is in heaven. I have witnessed too that he is fulfilling promises that he made to bishops, priests, or lay people and that he has not forgotten to fulfill them even after death. This makes me feel so humbled to be able to help him do all that he desires by taking him in his relic to where he wants to go and to whom he desires to touch. St. John Paul II is simply and will be simply remembered for everything he was and continues to be. Part of my mission is to keep alive his memory and legacy. The mission entrusted by the Lord and Our Lady to this simple servant has also become the mission of my spiritual daughters and sons. Our whole religious family and spiritual family have the gift and task of keeping the legacy of St. John Paul II alive in the heart of the Church and in the heart of the world. Maybe, just maybe, because of this task, we have been entrusted with the mission of taking the pilgrim relic of the blood of St. John Paul II through the continent of America on five occasions. It is not just a pilgrimage, it is a mission to teach, form, and remember the pastoral care he gave to this continent. After all, it was in America during his last trip after the canonization of St. Juan Diego, the visionary of Our Lady of Guadalupe, that he said before boarding his plane: "I go but I do not go; I leave but I do not leave because my heart will always remain." It is my joy and the joy of our religious family to be entrusted with the spiritual mission to keep his heart, person, mission, and magisterium alive for many to discover the great gift that the Holy Spirit gave to the Church through this son of Poland.

What do we need to build the civilization of love?

I would say that it is important to understand the role of culture in the life and formation of the human person. Culture is the "home" or environment that develops values, traditions, principles, and perspectives in the human person. A culture that loses this capacity corrupts the authentic development of the person and creates in him a sense of loss of meaning, purpose, and direction.

It is interesting to note that totalitarian systems have as their first purpose the destruction of the culture and the freedom of the society of a country; then, they move to destroy the family, to take away the liberty of the human person at all levels. Culture has been deeply affected by hidden agendas to change the makeup of humanity.

As St. John Paul II urged us so many times, we need to build a new civilization, or new culture, that returns to the power of principles founded on the truth about the human person, about family, and about authentic freedom to use our gifts in the service of society. A new civilization, at this moment, would require first of all that we make a commitment to reason with informed minds about all the slogans that are flooding society through so many channels as statements of truth. A new civilization would require strong characters and intrepid apostles to choose, as John Paul II did, not to allow the environment to determine choices but to freely choose what is good, to build a more humane society, a civilization of love.

John Paul II saw the horrors of the Nazi and Communist regimes, saw death all around him, saw injustice, antisemitism, imprisonment, concentration camps, the destruction of the education system, and persecution of the Church at all levels, creating a culture of fear and intolerance of truth. Before so much evil in all its forms, he did not become a man of hatred or revenge. He could have easily and even understandably become that kind of man. Nevertheless, he knew that the horrible actions that surrounded him, even though they affected him so profoundly, did not take away his freedom to choose the greater good: he chose to become a priest! A man totally given to serve his brothers and sisters, to teach the truth about the human person and the values of the Kingdom of God; to not fight with weapons that only foster the culture of death, but to fight with the power of love and truth, the only power that can change the human heart and the world. While prostrated on the floor during his ordination, when he saw himself being ordained alone and knowing that many of his companions had been killed, he prayed: "If I have been preserved, Lord, it is to donate myself." I will always be sustained and inspired by these words and by his choice to freely make of his life a total gift of self for the good of the Church and humanity.

MAESTRO PLÁCIDO DOMINGO

Recognized as one of the greatest living opera singers, Domingo is also a conductor, with over 600 opera and symphonic performances to his credit, and has been Honorary Artistic Director of the Centennial Festival of the Arena di Verona and General Manager of the Los Angeles Opera and the Washington National Opera. For over ten years, he performed in the concerts of The Three Tenors with José Carreras and Luciano Pavarotti. He has received 12 Grammy Awards.

What did St. John Paul II mean for you?

He was like a beacon, and since his election as pope in 1978 he enlightened the world. I will never forget his gaze, the incredible vigor of this man till the end of his days, despite his illness. He told us not to be afraid and he showed it with his own life, in every journey and in every trial he suffered.

When did you learn about Wojtyła's poetry? Is there any particular poem that is close to your heart?

I have always felt deep admiration for this man. He once declared: "The world of culture and art is called to build mankind, to support the human journey in the troubled search for truth, goodness, beauty." As a young priest in Poland he worked with children and loved Gregorian chant and other music. When he became pope, in addition to the physical vigour and passion for sport that brought him so close to young people and made him so unusual compared to his predecessors, Pope Wojtyła had a beautiful voice. While preparing the album *Amore Infinito*, I was able to delve into each poem, and it was the strength of his simplicity that moved me. In particular, in "Resound My Soul" I felt the gratitude to God and the bursting energy of the young man who had written it, and in "Mother" his melancholic emotion in front of the tomb of his mother, and those touching and faith-filled words: "from me, your son, you will have a prayer, a song, love that will live...."

How did you come up with the idea of recording songs inspired by the poems of Wojtyła?

The idea for *Amore Infinito* came after a special concert in Ancona, Italy, in 2004, where I sang the *"Canto di pace"* composed by Marco Tutino, who set to music words written Pope John Paul II himself. After the concert, I was received with my family in audience by the Holy Father and I asked him for the privilege of singing his poems. It was a meeting I have never forgotten, a meeting with such an extraordinary man who would be proclaimed a saint.

On the back cover of Amore Infinito *you commented: "These songs have enormous significance for me.... They will speak not only to religious people but to anyone who respects that uniquely great man, John Paul II, who chose to dedicate his life to the service of humanity and of God."*

I wanted to pay homage to the Holy Father. There were many compositions to choose from, and setting music and singing texts with a more theological or scriptural focus would have required a different approach. So we found the poems written by the "man" Karol Wojtyła: the profound humanity of these writings impressed me so much that I thought it would be wonderful to be able to use my voice as an instrument to share them and make them known.

Why did you decide to record this album? What kind of message did you want to share with the world?

With this album I wanted to transmit my boundless admiration for this man, then pontiff and now saint; I wanted to spread through music the profundity of his poetry.

The songs — in English, Spanish, and Italian — are based on poems Wojtyła wrote before his election as pope in 1978. What criteria did you use to select the poems?

I shared the idea for this album with my son Plácido Jr. Together we selected the poems and then called composers such as Maurizio Fabrizio, Antonio Galbiati, Fio Zanotti, Kaballà: it was a beautiful team effort. For me, this was the most important album of my entire career for its human and spiritual value.

You decided on poems without a specifically Catholic message. Why?

The message of these poems cannot be only for a few, because the love expressed by Wojtyła is a universal language open to all and knows no boundaries.

On Amore Infinito, *you sing duets with Josh Groban, Andrea Bocelli, Vanessa Williams, and Katherine Jenkins as well as with your son, Plácido Domingo Jr. Please briefly explain these collaborations.*

They are formidable artists and I have had a friendship with them for years. They enthusiastically signed up for this album, also admiring and fascinated by the depth and humanity of the poems of this extraordinary man. I have worked extensively with my son, and it has given me great joy to discover with him the richness of these pages.

What do we need to build a civilization of love today?

The historical moment we are going through leads us to think about the values of our civilization. I believe that mutual love is the most solid foundation on which to build any kind of relationship between human beings, in both public and private life. In daily practice we can apply the word "love" in its most concrete connotation: mutual respect. This is also the greatest teaching that I received from my parents and that I have tried to follow in my life.

HIS HOLINESS THE DALAI LAMA

His Holiness the 14th Dalai Lama describes himself as a simple Buddhist monk. He is the spiritual leader of Tibet.

What did Saint John Paul II mean for you?

His Holiness Pope John Paul II was a man I held in high regard. He was a determined and deeply spiritual-minded person for whom I had great respect and admiration. Right from the start of our friendship he revealed to me privately that he had a clear understanding of the Tibetan problem because of his own experience of communism in Poland. His experience in Poland and my own difficulties with communists gave us an immediate common ground. The first time we met, he struck me as very practical and open, with a broad appreciation of global problems. I have no doubt that he was a great spiritual leader. I also have deep appreciation for the Pope's mission to bring peace to the world.

ARTURO MARI

> *Started his professional career in the Vatican when he was 16 years old. He dedicated 55 years of his life to immortalizing the most important moments of six different popes. He accompanied Pope John Paul II for almost 27 years. He treated him as a friend and father and belongs to the "pope's family" of close friends and associates.*

You were there for nearly every day of John Paul II's pontificate. You took millions of photos of the pope. Is there any particular photo that you like the most?

I took the most important photo of John Paul II on his last Good Friday, March 25, 2005. It was during the Way of the Cross in the Colosseum. John Paul II was too weak to participate in the ceremony in person. He stayed at the Apostolic Palace. He prayed in his private chapel with the cross in his hands. I caught a gesture that went otherwise unnoticed: the pope took the cross, put it to his head, kissed Christ, and then pressed the cross to his heart. I think this is the photo that best describes his whole pontificate.

Do you remember your first meeting with Karol Wojtyła?

I met Wojtyła during Vatican II. I was friends with Cardinal Stefan Wyszyński, the Polish Primate of the Millennium, and he introduced me to Bishop Wojtyła. He had an extraordinary mind. He explained to me the entire history of Poland and her suffering. Then, I was able to experience it myself when I traveled to Poland, together with the editor-in-chief of *L'Osservatore Romano*, Dr. Trassi, and Mario Ponti, as part of John Paul II's first papal pilgrimage to Poland. There was great despondency in the air. I saw streets, houses, and long lines for food. I also remember a Mass at the Victory Square in Warsaw, where John Paul II breathed the spirit into Poles, giving them strength and faith. Do the Polish people know how much their life has changed since 1978? I want the Polish people to remember how much this man—Karol Wojtyła—did for their nation. What a radical change took place in Poland. Remember his words as pope: "Freedom cannot be owned; it must be constantly won." Remember that.

What was your reaction when Karol Wojtyła became pope?

I almost had a heart attack. I was so happy. I was outside the Sistine Chapel and they opened the door. I was going to go in when I saw him a few feet away. He looked at me, he smiled, and then he said, "Look how I am dressed." He hugged me and blessed me, and I hurried off to work.

You dedicated much of your life to the Church as a lay person, camera in hand. How did you view your service to John Paul II?

I wanted people to see the great work of the Polish Pope, his personality, humility, and simplicity. The charisma of John Paul II was very important to me. He was a man ahead of his time. He is the only pope I have known to beautifully emphasize the value of womanhood. Whenever he met women, he saw Mother of God within them. He saw a woman as the heart of the whole family.

What were your most memorable moments with John Paul II that you have not shared with the public?

I remember June 3, 1983. Martial law had been imposed in Poland. The pope met with Lech Wałęsa, head of Solidarity, in the Chochołowska Valley, in the Tatra Mountains. It was an unofficial meeting, behind closed doors, without photographers — except for me. The secret police was doing everything to stop me. I took photos of John Paul II with Lech Wałęsa, but they were never published. The pope's meeting with Wałęsa had a spiritual dimension, although it could be used for political purposes and possibly lead to bloodshed. Only after the death of the Holy Father did we decide to publish them.

Another time, during a papal pilgrimage, I went to the leprosarium. I wanted to get out of there as soon as possible because of the stench, but John Paul II kissed and hugged each of these people. I was crying behind the camera.

Let's return to the attempted assassination of Pope John Paul II on May 13, 1981. Could you reflect on that day.

I was standing in front of the Arch of the Bells. There were about forty thousand people in St. Peter's Square. It was a warm day. I managed to take a picture of a little girl whom the Holy Father took in his arms, lifted into the air, kissed, and handed back to her parents. Then I heard the first shot. The second shot immediately followed. The Holy Father collapsed into the arms of Fr. Stanisław Dziwisz. I was standing about two feet away from him. A grimace of pain appeared on his face. My world collapsed. Pope John Paul II, my father, was dying before my eyes. I started taking pictures — instinctively. I have no idea how I took all these photos. The Madonna must have guided my hand. I caught the moment when Fr. Dziwisz caught the falling pope. I took five or six photos.

The pope was brought to the Vatican clinic. His voice kept getting weaker. He was praying. I heard him saying twice: "Black Madonna, my mother." A red stain had appeared on his cassock. Fr. Dziwisz grabbed the Holy Father. He squeezed his hand. He saved his life. Before the nurses arrived, the pope might have been bleeding out. At that moment, I didn't take any photos. The struggle for the life of our father was ongoing. I was praying. I did not take any photo of the pope until a few days after his operation.

What image of John Paul II remains in your heart?

I was impressed by his humility and his mercy. His *Totus Tuus* for children, youth, the elderly, and the sick. *Totus Tuus*, Mary; all yours, Mary, for others. He taught me that and it changed my whole life. You don't need big words to speak about John Paul II. His example, his way of being, speaking, and acting are testimony enough. That's all I could see with my eyes or hear with my ears. I was aware that I worked in the presence of a saint.

I would like to emphasize his humility once again. Everything he did as a pope was based on his personal experience of a life marked from childhood by suffering. John Paul II showed us how to face suffering by embracing God and staying close to Mary. He carried suffering with him throughout his pontificate. For him, the most important things were prayer, suffering, and tireless work. I spoke with John Paul II many times during the 27 years of his pontificate, but it was the way he looked at me, and his life, that changed me and my family.

What did John Paul II leave behind for you and for all of us?

He left us his teachings. He showed us how to live. I hope we never forget his teachings, all he has done for us, his experience and teachings. We need to cultivate the values he fought to instill in us. We have to pray to him. As Pope Benedict said: John Paul II looks at us from heaven and blesses us. I know that he is not here with us on earth, but I do not miss him. I know he's still with me. I can feel his presence.

Is there a photo of you with John Paul II?

In 1982, Fr. Dziwisz joked: "Holy Father, poor Arturo photographs everyone, and nobody takes a picture of him." John Paul II immediately took my hands in his hands and Fr. Dziwisz took a picture of us.

You were present for the last earthly moments of the life of John Paul II.

We have seen the suffering of the Holy Father in last years of his life. His message to us was that we should love and understand suffering. I cried after his death, but I was happy in the sense that John Paul II achieved what he wanted in life. This message, which he preached to the end, was a message of love for one's neighbor.

What are your memories of your last meeting with the pope?

I was very lucky to be able to say goodbye to Pope John Paul II exactly eight hours before his death. I entered into his room and knelt down by his bed. Fr. Dziwisz told him: "Holy Father, Arturo is here." He was in his bed and slowly turned over. When I saw him, my heart leapt. He had a big smile, eyes I hadn't see in months. It moved me so much that I knelt before him. He caressed my head and blessed my hands. Then, he told me: "Arturo, thank you. Thank you." And with that smile on his face, he turned to his left side. It was already clear to me that he was ready for a much more beautiful journey. He was ready to go back to the Father's house.

Do you remember the last picture you took of the Holy Father?

This photo has never been published. John Paul II already lay in his coffin. I caught the moment when then-Bishop Dziwisz and Monsignor Guido Marini put a white scarf on his face, in accordance with protocol. It is a very touching moment that I will never forget.

MELANIA TRUMP

Melania Trump is the former First Lady of the United States of America, wife of 45th President Donald Trump.

Mrs. Trump, please explain the story of the rose named after Pope St. John Paul II which you included in a redesigned Rose Garden. Why did you decide to honor him in this way?

As a Catholic I was pleased to see that the Pope John Paul II Rose was planted at the Rose Garden to honor the pope's first visit to the White House in 1979. When the garden construction project began in July 2020 it was decided that the Pope's Rose single 4' shrub would remain in place. The rose was protected during the garden improvements, and it continued to bloom throughout the weeks of construction. A new companion "Pope John Paul II" rose was planted near the older shrub in August, joining over 200 newly-planted rose additions. Today, both "Pope John Paul II" roses are thriving in the renovated garden.

NORMAN DAVIES

Welsh historian of Europe and Poland. Professor Emeritus at the University of London, a Supernumerary Fellow of Wolfson College, Oxford, and the author of several books on Polish and European history. Mr. Davies holds a number of honorary titles and memberships.

Who is Karol Wojtyła to you as a historian? Who is John Paul II to you personally?

Personally, I regard John Paul II as one of the great figures of my lifetime, a personal inspiration, probably the greatest person to come out of modern Poland. He had a great significance in my life. As a historian, I have various reactions. I never studied him in detail. I told you that I was hoping to write his biography. I would have studied him and his documents and writings more thoroughly than I have. He seems to fit into so many different categories. Obviously, he was a great Church leader, probably the best that the Roman Catholic Church could have had. He was a great international figure. One of half-a-dozen people at most who conspired to bring down Soviet Communism. A great leader of the Polish nation, which was in serious trouble when he came onto the scene. Historically, he is a distinguished figure in European culture: in philosophy, theology, and literature.

How did you become interested in Karol Wojtyła?

It was hard not to become interested in him when he was elected pope in 1978. I met with him soon after the election and I was greatly impressed. In those days I was a budding historian and Polish history was my specialization. I've moved on to other things since then. But John Paul II could not have been otherwise than a major figure. He had a tremendous impact on Poland from the beginning of his papacy. I think we will talk a bit more about that.

Have you ever visited the places connected to Karol Wojtyła: Kraków, Wadowice, and so forth?

One reason I thought I was well qualified to write his biography is that I knew the part of Poland he was from, Wadowice and neighboring towns. I also knew Kraków and the Jagiellonian University very well. In the 1990s, there was no biography written by somebody who knew that part of the world. Most of what was written about him concerned his role in the Church, his philosophy and theology, not where he came from and what formed him. I was planning to write a biography about the first half of his life, before he went to Rome. I would not be so well qualified to study the politics of the Church and theology and so forth.

Do you think that knowing Polish culture and history as well as speaking Polish helped you understand John Paul II?

I had no Polish origins and in some ways I was an outsider, which in some ways gives one a good perspective. But the knowledge of the country, the cultures, the people, traditions, and so on is absolutely vital in understanding the person. Wojtyła was virtually unknown in the wider world until he suddenly stepped out on that balcony in the Vatican. I can share an anecdote which illustrates the world of non-understanding. On that day in October 1978, I was at a seminar in Oxford. I can't remember what we were talking about. There was a group of thirty or so people in the room. Then a secretary of the faculty entered and said: "Some may be interested that a new pope was elected." People asked: "Who is he?" She responded, "Well, he is called Wodge Tyler." "Wodge Tyler?" "What country is he from?" Sitting next to me was Włodzimierz Brus. He was a Polish Jew and a communist. He was a communist to the end of his days, absolutely unreformed. Brus stood up, put his hands up in the air, and exclaimed: "*Habemus Papam*!" [laughs] I caught on then. I knew Wojtyła because I had met him first ten years earlier, when he was Bishop of Kraków. The secretary read the name again and she still had no idea who it was.

What was your feeling?

It was very, very thrilling. We knew it was a tremendous event in the communist world. Poland was exceptional in having a Church which, although not fully independent, had a measure of autonomy. This was unheard of in the Soviet Bloc. The First Secretary of the Communist Party, upon hearing about the pope's election, exclaimed: "Wojtyła? *Jezus, Maria*!" Now that was the beginning of the end of the communist regime in Poland. There was absolutely no doubt about that. I was overjoyed at the election. I could not believe it. And there was a rapid series of consequences, not least when he went to Poland in June 1979, eight months after his election. That was an absolute bombshell. I was not there. I already had the proofs of *God's Playground*, a big book. I was plowing my way through it. I remember, I added two or three pages at the end to include the election of the pope. I did not actually, personally experience the pope in Poland. I went later that year. Extraordinary times! Extraordinary times!

Did you meet John Paul II in Castle Gandolfo in 1979?

No, as I have mentioned, I had met Karol Wojtyła first ten years prior. Here's another anecdote. I could not speak Polish properly then. In particular, I had no idea that one addressed a priest not as "you" — "*ty*" — but as "Thou" (*proszę księdza*). I did not even know how to say Dear Sir (*proszę pana*). I said everything with "*ty*." I was sent to the chancery to find some things. I was looking for room 9. I saw the back of a person walking a few steps in front of me, wearing a cassock. I ran after him: "Excuse me, do you know where room nine is?" In Polish: "*Przepraszam czy ty wiesz gdzie jest pokój numer 9?*" I used the familiar "you," which is overly informal, if not outright disrespectful. He turned around and it was Wojtyła. He laughed; he was quite pleased, and took me in the right direction: "*Bez problemu, tutaj na lewo*" ("no problem, you have to make a left") — So I was on familiar terms with the pope from the very beginning. Of course I did not really know him. But I did meet him once or twice when he was Bishop and then Archbishop of Kraków. I was very aware who he was. He did not know who I was then but he did later on.

I was wondering how it happened, but there is a picture in my study of me shaking hands with the pope. Somehow I went to Rome with a group of priests from Kraków. I can't even remember the name of the priest who invited me. It was more or less, "*Proszę Pana, jedziemy do Rzymu, proszę z nami*" ("Dear Sir, we are going to Rome; please join us"). I went to Rome on the train. We had this meeting at Castel Gandolfo. I have the picture of him dressed in white. The priest who introduced me said, "*To jest Pan Davies, który jest Anglikiem.*" ("This is Mr. Davies, who is English.") The pope started to talk English. I talked immediately to him in Polish quite well and he was confused. And he said: "*Aha, dziękujemy za obecność.*" ("Aha, we thank you for your presence"). That was really the first time I talked to him after he became pope. That was 1979; my book *God's Playground* was published in English in 1981. It was not available in Poland; I was on the blacklist of the communist censorship. He read it and invited me again to Castel Gandolfo, and I had a longer talk with him.

How do you recollect your meetings with St. John Paul II? What surprised you most about him?

He was very natural. The normality of the man was astonishing. He was very good-humored. He was used to talking to students, to young people. He did not have this distance that some prelates have. He was just himself, good-humored, always with a smile on his lips, waiting to see what you said to him. But he was very well informed. I could tell that he had read my book because he'd say: "You wrote this and what do you mean?" Of course, I spoke to him in Polish and he was very amused by all that. He was a very good linguist. English was his fourth or fifth language.

What was the impact of Galicia on Karol Wojtyła?

I think that Galicia and, in particular, his father were obviously a big influence on him, as his mother died early. His father was a Galician, a professional soldier in the Austro-Hungarian army. Western Galicia was very Polish, but it had a very different atmosphere from the Congress Kingdom — Russian Poland. Generally speaking, in late Galicia the Poles had a rather good setup. They did not have full autonomy, but they had a large measure of cultural autonomy. Polish schools and universities functioned in Polish and so did Polish publishing. People from all over Eastern Poland would publish things in Polish in Lwów and Kraków. But the people in Galicia were against the insurrectionary tradition. They were not for fighting the partitioning powers.

Unlike the Poles in Russia and Germany, Galician Poles were happy with their lot, if only somewhat. They had a lot of bad experiences. For example, in 1846 Polish nobles were massacred by Polish peasants. It showed that there was no Polish nation back then. Or, rather, that the Polish nation was only the nobles and educated people. Only after the serfs had been liberated did the whole of the Polish nation became conscious of itself. So Galicia was very strongly Polish culturally but not politically. I think this was something that was deeply embedded in Wojtyła, namely the primacy of culture, including religious culture. It is more important than politics and the state you live in and the regime and so on. Political regimes pass; they are ephemeral; they last a few decades. And then something else comes along. But culture is very long-lasting; it is very deep and very wide. That was the attitude he grew up in.

What would you say about the environment he grew up in in Wadowice, including his neighborhood?

Wadowice is a small town. It is situated on a railroad line between Kraków and Bielsko. Bielsko was the frontier. Wadowice was halfway along. Under Austrian rule, right before Wojtyła was born, there was a big military garrison there. There was also a considerable Jewish population. I do not know exactly, but about 10 or 15 percent of the population was Jewish. There were not as many as in eastern Galicia, as in Brody, where 90 percent of the population was Jewish. Wojtyła grew up in a world of cultural diversity; there were Austrians, too. His father was a professional in the Austro-Hungarian military. They would have been used to hearing German. The Jews spoke Yiddish. There were a lot of Ukrainians around, a bit further east. You did not have to go far in Galicia — already in Nowy Sącz there were the Ukrainian Lemkos. It was a world of cultural diversity but also of great religious devotion.

The town next to Wadowice is Kalwaria Lanckorońska. There is a famous monastery there. Pilgrimages take place. I have been there. Thousands of people walk up hundreds of steps on their knees to the sanctuary. In August, during the Feast of the Assumption, the celebrations last for days. It is a very deep, ancient religious culture in which Wojtyła obviously took part. As a teenager, he was an altar boy. In some ways, the Church was his second mother. He lost his mother. His father was very religious. He was brought up as a son of the Church.

The pope's father, Karol Wojtyła, Sr., was both a Polish patriot and a Habsburg loyalist. How did this affect his son's view of Polish national identity?

In late Galicia you could be Polish. All the courts, schools, and universities used Polish. There was no restriction on Polishness. The restriction was on political activities: you had to be loyal to the Habsburgs. Polish independence was out of the question, just as you could not support Czech or Hungarian independence. The father would have sworn an oath of loyalty first to the Emperor Franz Joseph and then to his successor Charles — Karol. To be loyal to this oath, you could not be in favor of Polish independence. Polish independence was one step too far. Still, on this view of patriotism, you could be a Pole, a Ukrainian, or a Jewish patriot. The Galician Jews were famously supportive of the Habsburg monarchy. They had it better there than almost anywhere else. But you could not be for national independence.

In his poem "Thinking My Country," Karol Wojtyła reflected on the concepts of nation and patriotism. How would you respond to his question: Can history ever swim against the tide of conscience?

He is really asking here whether people can take a different path from that which their conscience dictates. If for you loyalty to the Catholic Church was the main principle, then, for instance, you could not support the Polish Risings of the 19th century, you could not support violence. Catholic doctrine condemns violence. Although you may think that it is a noble thing to fight the Russians, to kill the Russians, it is violence. And Wojtyła was insistent upon nonviolence.

This was of course his position in the 1980s, when Solidarity appeared. Solidarity looked at first like another Polish Rising. There are two points to make about the Polish Risings. One is that they showed incredible bravery and courage. The other is that they always failed. Wojtyła was on the side of those saying, if you can restrain yourself from violence, from trying to fight the regime, then you are likely to win. But if you resort to killing people, even killing bad people, then you'll find that the odds are stacked against you. The Soviet Union and the Soviet Bloc were the most heavily armed part of the world. The United States had nothing like the forces of the Soviet Bloc. The NKVD secret police, the SS of the Soviet Bloc, if you will, was bigger than the British army. The police, the militia, not to mention the professional military, the tanks and everything, constituted a system based on control, enforceable control, and the only way to defeat it was to undermine its spirit. I think John Paul II was Lech Wałęsa's leading spiritual advisor. Solidarity's advisors, like Father Józef Tischner, had the wisdom of non-violence. Of course, the communists could not understand that. They were totally confused. They did not know how to oppose it. One-third of the Communist Party joined Solidarity. Then even the Party's First Secretary, General Wojciech Jaruzelski, lost faith in the system. It just died a natural death on its feet.

How would you explain the role of the Church in defeating communism in Poland?

The Catholic Church in Poland after 1956 was unique in the Soviet Bloc. There was an understanding between Communist leader Władysław Gomułka and Cardinal Stefan Wyszyński that they would exist alongside each other so long as neither interfered in the other's affairs. The

Party and the communist system would not interfere in the Church's worship and internal affairs on the condition that the Church did not openly oppose the political regime. This was something unheard of in the Communist world. Marxism-Leninism insisted on the complete control by the ruling party of all spheres of life. It did not apply in Poland.

My father-in-law was a very interesting case here. He was an educated man but politically he was left-wing; he had socialist sympathies. He was not hugely supportive of the Church. He went to Mass, but he never went inside the church; he stood in the back. There were always groups, mainly of men, standing in the back, smoking cigarettes. They were there but they were not there. My father-in-law spent most of the war in Dachau and other Nazi concentration camps. After the war, he would say, "Despite everything, this Church holds everything together. Without the Church we would be lost." I think quite a lot of Poles are in that category. They can be very critical of the clergy. But the Church is the institution that has preserved them. That did not happen in other countries such as Hungary or Czechoslovakia. The Polish Church was unique. Personally, I think that the Polish Church was at its best in the years of John Paul II. Things have gone wrong since then.

John Paul II was the catalyst of the anti-communist counterrevolution. How did his first papal pilgrimage to Poland impact Solidarity and the fall of communism?

The pope's first visit to Poland occurred before Solidarity, so did not influence it directly. Yet in a way, it created Solidarity. He created the national mood that made it possible. When he went there, it was absolutely electric. The communist media tried not to show how many millions of people flocked to see the great man in Kraków. The amazing thing is that he never said a bad word about the communist regime. Not a word! What he said was politically neutral: "Lift up your hearts," or "Be not afraid." Everybody knew what it meant. It did not mean, "Don't be afraid of the communist regime." He did not have to say that. This was an absolute mastery of the political language where politics was not mentioned. He was a diplomat, if you like. Or, rather, he was a great persuader, speaking in the unwritten code so that the people understood the message but the communist censorship could not have criticized him for anything.

Solidarity gave ordinary Poles the confidence to be themselves. It was not about shouting anti-communist slogans. Nobody was shouting,

"Down with Lenin!" They were demanding what the communist system had promised them. It was supposed to be a workers' state. So the workers said, yes, OK, we are workers, and we demand free trade unions. What's wrong with that? It was electrifying. It electrified people not only in Poland but throughout the Soviet Bloc. I had good friends in Estonia. They were watching this. And they said: "Gosh, if it can happen in Poland, then it may happen here someday." The Gdańsk strikes of August 1980 were inspired by this movement of liberation from toeing the party life, of being yourself, of making decisions by yourself. And that was the pope's doing.

You have said that there was no way to contest the Soviet power by force. It had to be contested by spiritual power. And John Paul II did it.

The communist system was based on brute force, on fear, on terrifying people into obeying the system, not speaking their mind, and so on. At every level the communist system had an overwhelming force at its disposal, from the workplace to the highest rungs of society. Nobody could have successfully opposed it by force. In the Stalinist period the communists were killing people in large numbers. Poland got off not quite so badly as other countries, not so badly as Russia or Ukraine. Nonetheless, communism was a murderous regime. It was known that it would stop at nothing if directly opposed. But when it was opposed by workers demanding things which appeared to be normal for workers, like workers' control, it was lost. It was totally baffled. It just did not know how to oppose this. Solidarity taught the communists that their regime was false, that so-called communist ideas were bogus, that it was a fraudulent, violent regime. And, subsequently, it collapsed under its own weight.

How was Karol Wojtyła shaped by history and heritage?

I told you about Galicia. Galicia was part of the Habsburg Empire and there were many nationalities there: Germans, Poles, Hungarians, Ukrainians, and Jews. Karol Wojtyła was very influenced by ethnic diversity. He was very much inspired by Polish culture, but he did not belong to the narrow "Poland for the Poles" camp. One of the really interesting events I attended, I think in 1988, again in Castel Gandolfo, was a historical conference about the old Commonwealth of Poland-Lithuania. John Paul II invited to Rome historians from every nationality of the Old Commonwealth: Lithuanians, Belarusians, Ukrainians, Poles, Jews, Germans, and so forth. One of the rules of the conference was that you could speak any language so long as it was a language of the Commonwealth. And the pope opened the conference speaking Latin. Naturally the biggest group was the Poles. But then it was the first time I heard Belarusian spoken. I could understand some. But then the Lithuanians stood up and, of course, nobody could understand a word. But that was the whole point: to recreate the atmosphere in one room of the old Commonwealth. He absolutely challenged us. That is what he liked: the multicultural Commonwealth. He was very much a protector of the Greek Catholic Church, which was banned in Russia. In fact, the Russians killed Greek Catholics where they could get hold of them. They were arguably more severely persecuted than Roman Catholics. But the Greek Catholics were protected in Poland. Kraków certainly had a Uniate Church, though I do not think there was one in Wadowice.

When he became Bishop of Kraków, the southern parts of the diocese, the Bieszczady region, saw deportations of the Lemko. Really, the Polish Communists pursued a sort of genocide. Thousands were killed and hundreds of thousands were deported. Their homes were razed to the ground. I went there for the first time in the 1960s with my father-in-law. The villages in the region were absolutely empty. Only graveyards and gravestones with Orthodox crosses were left. I know from various sources that Wojtyła gave support quietly to the Greek Catholic Church, which was of course illegal in communist Poland. The Russians or Soviets did not tolerate the Uniate Church. But it existed underground. Young people from Kraków would go in the summer to Bieszczady to tidy up the graveyards and clean up the villages until the inhabitants would return.

What do you appreciate about John Paul II the most?
I think the warmth of his personality. He was extremely warmhearted. He never posed as the big man. He was a friendly figure who came down to your level. He gave people confidence. He was never the prelate of the Church putting on the style. He was very human, a very Christian man.

What do we need to build the civilization of love?
Oh, dear, that is beyond me. Obviously, Wojtyła set a personal

example of love, compassion, reaching out to people, feeling for their problems, their difficulties, their pain. It is absolutely the opposite of what we see today: people getting rich when they can; making the most of every opportunity to get on; beggar my neighbor; a devil-take-the-hindmost attitude. Some people call it a capitalist attitude. I do not think that is precise. Capitalism is neither good nor bad.

MAREK JAN CHODAKIEWICZ

Kościuszko Chair in Polish Studies, head of the Center for Intermarium Studies, and professor of history at the Institute of World Politics. Professor Chodakiewicz is on the academic board of the Victims of Communism Memorial Foundation. He served as a presidential appointee on the United States Holocaust Memorial Council during the George W. Bush presidency and is the author of more than 30 books.

What did John Paul II mean to you?

It is hard to express myself about that because my appreciation of the Polish Pope has developed gradually. He was truly awesome on so many levels that someone very young could not have fathomed it. I was just a teenager when he was elected pope. I remember distinctly that when I heard the news of his elevation, I immediately told my father. He disbelieved me; we made a bet that I had heard right about the election of Karol Wojtyła and my father lost: 20 Polish złoty. So from my point of view my lot improved and the pontificate was off to a good start. He came to Poland soon after. I was amazed not so much by him and his papal authority as by the impact he had on my fellow Poles. I observed closely his visit in Warsaw and I saw people smiling, which was unusual under Communism. Further, it seemed that people stopped being afraid. I skipped school to watch him drive through the Old Town in Warsaw. The teachers either unconsciously or consciously spewed Communist propaganda that we would be trampled to death by the mobs. Instead, I witnessed enormous self-discipline and joy among the people. That really impressed me.

The pope did not say anything shocking to me, but I marveled at the impact his message had on the Polish people. "Fear not!" he said. "Let the Spirit descend and renew the face of this land. This land." He meant Poland. And the Spirit descended, resulting in the human solidarity which led to the eruption of Solidarity, an independent, anti-Communist trade union which masked a national liberation movement. That was directly the result of Wojtyła's influence. Again, my family and I were ready. My father and mother were dissidents; we were in the trenches of the war for freedom. But I doubt that without John Paul II's message our effort would have been successful. He mobilized millions of people against the Communists. It was simply amazing. I understood that then, though I had problems comprehending why people did not get the obvious before Wojtyła came to visit. I'm focusing on his first visit to Poland in 1979 because I experienced it firsthand emotionally, rather than intellectually. And I was able to feel and see plainly the results of it. The older I have grown, the more I have come to appreciate Wojtyła on many levels, but also to look critically at certain things he did. But the first impression of the first encounter with this towering personality has been etched permanently in my brain.

How did John Paul II understand culture? What role does it play in public and private life?

I believe that John Paul II restored culture to its rightful, central place in human experience. He distilled and universalized the message of Jesus Christ for us to love one another. But he also showed us, in a way much more accessible than T.S. Eliot did, what culture is and what role it plays. The word "culture" comes from "cult," i.e., religion. Without faith we miss out on culture, perhaps the most crucial facet of the human experience. Culture combines both faith and reason to reflect what is best in humanity. Culture naturally manifests itself in manifold ways and at various levels. Wojtyła had the uncanny ability to address our thirst for culture at all levels, from the most sophisticated to the most common, and he never cheapened his message, never compromised on its urgency. Man imbibes culture from his environment; he seeks it out to enhance his humanity, and then he returns the gift of culture, as he understands it and as he processes it, to the common national treasury of culture. But man also goes beyond a narrow national dimension of culture. Understanding how important the national flavor of culture is, Wojtyła taught us that we should share our individual and national cultural gifts with the whole of humanity. That is what truly makes for human diversity, and not some contrived, regimented leftist fantasies about nebulous "people" and "globalism"; culture is the synthesis of the individual, his nation, and the Christian world that man belongs to.

Was the elevation of Karol Wojtyła to the See of Peter a world historical event or just a fluke of history?

That's a tough one for a rigorous secular mind. But for a Catholic it is really simple. If God has a plan, and He does, then the plan develops accordingly to the Will of the Lord. Metaphysically, then, Karol Wojtyła was put on this earth to become Pope John Paul II. He was thus the right person at the right time in the right place: the Vatican. Of course, many intellectuals will disagree; a few will advance a theory of a Great Man in History; some will argue about the primacy of the material factors; others will point out the alleged machinations and conspiracies within the Holy See that brought Wojtyła to "power." But I firmly believe that there is a divine plan that ultimately drives our lives, even if, paradoxically, the Lord endowed us with free will and we are, thus, free to make our own choices, even to the point of rejecting our cross. When Wojtyła became the Roman Pontiff, he accepted the cross, a much heavier one than he had borne during the Nazi and Communist occupations of Poland.

What about his experience of Nazism and Communism?

The experience of Nazism and Communism was paramount in shaping him at many levels. He understood and assessed both totalitarianisms as equally evil. From his Kraków vantage point, he knew that Nazism was more murderous in a shorter time than Communism. Because of Stalin's victory over Hitler, Communism worked greater destruction over a longer period of time. Again, I am talking about Wojtyła's personal experiences. Naturally, as he grew up and learned, he understood that globally the Communists exterminated more people than the Nazis, but his Kraków experience allowed him to relate to both evils concretely and individually, rather than abstractly and collectively. For him the period of 1939 to 1945 was shockingly revolutionary, and the time from 1945 to 1978 mostly one of a gradual corruption of the soul by the Reds, but the years 1949 to 1956 approached somewhat the Nazi terror in the attacks against the Church and political opponents of the Soviet occupation regime. Wojtyła served the Church and her people (and Poland) faithfully, and many times he went well above what was expected of him to give witness in face of Communist oppression, as in 1960 during the famous "battle for the Cross" in Kraków's Nowa Huta suburb, where the steel mill workers clashed with the Communist police over the right to pray. Wojtyła intervened on their behalf intrepidly. All that shaped him as much as his experience as a forced laborer under the Nazi regime. Having suffered at many levels, John Paul II was able to relate to the suffering of others very well.

In what sense did Polish history shape Karol Wojtyła? How much of Polish history did he retain in his heart as John Paul II?

The impact of Polish history, by which I mean not just the past but also Poland's culture (including literature and poetry), was absolutely paramount. It stayed with Wojtyła throughout his life. It spoke through him. First, there was his personal experience, which I mentioned above. Then, there was the collective experience. This consisted not only of his education, starting in high school in Wadowice and later continuing in college in Kraków. It was a sense of belonging to a chain of generations that fought, bled, and suffered for Poland but also laughed, advocated, and worked for her. Wojtyła fully internalized this scheme of history; he totally identified with it. He was a nationalist (or as they say in Europe: a patriot). There is no doubt in my mind about it. Polish remained his preferred means of communication. It was an outstanding phenomenon: to remain a comfortable patriot while embracing the world. That is the mystery of Catholic Polish nationalism. And he embodied it.

Did John Paul II need Ronald Reagan to overthrow communism? If so, why?

Well, why not? If there was a divine plan, then Reagan must have been part of it. Therefore we can assume that he needed Reagan. Both were conscious agents of God. I say "agents," rather than "tools," for tools tend to be blind. But both men knew they were on a mission from the Lord to bring freedom to slaves; that entailed destroying communism. Each of them had a different assignment, but the same goal. Reagan's job was political. Wojtyła's task was spiritual. One drew from the other. John Paul II's mission was to preach the Good Word. Christianity in itself is antithetical to communism. The Word of God, if taken seriously by the slaves and their masters, had the power to destroy communism. The Polish Pope preached love, which was the contradiction of communism. And he prevailed because people believed the Word. That's the metaphysical explanation. But don't forget that President Reagan stepped in and the Word became Flesh. In other words, he physically destroyed the Evil Empire. And Margaret Thatcher helped as well.

What was the basis for the alliance of Ronald Reagan and the Polish Pope against the Soviet Union?

Ronald Reagan always told the truth about Communism. That was indispensable to the success of his alliance with John Paul II, who also spoke truly about this leftist ideology. Further, Reagan was an actor, and so was Wojtyła. As I learned from your own work long ago, they both understood the power of the spoken word. Reagan appreciated the need to communicate his message of liberation to the people and win them over. That is a classical missionary approach. Wojtyła practiced the same. So they jointly understood the need to proselytize before striking evil, the need to communicate the message clearly. For Reagan, the fight against communism was primarily a moral imperative. The same goes for Wojtyła, although, naturally, he related to it more theologically and spiritually. Overall, the president and the pope were a match made in Heaven. They were usually on the same page.

What were the defining moments of the pontificate of John Paul II?

If we are talking about communism, it must have been his first trip to Poland; his chastisement of liberation theologians, including in Nicaragua; and his deft and compassionate handling of Mikhail Gorbachev. Going beyond communism, his most important contributions, which make him a towering giant in history, were, first, his multiple pilgrimages virtually to every corner of the world; and, second, his concern for young people, which expressed itself best in so-called World Youth Days, virtual festivals of Catholic faith with millions of young people participating. It is too bad that his successors cannot seem quite able to replicate John Paul II's rapport with the young and find it difficult to continue this crucial missionary endeavor.

What elements of John Paul II's thought should apply in politics today?

Well, not just his thought. His entire persona is missing in today's politics. I'm talking about his intellect, his example, his kindness, his leadership, and, first and foremost, his moral clarity. True, Wojtyła was put on this earth under specific circumstances, which entailed particular challenges. However, much of what he gave of himself to meet the adversity was universal. So we should learn about John Paul II's universality and apply it to the challenges that face us today, if possible.

What do we need to build a civilization of love?

We must start loving ourselves so that we may love each other. We must restore the world in congruence with our beliefs to make it lovely and, upon victory, we must be able to forgive our enemies. We should understand our life as a good fight, whether it involves a crusade, a counterrevolution, or any other endeavor, including writing books. God has promised us that the gates of hell shall not overcome the kingdom of heaven. That means that in the end we win. Meanwhile, however, the Lord does not guarantee that we shall triumph in our lives. We are here to fight a good fight now until we die. That's the way to build a civilization of love.

I come before you as a witness: a witness to human dignity, a witness to hope, a witness to the conviction that the destiny of all nations lies in the hands of a merciful Providence.

John Paul II

GEORGE WEIGEL

Author, political analyst, and social activist. He currently serves as a Distinguished Senior Fellow of the Ethics and Public Policy Center and is the author of a best-selling biography of Pope John Paul II, Witness to Hope, *and other publications.*

When and where did you learn about Karol Wojtyła for the first time?
I began to study his life seriously after his election and especially after being impressed by his first encyclical, *Redemptor hominis*.

"In the designs of Providence, there are no mere coincidences." How did the events of your life prepare you to be John Paul II's biographer?
This is described in detail in my memoir *Lessons in Hope: My Unexpected Life with Saint John Paul II*. Some of the key "preparations" included my academic work in philosophy and theology and my work on human rights issues behind the Iron Curtain, especially religious freedom.

How did the time you spent with John Paul II shape your life?
I hope it made me a better Christian. It certainly, and unexpectedly, made me into a media "expert" on the papacy.

What were John Paul II's greatest achievements in geopolitics, human rights, theology, and ecumenism?
(1) The nonviolent collapse of European communism in 1989; (2) his persistent defense of religious freedom as the first of human rights, beginning with his first UN address in 1979; (3) *Redemptor hominis*, *Veritatis splendor*, and the Theology of the Body; (4) the Joint Declaration of the Holy See and the Lutheran World Federation.

Let's talk about John Paul II's first papal pilgrimage to the United States in October 1979. How did the Polish Pope contribute to American Catholic life?
The really important and decisive visit was World Youth Day in Denver in 1993. That ignited the New Evangelization in the United States and the effects can still be felt today. As for 1979, I think the pope learned that the U.S. Church was much more alive than he had found it to be during his previous two visits as a cardinal.

What are your thoughts on the role of Ronald Reagan and John Paul II in defeating Communism?

They were working on parallel tracks and respected each other's unique competence and sphere of influence. There was no "holy alliance." Both believed that communism would die of its inherent implausibility.

Which of the encyclicals of John Paul II is the closest to your heart and why?

I'm much less interested in my heart than in my brain! *Redemptor hominis* is crucial as the "program" for the entire pontificate. *Redemptoris missio* is the charter of the New Evangelization. *Centesimus annus* is the most developed statement of the classic Catholic social doctrine tradition. *Evangelium vitae* is a crucial warning to modern democracies that wrongs-declared-to-be-rights lead to the dictatorship of relativism. *Fides et ratio* is a powerful challenge to western intellectuals.

How did John Paul II define nation and culture, and their role in the life of a nation?

He certainly believed that culture is the most dynamic force in history, rather than politics or economics, and he deployed that conviction in his efforts to help east-central Europe self-liberate from communism.

Recent history and tragic events provide evidence of the evil use of freedom. John Paul II said: "Freedom is for love." Following his teachings, what does freedom consist of and what purpose it should serve?

The "virtue" of freedom for the individual is a matter of freely choosing the good (which we can know by reason and revelation) and doing so as a matter of moral habit. Freedom in public life is a matter of having the right to do what we ought, as John Paul II put it in his homily in Baltimore in 1995.

What is the significance of Pope John Paul II's defense of religious freedom in Redemptor hominis?

It set the table for his developed defense of human rights throughout the pontificate.

Pope John Paul II once remarked: "They try to understand me from outside. But I can only be understood from inside." What was this "inside" of Karol Wojtyła?

He meant that his actions could only be understood as an expression of his convictions, formed by prayer. That intense life of prayer — of conversation with the Lord — was the "engine" of his ministry.

In your book The End and the Beginning, *you wrote: "Yet even his critics had to concede that he had become a global moral reference point — a man whose thought mattered, even to those who opposed it and opposed the Church he led." How had John Paul II come to this point?*

By being true to his convictions, living them himself, and demonstrating that a life of fidelity to Christ and the Gospel was a great adventure in human liberation.

What lessons from John Paul II's pontificate are most applicable now?
Be not afraid!

What do we need to build a civilization of love?
Conversion to Christ.

JOHN RADZILOWSKI

American historian and author of numerous books and articles. He received the Cavalier's Cross of the Polish Order of Merit, among other awards. He is Director of the Polish Institute of Culture & Research in Orchard Lake, Michigan.

What was the political thought of John Paul II?

His politics grew organically out of his deep faith, Polish culture and history, and a profound encounter with Catholic theology and philosophy. Elements of each of these are visible in his politics. There is a tendency even among admirers of John Paul II to think of him simply as the pope who started the collapse of communism in Europe. While that is certainly important, such a view confines John Paul II's political insights to the past. Yet his ideas are highly relevant today.

John Paul II instructs us on the proper ordering of politics as part of human life and human societies. By "ordering" I mean more than simply "priorities" or a ranking of things by importance, but establishing the proper relationships among different elements of human life. I would avoid the term "ideology," since he espoused more than a particular political program. Politics for John Paul II is never an end in itself, but rather it exists to serve mankind and to bring men and women and human society closer to God. In other words, the goal of politics is human thriving in the sense of St. Irenaeus's remark: "The glory of God is man fully alive."

John Paul II's politics are a stark departure from nearly all forms of modern political thought, especially in the past century and a half. Whether it is communism, fascism, post-modernism, or even the statist democracy that is common in Europe and North America: all place man in service to politics, which reverses the proper order of things. While professing high ideals, these approaches to politics quickly devolve into some form of enslavement, whether literal enslavement as in the Soviet Union or a form of the spiritual enslavement more common in the West today. From the 1960s in the U.S., politics increasingly became an end in itself. It was the feminists of the 1970s who coined the phrase "the personal is political," heralding the intrusion of political ideology into the most intimate aspects of family and human life. In America and Europe, we increasingly see people dividing themselves by political party or ideology, even separating from family and friends over political differences. (Not only has the personal become political, but the political has become personal.) This has caused deep dysfunction in our time, to the point where no one is immune from becoming the means to achieve some political end. Even the value of human life is a political commodity. John Paul II points us in the opposite direction.

John Paul II's critique of modern politics mirrors his approach to economics. Economies and markets exist to serve mankind, not to be served. His critique of communism was rooted in the same principle as his critique of what he considered unrestrained capitalism. To put it more simply, man exists to love and serve God, and all that man has, including politics, should be ordered to that end. Without this proper ordering, even with the best of intentions, politics can become and has become a form of idolatry. Therefore, understanding the political thought of John Paul II remains as relevant today as in 1978.

Please reflect on St. John Paul II's reception in the U.S., in particular with regard to his foreign policy.

His reception in the USA was generally very positive, though there were exceptions. Most people, including non-Catholics, were fascinated by him even if the nuances of his message were "lost in translation." Prior to John Paul II, popes were very austere, distant figures. Pope Paul VI had begun making the papacy more visible throughout the Catholic world, and John Paul II continued this and amplified it to the world at large, becoming one of the most visible world leaders ever. He was tremendously charismatic, with an ability to relate to anyone, but also a man of great holiness and authenticity, something which people hungered for then as now.

That said, there were also many who disliked or even hated the pope. Liberal Catholic circles in the U.S. were particularly opposed to him and made no secret of it. It was quite common even among some clergy to openly say they were praying for John Paul II's death. This was directly related to his strong affirmation of the Church's teaching on the sanctity of life, the truth of Pope Paul VI's *Humanae vitae*, and the priestly vocation. However, this opposition also found its way into foreign policy, since many of the Catholics who opposed him on these issues were also distinctly favorable toward Marxist regimes, especially in Latin America, and, of course, to so-called Liberation Theology. "Anti-communist" was considered a slur among "educated" people, both inside and outside the Church. All of this was linked to his being Polish. It was (and to some extent remains) a common prejudice among Americans, especially elites, that Poles are backward, ignorant, emotional, and superstitious. These prejudices extend back to the nineteenth century but were revived in the 1960s, when being too patriotic and too religious were seen as a sign of a defective personality (the so-called Authoritarian Personality). Poles were (and remain) in this view overly attached to faith and nation and thus out of step with the modern world. So we read in the press from that period dismissive comments such as, "of course he's anti-communist... after all, he's from Poland."

Was the election of a pope from communist Poland convenient for the United States? How did America perceive Poland in 1978?

For those who had been directing American foreign policy up until then, he was inconvenient. But we have to remember the intense opposition and fear that Ronald Reagan also faced in the field of foreign policy. There was a strong bias in favor of the status quo and a real fear of "provoking the bear." While today the Solidarity movement has a cherished place in history books, in 1980 there were many in the West who were alarmed by the strikes in Gdańsk and by the pope's stance against Marxism. The Soviet Union was after all a permanent fact of life in the world (or so most believed), so confronting it was seen as a form of madness. We also recall that many Western institutions were rather friendly with communist regimes. This included many banks which — with the support of their governments — had loaned the communist regime billions of dollars by 1980. Along comes John Paul II, Solidarity, Ronald Reagan, and Mrs. Thatcher... well, you can imagine how they would feel! This is part that often gets left out of history books.

Americans had a very poor view of Poland in 1978. There was quite a bit of anti-Polish prejudice, which I experienced frequently growing up. It was abetted by the American popular media. Some few remembered Poland's history of standing against Nazi Germany and Soviet communism, but even that resistance was often viewed as futile or hopeless. Here the myth of Polish cavalry charging German tanks proved useful, and this story appeared in all school textbooks. (In school we often read aloud from our books in class, and since I was the only Polish kid in my class, the teacher made me read aloud the section about the Polish cavalry being slaughtered by the German tanks, much to the amusement of my classmates.) Many Americans viewed Poland as part of Russia or as existing in a place called "eastern Europe" which was virtually part of the Soviet Union. For American Polonia, the election of John Paul II was a true miracle. Along with the Solidarity movement, it marked a major change in how Americans perceived Poland and the Polish people. To this day, I can still remember where I was when I heard the news of John Paul II's election when it was announced on the radio in our small town. For many Polish Americans it remains one of the greatest moments in history.

John Paul II interacted with five different presidents of the United States. Why did he work so well with Ronald Reagan?

The two men had a common interest in stopping and rolling back Soviet and communist power in Europe and in other regions, e.g., Latin America. This is obvious. But there was also a deeper dimension. In the 1970s and 1980s, most political leaders and foreign policy experts — and indeed most people — assumed Soviet power was a permanent feature of the world scene. Yet here were two leaders who were certainly not naïve (in fact, both were quite realistic in their politics) but did not take such a grim reality for granted. Instead, they could see possibilities beyond what seemed an insoluble problem. Both President Reagan and St. John Paul II were optimists, but on a deeper level we can see that they shared the virtue of hope. This was the bedrock on which their partnership was founded. While the Holy Father had warm feelings for other U.S. presidents and the U.S. more generally, none of the other presidents he interacted with came as close in outlook to him as Reagan did.

During the Cold War, America helped Poland defeat the evil of communism. Can Poland with its strong Polish Catholic faith help America to defeat the evil of our times?

Not directly. America's toughest battles are against the evils that come from within. This is also true of Poland. We cannot be complacent about the strength of the faith in Poland. While it is certainly stronger than in western Europe, if we look at trends since 1990 in terms of regular Mass attendance, birth rates, etc., we see a disturbing picture. Of course, there are many positive elements as well, but the "soul" of Poland hangs in the balance and it remains to be seen whether she will end up like

Ireland or will chart a different course and maintain it in the decades to come. Becoming a model for a different kind of society where human thriving is not completely subordinate to politics or economics would be a great victory, not only for Poland but as a beacon for Americans. Many Americans — primarily but not only conservatives — have looked to Hungary and Poland for a different approach to politics, culture, and national identity. Poland's example could be quite important in this respect. Likewise, Poles should learn from what is happening in the U.S., both positive and negative.

This is not to minimize the threats from countries like Russia and China. China, for example, is quickly becoming the 21st-century version of President Reagan's "evil empire" and may soon pose a far greater threat to the world than the Soviet Union did during the Cold War. Soviet culture had no appeal to Americans; China clearly understands the importance of culture and has devoted massive resources to controlling and manipulating culture, education, and public information in the United States. Americans' loss of national identity and self-confidence, the result of years of bad education in our schools and corruption in our politics, provides an opening for China that it is exploiting. In this sense Poland and the U.S. are in a parallel situation where their greatest challenges come from internal moral and cultural forces, but internal problems create weaknesses foreign adversaries can exploit.

How do you see the present relationship between the U.S. and the Vatican? How has it changed since John Paul II's times?

It has changed a good deal. At the Vatican we have seen a return to some form of accommodation with regimes such as China, as characterized Vatican diplomacy before October 1978. The current Holy Father has a very different view of the papacy and its role in the world — and a very different way of communicating that view — than his two predecessors. Many people disagreed with John Paul II or Benedict XVI, but I cannot recall anyone coming away confused at the message either pope was conveying or claiming that they had been mistranslated by the media. We should also remember that the strong papacies of John Paul II and Benedict XVI made the Church and the Vatican a target for forces in the West strongly opposed to Church teaching on fundamental moral issues such as abortion. Prior to October 1978, the Church and the Holy See simply were not important enough to merit such sustained attacks. When American governments promote abortion or champion gay marriage internationally, it places the U.S. and the Vatican in direct opposition to one another even if figures on both sides try to paper over the differences. American politicians on the left and even some so-called moderates are often intensely anti-Catholic, and when they are in power, American policy follows suit. (As an aside, the fact that some of these politicians are themselves baptized Catholics is irrelevant to their intensive opposition to what the Church teaches. They have mastered a form of "dialectical" thinking that allows them to simultaneously proclaim two or more things that are entirely contradictory without the least embarrassment or sense of hypocrisy.)

As John Paul II said, "democracy ... [is] understood not only as a political system but also as an attitude of mind and principle of conduct." How do you see the place of America in the world in light of that statement?

How I wish more American leaders had remembered these words when setting policy towards Afghanistan, Iraq, and Syria! Democracy is not merely a process or set of procedures, but a culture and a set of habits and social practices. We Americans forget that it took generations after the founding for our system to function smoothly. Many early elections, especially in major cities, often resembled riots. We even fought a civil war to restore a proper understanding of the meaning of the Declaration of Independence.

John Paul II understood the American founders very well. John Adams said, "Public virtue cannot exist in a nation without private virtue, and public virtue is the only foundation of republics." In 1997, the Holy Father echoed this in an amazing discourse on the American ideal to the newly appointed U.S. ambassador to the Vatican, which should be required reading in schools. In it, he lays out why America plays a unique and consequential role in the world, and it is not due to economic or military power. America, he said, was based on

> a freedom designed to enable people to fulfill their duties and responsibilities towards the family and towards the common good of the community. [The founders] clearly understood that there could be no true freedom without moral responsibility and accountability, and no happiness without respect and support for the natural units or groupings through which people exist, develop and seek the higher purposes of life in concert with others.

America's gifts and its founding ideals, the Holy Father believed, were ordered toward fostering a culture of life and love that would truly serve as a beacon for the world. We are quite far from that ideal today, but we have to face the challenges of living up to it with hope.

Since John Paul II's death in 2005, many changes have taken place in the U.S. and Europe that push the Church to adapt to new cultural realities. What is essential to Catholic identity in today's world?

The beauty and glory of the Catholic Church is that it maintains the splendor of Truth unchanged through the ages. Throughout history, it did not reject the cultures it encountered but rather baptized and Christianized them. It sought to creatively retain what was best in those cultures in a Catholic idiom. So when we talk of the Church "adapting to" a new cultural reality, we are looking at the problem backward. Instead, we should ask how the Church will adapt the cultures of the world to the Truth it proclaims. The Church has to stand as a "sign of contradiction" to the world, and when it fails to do so, it fails in its mission.

Catholics—especially in the U.S. and Europe—have acquiesced far too much to a version of modern secular culture that is akin to *laïcité*. We've adopted a sense of Catholicism that treats faith as a separate element of identity sealed off from our cultural, political, or economic life. This is disordered and not sustainable. Catholicism thrived in the U.S. for decades because the cultural underpinnings of American life were—broadly conceived—Christian. But now we are approaching a "post-Christian" period where the underpinnings of our society resemble a kind of Nietzschean or materialist paganism. Our challenge, though, remains the same: to be in the world but not of the world. We must live in, be in dialogue with, and evangelize the culture in which we live without becoming subsumed by it.

What do we need to build a civilization of love today?

In a word: God.

The past century-and-a-half was full of efforts to create ideal human societies or communities, whether Christian or secular, all ending in failure and in some cases massive bloodshed. No such thing can be created on earth by human power, and certainly not by political means. As C. S. Lewis pointed out, a Christian political party is a contradiction in terms, since true Christianity can never yield effective politics and effective politics can never result in true Christianity. Instead, we have to recall Matthew 22:37–39 and render unto Caesar what is due to Caesar: nothing more, nothing less. Our true kingdom, the true civilization of love is not of this world. Our task is to help get as many of us as possible to our true home. This is why we need the Church, Scripture, and the sacraments: we can't do it unaided.

Our world has a very disordered notion of love. In the realm of politics, we have ideologies that claim to love the working class or "the people," and movements that claim to love "people of color" or "LGBTQ" people. But these terms are abstractions. It is not possible to love an abstraction: we can only love a real human person. Once we transfer our love from the real to abstract, all manner of evil results. This is why Marxists proclaimed their love for the abstract idea of the working class while murdering real workers, or why BLM proclaims its love for "Black people" while pursuing policies that cause devastation for real Black families and individuals. "Love your neighbor as yourself" is the Samaritan dressing the wounds of the real stranger by the side of the road, not a theoretical neighbor.

A healthy civilization would eschew the abstract for the real. It would value families as a fundamental building block, embracing them with all their human failings and imperfections. It would rightly order politics and economics to serve the goal of human flourishing. It would most of all be humble in what it sought as ends and prudent and humane in the means it used to pursue those ends. We don't live in such a civilization, but this does not free us from the obligation to love the world we have or from the duty to hope for salvation.

Yes, you need to teach freedom, you need mature freedom. Only on such a basis can society, the nation, and all areas of its life be founded. We cannot create fictitious freedom which supposedly liberates man but, in fact, enslaves and depraves him.... It is much easier to destroy than to rebuild...

John Paul II

JAN ŻARYN

Historian, professor, politician, author, and lecturer. He is the director of the Institute for the Legacy of Polish National Thought in Warsaw.

Tell us about your relationship with St. John Paul II.

Mine are very private recollections. When John Paul II was scheduled to arrive in Poland in June 1979, I attended a "post-secondary" school, where the instructions took place also on Saturdays (the day of the Holy Father's arrival). I signed up at my parish to keep vigil on Saturday, first in the center of Warsaw to welcome the pope and then at Victory Square. On the Friday, the school principal asked whether anyone would dare call in absent on Saturday. I was the only one in my class (and, I hear, in my entire school) who stood up and announced that, yes, I would be absent because I intended to be with the pope and not at school that day. The principal was furious, but I insisted stubbornly enough that she gave in. I was the only one who was permitted to go, but the rest of the students simply played hooky anyway.

I could not get enough of the pope, so after his departure, when summer vacation started, I hitchhiked to Rome. I applied for a passport and obtained an Italian transit visa for five days, which the Italian embassy issued to me without a hitch. I traveled to Italy with an Italian citizen, so at the border no one asked for my own passport. I remained in Rome for ten days. I met some wonderful people there, such as the recently departed Fr. Kazimierz Przydatek, SJ, who took care of all the Polish pilgrims, especially students; he got us a discount at a campground. Announcing "I am Polish" and my Polish flag opened the doors of many a car.

How did you come to meet the pope in person?

I met the pope personally several times, as a teacher and a Catholic activist in Włocławek. The most important meeting was a family affair, with my wife Małgosia and our children: Ania, Staś, and Krzyś. I remember that I was nervous speaking to the pope, or rather I slipped into a nervous monologue. I presented to him my book *On Polish History*. There was a picture of John Paul II on the cover; I told him the book was about the greatest Poles. He finally grabbed my hand, interrupted me, and said: "Good, that is important, but look there, you have such splendid children!" We talked for about ten minutes. He asked me what we did and where we worked. He asked all of us: the entire family. I remember this because the pope was spot on. Family is the basis of our individual and national sense of life. When we are, even without our fault, outside its field of interaction, we are away from the action of love.

What kind of mood prevailed at the Central Committee of the Polish United (communist) Workers Party (PZPR) after the election of Karol Wojtyła as pope?

On October 16, 1978, from Książecka Street, we could see lights on in the headquarters of the communist authorities. I was told the lights stayed on all night long. We know now that the members of the Central Committee of the PZPR were quite depressed. Finally, Comrade Józef Czyrek, foreign minister, calmed everyone down. He said that at least "Wojtyła will not be in Poland anymore." Cardinal Wyszyński, in a small circle of confidantes, some of whom were not discreet, had told Wojtyła that he saw him as his successor. Communist propaganda presented the election in its newspeak as, "Look what a Pole can do!" Therefore, the regime granted permission to broadcast the Mass inaugurating the pontificate. According to polls, the results of which were kept secret at the time, 96% of all Poles watched it on TV. From the beginning the communists realized that the first consequence of this would be a desire of John Paul II to visit his motherland. And they were afraid of that.

It was Cardinal Stefan Wyszyński who invited John Paul II to Poland. How did the regime react to the fact that a "private" person, not an official from the Foreign Ministry, and without consulting with the communists, invited the head of a foreign state to Poland? What was the reaction of the Kremlin to John Paul II's visit? What ultimately made First Secretary Edward Gierek grant permission for the pope to come to Poland?

Secret party documents reveal a picture of terribly scared functionaries. Whichever way things would go, it was always considered bad. One could not deny the pope his visit because he was a Polish citizen. However, if he were allowed in, he would threaten the entire Warsaw Pact. Pope Paul VI was denied entry at least twice, including in 1966 for the millennial celebrations of Polish Christianity. But Paul VI was an Italian. Finally, in January 1979, during a conversation with the Primate of Poland, Gierek consented to the establishment of a joint government-Church commission to arrange a visit, but that did not guarantee a visit in May 1979, the 900th anniversary of the martyrdom of the bishop St. Stanislaus, patron of Poland. The bishop was murdered by the royal government, or, more precisely, the king's men, and he is buried in the pope's city, Kraków. The communists feared historical analogies. Therefore they insisted on a visit in 1982, which would be the 600th anniversary of the installment of the painting of Our Mother of Częstochowa at Jasna Góra. Of course, that would be quite a long time away and much could happen, e.g., a successful assassination attempt on the pope. Finally, however, they agreed to a papal trip in June 1979.

On the other hand, Moscow advised Polish communists not to grant permission for any such visit, because the Kremlin correctly predicted that it would mean an ideological loss for the communists. In March 1979 the entire Communist security apparatus under General Bogusław Stachura commenced Operation Summer 1979. Thousands of secret policemen and other agents participated throughout Poland. Their aim was to minimize, via legal and extralegal activities, as they used to say, the negative consequences of the visit. It consisted of surveillance, detention, searches to discover illegal printing houses, and so forth. The communists were afraid of the activities of the democratic opposition, whose activists also wanted to meet with the Holy Father. At the same time, however, the joint regime-Church commission commenced operation, also at the local level, wherever the Holy Father was scheduled to visit.

What was the atmosphere in Poland during the papal visit? How did the regime react to the millions of faithful participating in Holy Mass with the pope?

In the span of those eight days in June (2–10), 1979, the public space in a totalitarian and atheist country belonged to the head of the Catholic Church. The pope addressed us and he also spoke for us; he said in Warsaw that one could not understand Poland and the Poles, our culture, without Christ. He exhorted us in Kraków to protect our Polish heritage, even if that required sacrifice. On June 5, in Jasna Góra, he met with the Episcopate of Poland to discuss relations between Church and state. He characteristically asserted that the Communists would first have to fulfill all conditions necessary for a full development of a Catholic society and its Church before establishing diplomatic relations with the Holy See. *De facto*, that meant that without a Free Poland, the Church would not legitimize the communist regime. John Paul II, together with Primate Stefan Wyszyński, stressed that his elevation to the Throne of St.

Peter was also an elevation of the Church in Poland, and an acknowledgment of its achievements in the struggle against communism. At the same time the pope and the bishops stressed that all this meant that the Universal Church needed a strong presence in Poland, which, therefore, had a mission to fulfill. John Paul II meant not only the liberation of the half of Europe behind the Iron Curtain from inhuman Bolshevism, but also that of Western Europe from an inferiority complex vis-à-vis Communism. Catholicism in Poland was strong.

The Poles stepped up to the plate. The attempt at total atomization of society failed. And the nation quite openly started speaking in a common cultural code. Furthermore — as a member of the Council of State, a communist dignitary but also a good sociologist, Professor Jan Szczepański, noted himself — the communists effectively stopped ruling the nation, leaving only the Primate of Poland standing. Marxism as a doctrine came crashing down.

The pope told not only the faithful but also the regime that, among other things, "Christ can be excluded from human history in no place on earth." How did the regime react to his words?

The Primate of Poland spoke to Gierek on behalf of the Church and also the nation: "I'd like to ask for the [communist] Party to undertake some kind of reorganization, so there can be a moral healing of the people, because in its current predicament in the [Soviet] Bloc the Party cannot be replaced. So they [the communists] must endure. To endure, they must undertake a moral renewal among themselves. I spoke like that for two and a half hours."

In his diary for June 2 [1979], an hour before the landing of the pope, the Primate wrote: "Great days commence for Poland today. We are awaiting the arrival of the Holy Father in Warsaw." The Primate realized that the public preaching of the Gospel would lift up the nation. To join him in the state of joy he also invited Gierek during a conversation he held with him at the end of May, a few days before the papal trip. Confidentially, Gierek claimed that he needed the backing of the Holy Father and the Primate because not everyone on his side, and Moscow in particular, would like the pope to visit Poland. So on the one hand we had full freedom, and on the other fear and slavery.

During his first pilgrimage to Poland, John Paul II spoke memorable words: "Let the Holy Spirit descend and renew the face of the land. This land!";

"Fear not!" They meant a lot for Poland. Would there have been Solidarity or the eventual toppling of the communist system without this visit?

Scholars studying the history of the Catholic Church in Poland agree that if there had been no generation saved from the Sovietization by means of the Nine-Year Program of the Great Novena and the millennial commemorations (1957–1966), there would not have been Solidarity as a Christian movement. Further, if it were not for the election of the Polish Pope and his visit to Poland, Solidarity would not have arisen after the strikes in July and August 1980. The strikes were a function of the influence of the Church, in particular as far as the shipyards of the Baltic Coast were concerned. According to the positive (Communist) law, the strikers were of course illegal. The communists, who in the West — in the capitalist world — had their own strong trades unions, in the nations they ruled without any limitation, on the other side of the Iron Curtain, had liquidated true unions back in the 1940s, and they replaced the right to strike with the so-called socialist labor competition and fake unions staffed by activists appointed by the Political Bureau of the Central Committee of the PZPR.

In August 1980, the workers realized that above positive law and coerced organization of labor there is moral and natural law, which are guaranteed by the Church and its social teachings. They did not have to verbalize that. It was taken for granted. On the gate of the Lenin Shipyard in Gdańsk there were pictures of the Black Madonna and John Paul II; and on Saturday, August 16, 1980, when a strike began there, a delegation of workers led by Anna Walentynowicz arrived before the local bishop, Lech Kaczmarek, with a request (or demand?) for a Holy Mass in the shipyard the next day. Priests began to enter a space which hitherto had been managed exclusively by communist party flunkies and managers. There was mass Confession, mass reception of Holy Communion. The strikers did not know whether on that day, August 17, the strike would end just as it did in December 1970, with a communist police pacification, when 40 people perished, also in Gdańsk.

The papal exhortation to "fear not" allowed the workers, as well as other Poles, to trust their ability to build their own communitarian and national narrative. The Solidarity movement embraced about 9.5 million people, including Party members. Solidarity cells began to enter power structures, such as the police or the Citizens' Militia (MO). The communist system was paralyzed from below. At the same time, a so-called self-limiting revolution was taking place with the active cooperation of the Church, starting with the Primate, all the way down to religious, diocesan priests, and the laity. Having been both a theoretician and a trade union activist in the interwar period, Cardinal Wyszyński became one of the most important advisers to the leaders of Solidarity. At the same time, along with other bishops, he forced the regime to yield (for example, by applying pressure to get the communists to permit individual farmers to create their own free unions). Priests blessed union banners, offered Mass, and opened up parish centers so the unionists together with lawyers could put together basic union documents.

Which words of John Paul II mean the most to you and why?
The words and thoughts are so many; today I believe that it is worth recalling his worries about our egotism and desire to "liberate" ourselves not only from communism but also from values and duties, such as the protection of life from conception to natural death, or taking care of the family, motherland, and commonwealth. I would certainly repeat his warning from 1991:

> It is my mother, our motherland! These are my brothers and sisters! And do understand, all of you who thoughtlessly treat such matters, do understand that such matters cannot but concern me; they cannot but hurt me. The destruction has been going on for too long! Now we must intensify the effort to rebuild! We cannot thoughtlessly destroy.

Today, young generation of Poles have submerged themselves in the swamp of skewed concepts, lies, and pernicious definitions of real values — a reality which it will be difficult to free ourselves from.

Once you said, "the pontificate of Karol Wojtyła paved the way to Poland's independence.... He gave wings to the Polish nation." Could you elaborate.
It was John Paul II who spread our wings, for my generation, the "JPII generation." Perhaps his strongest statement came at Westerplatte, where in 1939 Polish soldiers had opposed the German invaders, who vastly outnumbered them: "Each one of you, my young friends, finds in his life some kind of a 'Westerplatte'; a dimension of tasks, which he must take up and fulfill; a just cause one must fight for; some kind of a duty, an obligation, that one must not duck. One must not 'desert.'" He also said that even if no one demands that from us, then we should demand it from ourselves. The pope sought to make us better than we

were. He uplifted us, while the communists cast us down from the throne of man, who was created in the image of God himself.

What kind of message did John Paul II leave for our world?

For the contemporary world, Europe in particular, perhaps the most important message is something he learned from his Polish home, and Polish historical experience, and wrote about in *Memory and Identity*:

> Yet it still seems that nation and native land, like the family, are permanent realities.... Every society's formation takes place in and through the family: of this there can be no doubt. Yet something similar could be said about the nation. The cultural and historical identity of any society is preserved and nourished by all that is contained within the concept of nation.

It appears that in family the individual discovers his capacity for limitless love, and when one loves the motherland, he is capable of defending her culture and the heritage of the past generations. Without this harmony in the public space embraced by the national community, a man will not be able to find in himself enough love to embrace the entire world and its needs.

What do we need to build a civilization of love?

To build a civilization of love we need constant work on our conscience. Work frees a man. I do not want to sound like I am preaching a sermon, but in the past people who sinned had enough honor and dignity to suffer the consequences of their weakness. Now, as they say, sinners would like to have their cake and eat it too, without noticing the costs. This attitude is visible everywhere in the world, with for instance abortion and euthanasia. But such evil will spread if we do not control it. Killing of the unborn for eugenic reasons is the first step in building a "pure race" and seeking to eliminate the "useless." How can a man make such a decision? But love is difficult and demanding because it embraces one's enemies; we are called to love those who hate us.

ZBIGNIEW STAWROWSKI

Professor of philosophy at the Institute of Political Science at Cardinal Stefan Wyszyński University in Warsaw, co-founder and director of the Józef Tischner Institute in Kraków.

Professor Stawrowski, how did your fascination with John Paul II start?
It all started on June 3, 1979, in Warsaw. I was a young and confused man. I had lost my faith, and kept my distance from the Church. I stumbled into a Holy Mass celebrated by the pope for students. I heard him preach that while it was very important for us to complete university and enter a profitable profession, it was even more important that our lives should become the revelation of God's sons and daughters. It was not an easy language for me to hear at that time but I understood one thing: I was not just anybody; I belonged to God's family; I had my dignity and my life could make sense. Years later, I realized that everything I had experienced that day at the church of St. Anna in Warsaw was the effect of the Holy Spirit's work. Incidentally, it was the very day of Pentecost. From then on, John Paul II would become my own guide and a point of reference for me. I absorbed his teachings. I regularly tried to read all his encyclicals and homilies.

Which Wojtyła is closest to you heart: philosopher, pope, patron and champion of Solidarity?
Definitely: he is closest to me as a pope because he came to me preaching the Good News. It was, after all, his main endeavor. His philosophical formation, of course, facilitated that greatly. However, it was not his philosophical inquiry that finally changed the world. His support for the Solidarity movement in Poland also resulted from his pastoral work. Ultimately, every form of interpersonal solidarity grows out of brotherly love and should be a natural Christian attitude towards people in need.

Which words of John Paul II are closest to your heart?
The closest to me remain those I heard during his pilgrimages to Poland during the communist era. They were reaching people, especially young ones, because they were direct and uncompromising: "You must demand from yourself, even if others do not demand of you"; and also: "Freedom is given to man as a measure of his humanity. However, it is

also entrusted to him... [in order] to build, not to destroy"; and, finally, the most beautiful and moving words:

> Every one of you, young friends, also finds in his life his own ... task to be undertaken and fulfilled, some just cause that you must to fight for, some duty that cannot be avoided, cannot be deserted. Finally, a set of truths and values that must be "maintained" and "defended," ... for yourself and others.

Would the Polish Solidarity movement have been possible without John Paul and his teaching?

I think that without the teachings of John Paul II during his first pilgrimage to his homeland in 1979, the mass strikes and protests of the following year would have taken a completely different course, if they had happened at all. The Holy Father awakened a sense of human dignity in hundreds of thousands of people, giving them strength and inner peace, and preventing them from resorting to desperate actions. The communist authorities also needed to consider that the Polish Pope was the successor of St. Peter, and any use of force against the strikers would prompt a strong international reaction. This is how the Solidarity movement was born. It connected people of good will with a sense of responsibility for the entire community.

What was the idea behind Solidarity?

It was most aptly expressed by Fr. Józef Tischner, who recalled the words of St. Paul: "Bear one another's burdens, and so fulfill the law of Christ" (Gal 6:2). In Tischner's book *The Ethics of Solidarity*, we read:

> Solidarity does not need to be imposed on a person from outside by means of violence. This virtue is born all by itself, spontaneously, from the heart.... Solidarity is born of goodwill and awakens goodwill in people. Solidarity is like the sun's warm ray; wherever it falls, it leaves a warmth that radiates on without violence.... A Solidarity born of the pages and the spirit of the Gospel does not need an enemy or an opponent to strengthen and develop. It is addressed toward everyone, and not against anyone.

Once the Solidarity movement was established, the Holy Father faithfully accompanied his spiritual child. He was her patron and champion. How did John Paul II protect Solidarity from losing its evangelical spirit?

He addressed Poland through the Vatican Radio and other Church media. However, protecting the spirit of Solidarity became a burning issue only upon the introduction of martial law by the communists in December 1981. Among those who were persecuted, imprisoned, fired from work, expelled from universities, or forced to emigrate, a temptation to take revenge or to resort to violence could arise. The answer to this temptation was John Paul II's message during his second pilgrimage to his homeland in 1983: "Do not be overcome by evil, but overcome evil with good" (Rom 12:21). The Holy Father asserted that the most important task of that time was "the Gospel's program. It was a difficult program — but possible." How difficult this program was and what price one could pay for it the martyrdom of Fr. Jerzy Popiełuszko demonstrated soon after the papal pilgrimage.

How did John Paul II situate Solidarity within Catholic social teaching?

The Holy Father immediately understood that the Solidarity movement was an "embodied idea," which in a new and surprisingly attractive form expressed essential aspects of the Christian message. From the encyclical *Dives in misericordia* (1980) to his last documents, John Paul II made solidarity the basic category of Catholic social teaching. He constantly returned to it and always revealed its deepest theological meaning: "God's solidarity with man is the origin of all human solidarity. God's solidarity with man stems from the fact that He sacrifices himself." It is enough to refer to the encyclicals *Sollicitudo rei socialis* (1987) or *Centesimus annus* (1991), where John Paul II explicitly says: "The principle of solidarity, the validity of which both in the internal order of each nation and in the international order I have discussed in the Encyclical *Sollicitudo rei socialis*, is clearly seen to be one of the fundamental principles of the Christian view of social and political organization." His successors have not relied on this concept, returning instead to other concepts present in the tradition of the Church. Pope Francis, in his encyclical *Fratelli tutti*, prefers to use the idea of brotherhood.

You once said: "This relationship was not one-sided at all, because Solidarity also gave the pope something and taught him something." What did John Paul II give to Solidarity, and what did Solidarity give to him?

The pope sowed the seed of the Gospel during his first pilgrimage to Poland, and the seed fell on good soil and produced a bountiful harvest.

The Holy Father's eyes could see how the word was made flesh — precisely in the Solidarity movement — and with its power it began to transform not only Poland, but soon the whole divided, hostile world.

What should the world learn from the Solidarity movement in Poland?
Certainly, there are things in the world that philosophers, and political scientists, have never dreamt of. They fail to grasp that the impossible can become possible; and that the power of the spirit, and the power of love, can be stronger than the strength of the enemy tanks. But also it is obvious that these spiritual struggles will never be definitively over, and the call to bear each other's burdens remains valid.

Once John Paul II said: "There is no solidarity without love." Do you agree with him?
Certainly, there is no solidarity without love. Yet this does not mean that solidarity is a form of love. Solidarity is something more, something that is built on love. Solidarity is a bond that connects people who know how to love others and those who have courage to offer their help and sacrifice to those in need. The bond between the helping person and the one who needs help is called love. The bond that connects people who help each other is solidarity.

Please reflect on the Holy Father's position regarding the fundamentalist secular state that dominates the West, especially in the European Union. How would you explain these situations in relation to solidarity?
I would probably follow his words in the encyclical *Centesimus annus* (46): "A democracy without values easily turns into open or thinly disguised totalitarianism." On the other hand, solidarity is founded on the value, fundamental for every well-organized political community, of human dignity. You cannot be in solidarity with another person in need without noticing that he or she deserves not only absolute respect, your time and strength, and sometimes even your very life.

What do we need to build a civilization of love?
To build a civilization of love, you must be aware that you are loved by a loving Father. Only then can you live with love every day and radiate it to others. So it all commences with the experience of love in our hearts. This further gives rise to sensitivity to others, the desire to change the world for the better, the courage to act, and the

experience of a bond of solidarity that unites people who can love each other with brotherly love, who are always ready to help others bear their burdens.

JOHN HITTINGER

Professor of philosophy and director of the St. John Paul II Institute at the University of St. Thomas in Houston, Texas. He founded the Pope John Paul II Forum for the Church in the Modern World in 2009 and has published books and articles on a variety of topics.

How did your journey with St. John Paul II start?

I met Cardinal Karol Wojtyła at the Catholic University of America in 1976. I was a graduate student in the philosophy program at the time. He was attending the Eucharistic Congress in Philadelphia and was invited by Jude Dougherty of the School of Philosophy to come to Washington, D.C., and deliver a paper. He presented, in English, a now-famous paper on transcendence and auto-teleology. I was deeply impressed by his work — I still have a copy of the manuscript that he used that day. I had an opportunity to meet him afterwards; he quipped that the "Marxist-Christian dialogue" (so popular at the time in the West) was much more of a "monologue." I have been deeply attracted to his work ever since that day in the summer of 1976. Cardinal Ratzinger said it best during the 20th anniversary of John Paul II's election as pope: "It is a way of thinking in dialogue with the concrete, founded upon the great tradition, but always in search of confirmation in present reality. It is a form of thought that springs from an artist's gaze and, at the same time, is guided by a pastor's care." His life and work continue to surprise me with their illuminating power and rejuvenating influence.

John Paul II said: "Man lives a truly human life through culture.... Culture is that by which man as man becomes more man, is more, enters more into 'being.'" What's going on with our culture?

Culture extends through many fronts and venues, primarily through education according to John Paul II. Many venues of culture today are sick or superficial because they have cut off the search for God, which is the root of culture. Culture has become nothing more than the construction of a bubble around human fears and appetites. In *Fides et ratio* John Paul observed sadly that "those whose vocation it is to give cultural expression to their thinking no longer look to truth, preferring quick success to the toil of patient inquiry into what makes life worth living."

Yet the creative impulse still shows itself. As John Paul II wrote in *Redemptor hominis*: "In this creative restlessness beats and pulsates what is most deeply human — the search for truth, the insatiable need for the good, hunger for freedom, nostalgia for the beautiful, and the voice of conscience." The Holy Spirit is always at work in the depths of the human heart and in the creative impulse.

Today, we are in a historic battle between a culture of life and a culture of death. What went wrong with our civilization?

The root cause of perdition and our demise is now and always has been the turning from God and the exaltation of self, the city of man as opposed to the City of God, as explained by St. Augustine. In the modern world we also see the tremendous works of our own making turning back against us and seducing and ruining the very mind and will that hoped to prosper by them; again to quote *Redemptor hominis*: "The man of today seems ever to be under threat from what he produces, that is to say from the result of the work of his hands and, even more so, of the work of his intellect and the tendencies of his will.... [I]t turns against man himself, at least in part, through the indirect consequences of its effects returning on himself." We have magnified our minds and our will — we have seized tremendous power — only to find that we are unable to use them well or to sustain a moral and spiritual growth. We lack wisdom and social love, so we are more imperiled today than ever before. The external threats to human dignity are obvious, but the many forms of voluntary self-degradation are often celebrated as a true freedom.

What did John Paul II mean by a civilization of love?

The civilization of love is a new term for the City of God — a bond between persons based upon love, the love of God and neighbor. It is not a plan for utopia, but a concrete reality found in the daily life of many people and associations striving to live in friendship and love. Love is mutual self-giving. The communion of persons is rooted first in conjugal love, the marriage of a man and a woman open to new life. It springs from the law of free giving, self-sacrifice; it is blessed by a joy in truth and goodness. Of course, baptism in the Lord Jesus Christ empowers fallen human beings to sustain a life of moral and spiritual growth in the Church. Through solidarity it radiates through all associations for the renewal of temporal society.

Is the civilization of love a bracing call to a new American revolution: a revolution of virtue?

Yes, there is a revolution underway, and John Paul II continues to inspire its faithful conspirators — to say "yes" as Mary did to the grace of God in our hearts, "for the love of God has been poured into our hearts by the Holy Spirit" (Rom 5:5). The demands of the Gospel present formidable personal and social challenges, but John Paul II frequently urged us, "Be not afraid." In *Crossing the Threshold of Hope* he said:

> To accept the Gospel's demands means to affirm all of our humanity, to see in it the beauty desired by God, while at the same time recognizing, in light of the power of God Himself, our weaknesses: "What is impossible for men is possible for God" (Lk 18:27). These two dimensions cannot be separated: on the one hand, the moral demands God makes of man; on the other, the demands of His saving love — the gift of His grace — to which God in a certain sense has bound Himself.

Our age is marked by a "crisis of truth." Why is the "splendor of truth" so important?

As a teacher, pastor, and scholar, John Paul II vigorously sought truth and promoted its expression. We recall that John 8:32 was his favorite scripture passage: "You will know the truth and the truth will make you free." The intimate connection of truth and freedom lies at the core of his teaching. In *Redemptor hominis* he wrote that truth stands as a fundamental condition of freedom, and it serves as a warning to us in exercising it. Without truth we fall prey to superficial and often degrading forms of life. With the truth we discover our true greatness and the call to greatness of each human being. "The name for that deep amazement at man's worth and dignity is the Gospel, that is to say: the Good News." How can we rise to the full stature of our being without a regard for the whole truth about the human person?

In his encyclical Evangelium vitae, *Pope John Paul II condemned a growing and widespread "culture of death." How did he define this "culture of death"?*

The culture of death is manifest in the unbridled freedom to take the lives of others, and even to claim a right to commit suicide. The deepest root of the culture of death is the loss of God:

The eclipse of the sense of God and of man, typical of a social and cultural climate dominated by secularism, which, with its ubiquitous tentacles, succeeds at times in putting Christian communities themselves to the test. Those who allow themselves to be influenced by this climate easily fall into a sad vicious circle: when the sense of God is lost, there is also a tendency to lose the sense of man, of his dignity and his life; in turn, the systematic violation of the moral law, especially in the serious matter of respect for human life and its dignity, produces a kind of progressive darkening of the capacity to discern God's living and saving presence.

Rather than an amazement at the gift of life, rather than a celebration of God's good creation, rather than a life of reconciliation and forgiveness, we find poisonous seeds of hatred, anger, and lust: "For from the heart come forth evil thoughts, murders, adulteries, fornications, thefts, false testimonies, blasphemies" (Mt 15:19). These seeds are constantly cultivated by popular culture, encouraged by modern ideologies, and readily embraced by individuals, to the perdition of many. So now the culture of death leers out at us through most venues of culture, education, and politics.

How do parents go about raising their children in a radically secularized world where wokeism and cancel culture contradict the civilization of love?

We must always cultivate a sense of responsibility and conscience in our children. We must always encourage the "search for truth, the insatiable need for the good, hunger for freedom, nostalgia for the beautiful, and the voice of conscience." Most of all, the child must be introduced to the person of Jesus Christ and encounter his saving word at various stages of life. But we must anticipate heartrending setbacks and losses; at times we may sow in tears, with hope for a future of reaping with joy. To those pulled into the cancel-culture mindset we should repeat the counsel of Alyosha to Ivan in *The Brothers Karamazov*: "Be resurrected in the truth or perish in your own hatred."

How do we save our culture? Or is it not redeemable anymore?

John Paul II was a man of authentic faith, tremendous hope, and intense charity. There is always hope, given the power of the Holy Spirit and the "restlessness of the heart." We light our candle rather than curse the darkness. John Paul II named Maximilian Kolbe the saint of the difficulty 20th century because he witnessed to love amid utter hatred and degradation of the human person. Quoting St. John the Apostle — "This is the victory that overcomes the world, our faith" (1 Jn 5:4) — John Paul II proclaimed: "The victory through faith and love was won by him in this place [Auschwitz], which was built for the negation of faith — faith in God and faith in man — and to trample radically not only on love but on all signs of human dignity, of humanity. Father Maximilian won a spiritual victory like that of Christ himself."

What do we need to build the civilization of love today?

As always, two things are necessary — prayer and contemplation. In *Evangelium vitae*, Pope John Paul II says we need first to foster, in ourselves and in others, "a contemplative outlook." Such an outlook should form us to be those "who see life in its deeper meaning, who grasp its utter gratuitousness, its beauty and its invitation to freedom and responsibility." For people so educated do not "give in to discouragement when confronted by those who are sick, suffering, outcast or at death's door. Instead, in all these situations one feels challenged to find meaning, and precisely in these circumstances one is open to perceiving in the face of every person a call to encounter, dialogue, and solidarity." I think that too many American pro-life Catholics are tempted by activism and seek political solutions alone. Large amounts of money are poured into political campaigns and centers of prayer, while educational programs receive meager support. John Paul II was very keen on what he called "self-education" — each person should make a plan for reading and studying, using both faith and reason, to deepen his own understanding of truth, and to broaden awareness of the whole truth about man and God. This is the seed for the civilization of love.

Venerable and beloved Cardinal Primate [Stefan Wyszyński], allow me to tell you just what I think. This Polish pope, who today, full of fear of God, but also of trust, is beginning a new pontificate, would not be on Peter's chair were it not for your faith which did not retreat before prison and suffering. Were it not for your heroic hope, your unlimited trust in the Mother of the Church! Were it not for Jasna Góra, and the whole period of the history of the Church in our country, together with your ministry as Bishop and Primate!

John Paul II

RAFAŁ ŁATKA

Historian with a focus on the relationship between the Church and communist states. Professor at the University of Cardinal Stefan Wyszyński in Warsaw. Lecturer. He works at the Institute of National Remembrance in Poland.

After the end of World War II, Poland failed to regain her independence, instead finding herself under Soviet domination. What was the situation of the Church in Poland under the communist regime?

The Church was struggling with high personnel loss among the clergy during World War II. As a result of the actions of the German and Soviet occupiers (as well as the Ukrainian nationalists), about 20 percent of all Polish Catholic priests were killed. At the same time, however, the Church enjoyed significant social and moral authority. This reflected the appreciation for the steadfast attitude of priests in 1939–1945, which, among other things, involved maintaining the Polish national identity. After the Communists took power, the Church was under surveillance and the authorities, installed by Moscow, prepared to subordinate or even destroy it. The goal was not achieved, despite the work of the red terror apparatus and the communist Office for Religious Affairs. The latter institution, established in 1950, was responsible for administratively harassing the Church in Poland. The Church survived the most drastic repressions of 1949–1955, when priests were arrested, including Primate Stefan Wyszyński — imprisoned from 1953 to 1956. After returning to his see in October 1956, Cardinal Wyszyński began implementing his most important pastoral program, the "Great Novena," which lasted from 1957 to 1966. Its culmination was the celebration of the Millennium of Poland's Baptism, her Latin Christianity, in 1966. This deepened the faith of Poles and brought them closer to the Church. In the seventies, academic chaplaincies became more prominent. Thanks to them, young people adhered more closely to the Church.

In 1978, Cardinal Wojtyła became pope, and a year later he went on pilgrimage to Poland. This further enhanced the moral authority of the Church in Poland and became a key factor in the beginning of the Solidarity revolution in 1980. The Church backed the people in their quest for social rights and freedoms. John Paul II played a special role during the martial law period, powerfully supporting the repressed. The bishops also helped facilitate a peaceful political transformation in 1989.

What role did Cardinal Wyszyński play in Communist Poland?
Wyszyński, the "Primate of the Millennium," was a true leader of both the Polish Church and the Polish nation. In this respect, he filled the axiological void created by the communist system, which had never been supported by the majority of Poles, and the void of a flawless authority figure. The Primate lived up to these expectations, although he was never afraid to take the position he believed was right even if it went against public expectations. He showed courage not only in managing the Polish Church, but also was able to look at the political situation objectively. Whenever he believed that the state authorities, in some way, acted for the common good and, in some way, cared about the fate of society, he supported their activity, as in the fight against social pathologies — especially alcoholism.

How would you describe the relationship between Primate Wyszyński and Cardinal Wojtyła?
The Primate was, for the young bishop Karol Wojtyła (consecrated a bishop in 1958), a model to follow and a leader of the Catholic Church. Their relationship matured over the years, in particular during the Second Vatican Council, when Cardinal Wyszyński saw Bishop Wojtyła as an outstanding intellectual who was able to speak on behalf of the entire Polish Church. After receiving the nomination as Metropolitan Archbishop of Kraków, Karol Wojtyła gradually became one of the closest collaborators of Cardinal Wyszyński. He was made a cardinal in 1967. He became vice-president of the Polish episcopate two years later. Cardinal Wyszyński saw him as his successor in the role of Primate of Poland.

After Karol Wojtyła was elected pope, Primate Wyszyński said, "In Poland, everyone is happy, including our red brothers [i.e., the Communists], because I think that Poland is not so bad at all and things are not so bad in it, since the pope emerged from it. Perhaps it is more sad for me — the Primate — because I have lost for Poland my bravest and closest associate and assistant. For the Church of God, for the deepening of the spirit of God, for the living faith in the universal Church, I must rejoice. And I'm glad." How did Primate Wyszyński help to facilitate the election of Cardinal Wojtyła as the Supreme Pontiff?

Without the activity of Cardinal Wyszyński as the leader of the Catholic Church in Poland and even as a leader of the nation, Cardinal Wojtyła would not have been elected pope. After assuming the throne of St. Peter, John Paul II clearly emphasized the role of the Primate. Cardinal Wyszyński probably contributed directly to the decision of the conclave, as he persuaded some members of the College of Cardinals to vote for Cardinal Wojtyła. The election of Wojtyła as pope did not change their close relationship; moreover, John Paul II consulted Cardinal Wyszyński on important decisions, for example in the area of the Holy See's Eastern policy. The Primate played a key role in the preparation of the Holy Father's first pilgrimage to Poland in 1979. Wyszyński's emotional reaction to the assassination attempt of John Paul II on May 13, 1981, testifies to the closeness between the two. The Primate asked the faithful not to pray for him (he was already seriously ill then, and died 15 days later), but instead for John Paul II.

Would there not have been a "pope from a faraway country" without the Primate?

Undoubtedly, there would not have been Cardinal Wojtyła on Peter's Chair had it not been for Cardinal Wyszyński. It is thanks to the Primate who rebuilt a strong Catholic Church in Poland that Cardinal Wojtyła was able to appear at the Second Vatican Council and become a figure recognizable to bishops all over the world. He represented one of the strongest parts of the Church: the faith of the Poles waxed continuously, while it gradually waned in the West.

How did Wyszyński influence Wojtyła?

Cardinal Wojtyła was an outstanding and original thinker. From the teaching of Cardinal Wyszyński, he took the notion of a strong bond between the Church and the nation. Both clergymen were concerned about the moral level of the Catholic family as a primary social unit, as well as the inherent dignity of the human person and the sanctity of every human life.

What were the success and strength of the cooperation between Karol Wojtyła and the Primate of the Millennium?

Their success was primarily in mutual understanding and rational care for the Church and the Polish nation. Their strength derived from the fact that Cardinal Wojtyła was aware of the need to support the Primate in his mission, and to prevent sowing divisions between churchmen.

How did Cardinal Wyszyński contribute to the success of John Paul II's first pilgrimage to Poland?

Cardinal Wyszyński contributed significantly to the success of John Paul II's first pilgrimage to Poland in 1979 by taking care of some of the toughest organizational issues. He negotiated with the government himself, leading the First Secretary of the ruling Polish United Workers' Party — Edward Gierek — to grant permission for the pope's visit.

At the center of the moral vision of your founding documents is the recognition of the rights of the human person, and especially respect for the dignity and sanctity of human life in all conditions and at all stages of development. I say to you again, America, in the light of your own tradition: Love life, cherish life, defend life, from conception to natural death ... At the end of your national anthem, one finds these words: "Then conquer we must, when our cause it is just, / And this be our motto: 'In God is our trust'!" America: May your trust always be in God and in none other. And then, "The star-spangled banner in triumph shall wave, / O'er the land of the free and the home of the brave."

John Paul II

MARGARET MELADY

Former President of the American University in Rome, she served as the elected President of the Federal Association of the Order of Malta. She is married to Thomas P. Melady, former U.S. Ambassador to the Holy See.

Dr. Melady, how did your journey with St. John Paul II start?
Like many Catholics, I was excited about the election of a pope from Poland in October 1978 — as the first non-Italian pope in four centuries. I was living in Connecticut at that time, and had been active in helping to organize the many ethnic groups in the Bridgeport area. The Polish Catholic community was ecstatic. Prior to his election as pope, Cardinal Wojtyła had traveled to the United States visiting Polish communities and raising funds for his diocese back in Poland. My husband Tom, then president of Sacred Heart University, had invited him to receive an honorary doctorate on one of those trips. The cardinal had scheduled a trip to Boston and agreed to come to Connecticut to participate in the ceremony. But the cardinal's schedule became very busy and he called Tom to see if the university could confer the degree in Massachusetts. My husband had to tell the cardinal that, unfortunately, the university only had the power to confer this degree on-site. The cardinal promised that on his next trip he would come to Bridgeport, Connecticut. Of course, that never happened. And the pope showed his sense of humor when my husband Tom presented his credentials as the U.S. Ambassador to the Holy See in 1989. Pope John Paul II asked jokingly, "what about that honorary degree you were going to give me?"

What fascinated you about the Polish Pope the most?
John Paul II had such diverse experiences before becoming pope. And those experiences influenced his papacy. He labored as a worker. I remember his hands being so strong and large when he greeted people. He therefore could empathize with those making their living as farmers, construction workers, factory workers. He was also a poet, a dramatist, and an actor. As a poet he had an ability to seek deeper meanings and as an actor, he took advantage of communicating through symbolic action to convey a story. Of course his encounter with the Polish political scene — its communist leaders and their attempts to dampen religious expression — allowed him to understand the complex road to religious freedom.

Why did you choose John Paul II as the subject of your doctorate?

I was studying for my doctorate in Social Communications at the Pontifical Gregorian University in Rome and was particularly interested in the Church's rich history of using new methods of communication to evangelize. During the nineteenth century, the growing urbanized and industrialized populations became less dependent on the pulpit for information to guide their everyday decisions. These increasingly pluralistic societies were serviced by cheap newspapers aimed at the masses. At first, the Church seemed to fear the growing influence of the press and its role in stoking democratic expression. Then, Pope Leo XIII employed a new approach by issuing the first of a long series of social encyclicals addressed to a much wider audience of rich and poor, capital and labor, Catholic and non-Catholic. He warned that it would be a mistake to leave out the Church in this public discussion.

During World War I, the Vatican pursued a policy of neutrality which culminated in 1929 with Pope Pius XI renouncing the Church's territorial claims in exchange for a sovereign and independent Vatican state. Two years later Pius XI broadcast Vatican Radio's first message over transmitters built by the inventor of radio, Marconi. By the outbreak of World War II, people from all parts of the world listened to Vatican Radio, and especially Pope Pius XII's Christmas messages, which became important rhetorical milestones. After the war, Vatican Radio, broadcasting in many different languages, became a vital link with local churches that had been forced underground by communist, atheistic governments.

In 1962 Pope John XXIII opened Vatican Council II and set up a press office to meet the demands of both the religious and the secular press for information. He also began to venture outside the Vatican walls to visit hospitals, churches, and prisons. These visits were seemingly unplanned, stopping on the way to mingle informally with the people. Vatican Council II continued under the pontificate of Paul VI, who enthusiastically embraced the council's mandate. Closely collaborating with bishops from many parts of the world, he understood the global reach of the Church and thus he began a new era of international papal travel. He made nine trips outside of Italy over seven years. Many of these trips were to attend single events, such as international meetings of the United Nations or International Eucharistic Congresses. His last visit, to several Asian countries, could be considered more pastoral and prefigured those of John Paul II. Undoubtedly, the latter took Paul VI's model and made it a major part of his papacy. These visits employed public discourse as a persuasive technique. Most importantly, this communicative papacy of John Paul II presented endless possibilities, and as my dissertation director remarked, I was in a unique position to use original research in my study.

John Paul II established himself as a "great communicator." What tactics helped him to succeed?

When John Paul II became pope, the Church was part of an increasingly diverse and pluralistic world. Already, institutions and tradition had become suspect. Self-cultivation and individualism threatened communal ties. Sacred vocabularies often seemed to be unconnected to everyday pragmatic decisions. One of his most important communicative tactics was to move out into the world to give the Church and those encountering her a way to experience the sacred in community. He did not do this through small personal meetings behind closed doors — but rather in public events most often massive in numbers. The large gatherings in stadiums and open fields were designed to touch and inspire members of the Church from all sectors of the population. Attending these events were people who could not necessarily make the pilgrimage to Rome or Jerusalem. For them, it was a once-in-a-lifetime experience. The papal visit was missionary in that it aimed to build up the Church. Not only did people experience this through their participation in these crowded venues, but media coverage transmitted images of the events throughout the world.

Another important tactic was for the pope to move through the crowd, kissing babies, hugging children, bantering with young audiences, stroking the elderly and disabled — all with a caring and approachable demeanor. John Paul II became an ordinary person with the same human qualities as his interlocutors. It was a mixture of ordinariness and extraordinariness — the same tension that allows us to experience the sacred amid the secular.

John Paul II was particularly sensitive to the influence of culture. He was invited by many countries, and once a decision was made to accept an invitation, the local Church became involved in the planning. The planners at the Holy See sought the suggestions of local Church leaders for the itinerary, specific sites for events, themes, and even points of discussion. Certainly that was evident in visits to the United States, where our religious landscape includes ethnic and racial diversity as well as a well-formed tradition of working with people of all faiths.

Each pope brings his own style to the Church. How did John Paul II's style shape his pontificate?

Pope John Paul II's style was intimate and personal. First, he frequently used the singular personal pronoun—no longer the "we" of past popes. Sometimes he would recall his Polish heritage, or recall a song from his youth. He exhibited spontaneous moments as a relief from the more formal, scripted portions of his visits. In those moments he demonstrated his native personality. I remember such a moment: when he came out of a meeting with President and Mrs. Reagan, I told him that my husband and I had just returned from Poland, where we visited his boyhood home. He stopped and let out a boisterous laugh, remarking how amazing it was that his simple home had been turned into a museum. The expert papal photographers captured that moment, and I now have the picture framed on my desk.

Did Karol Wojtyła's experience in the Rhapsodic Theatre help him carry out his mission as pope?

John Paul II had a powerful stage presence. He was always aware of being captured by camera. Pastoral visits normally included an opportunity for young audiences to gather with him. Once he jumped off the stage and ran to an armless boy who was strumming the guitar with his feet and hugged him, calling him by name: "Tony, Tony." He humbled himself before this courageous youth, displaying his emotions and bringing the audiences to tears.

How did John Paul II use rhetoric in his pontificate?

His pastoral visits consumed much of his papacy. Through these he attempted to demonstrate that the Church as a community was not dead—but very much alive in all parts of the world. Religious language cannot be entirely clear because a sacred vocabulary is not grasped only as a scientific, rational concept. Therefore, the visits were mediated and visual in character, encouraging dramatic production of sacred symbols, with emotion and a sense of intimacy.

What does the rhetoric of John Paul II mean for the world and the Church?

I believe that much of Pope John Paul II's style of communicating is and will be continued by future popes. As the successor of Peter, a pope bears all the splendor and majesty of the office. And yet we crave a pope who is approachable. John Paul II sometimes spoke as an "approachable uncle." We were also surprised by his spontaneous moments of unscripted remarks or unplanned actions that were in contrast to the known and predictable formulas of ritual. At times these spontaneous moments produced emotional reactions. They showed that the sacred can be fun, sorrowful, and frightening by turns. Now we see some of those same rhetorical traits in Pope Francis.

In The Rhetoric of Pope John Paul II *you said: "He is the first pope to use the international visit as a new form of communicating with the far reaches of the Catholic Church, contributing a unique character to the development of the modern rhetorical papacy." Could you elaborate on this.*

Pope John Paul II was not the first modern pope to travel outside the Vatican and Italy. Yet he was the first to make this a major part of his papacy. The pastoral visit has become a central part of the papacy. During John Paul II's papacy, much effort was given to planning for pastoral visits. In my research, I was able to show how the planning was not just top-down from the papacy to the local Church, but the local Church was asked to provide guidance — not only on sites and special audiences but also on content of texts. This counsel greatly influenced the character of the visits. John Paul II adapted to his audience, whether in rural Africa or in urban Europe. He spoke using a mixtures of symbols that resonated with those at various points of the continuum of resistance or accommodation to the secular world. He presented without question the essentials of the Christian faith, but he also led his audience to experience the complexity of a deeper and mystical faith.

What was Karol Wojtyła's greatest strength as a teacher?

During the time when my husband was U.S. Ambassador to the Holy See, we often had guests in Rome. Sometimes we would receive a call from the pope's secretary saying that our guest was expected to have lunch with the pope. Of course, we would grill these guests afterwards; often it was not what the pope said but what topics he most wanted to discuss that proved especially interesting.

When we made our last call on the pope before leaving Rome, we thought it would be a formal farewell ceremony, but instead we were invited to sit down at his desk and just talk. I was working on the beginnings of my dissertation then, and so posed a few questions to the pope. He never answered, but rather turned the question to me, asking me what

I thought. And that was the experience of most of our guests who had lunch with him: he invited them to his table to ask them questions and explore their thoughts. So as a teacher, he was a listener and a learner.

What do we need to build a civilization of love?

Woven through John Paul II's visits was an optimism drawn from a strong faith in human potentiality to reach holiness. In his life as well as in his written and oral communication, John Paul recognized that the way of holiness sometimes requires venturing into unknown and unchartered domains. He often highlighted those who suffer, extolling them for their courage and showing how compassion can form a community. He publicly dramatized messages of love and compassion. Hugging a baby with AIDS, softly touching an elderly patient, and visiting his assassin in prison conveyed a message that life's bumps, bruises, and disagreements can be opportunities for people to leave their frightening solitude and reach out lovingly to others. We remember St. John Paul II's famous exhortation to "Be not afraid."

When I think my Country — I express what I am, anchoring my roots.
And this is what the heart tells, as if a hidden frontier ran from me to others
Embracing us all within a past older than each of us;
And from this past I emerge when I think my Country, I take her into me as a treasure,
Constantly wondering how to increase it, how to give a wider measure to that space it fills withal.
... Freedom has continually to be won, it cannot merely be possessed.
It comes as a gift but can only be kept with a struggle.
Gift and struggle are written into pages, hidden yet open.
You pay for freedom with all your being, therefore call this your freedom, that paying for it continually you possess yourself anew.
Through this payment we enter history and touch her epochs.

John Paul II

LEE EDWARDS

Scholar, journalist, historian, author, founder of the Victims of Communism Memorial Foundation.

What lessons do we learn from John Paul II and Ronald Reagan?

There are certain lessons to be learned.

Ideas matter. They do matter. They made a difference in the minds of both John Paul II and Ronald Reagan.

Friends and alliances matter. You cannot do it alone. Both John Paul II and Ronald Reagan realized that it cannot be a single power, even a great, mighty USA, that overcomes communism.

God matters. He mattered to John Paul II, Ronald Reagan, and people around them.

Morality matters. Both John Paul II and Ronald Reagan understood that what was involved here was a moral struggle.

Leadership matters. You must have the right leaders. You must have women and men who speak up against the tyranny. You must have leaders who are both charismatic, and courageous, and driven not just by their own place in history but try to change history for everyone.

> I recall with deep gratitude the late president's [Ronald Reagan's] unwavering commitment to the service of the nation and to the cause of freedom as well as his abiding faith in the human and spiritual values which ensure a future of solidarity, justice and peace in our world.
> *John Paul II*

MICHAEL REAGAN

American political commentator, journalist, former talk show host, and author of many books. He is the son of Ronald Reagan.

You were raised in a politically involved family. You knew Ronald Reagan better than anyone else alive today. How about John Paul II? When did you first hear of the Polish Pope?

I was raised Catholic, so I heard of the Polish Pope probably before my father did. My mother, Jane Wyman, an actress, converted to Catholicism. Maureen (my sister) and I were a part of the package, as we were all baptized in 1954 at the church of Good Shepherd in Beverly Hills on the same day as our mother. I had heard of John Paul II, the Polish Pope, before he really came on my dad's radar screen. It was interesting to have John Paul become the pope from Poland at the time he did, with everything that was going on in Eastern Europe.

When did your father first mention John Paul II to you? Do you recall a particular conversation?

I do not recall any particular conversation with my dad about Pope John Paul II. But I was thinking about their relationship way back in the 1980s. I spoke to Margaret Thatcher about it after his funeral in 2004. We happened to be staying at the same hotel in Bel Air. She said, "Oh, Michael, think how things would have been different had your father been elected in 1976. Think about how much we could have done." I responded, "Lady Margaret, had my dad been elected in 1976, the Berlin Wall would still be up and the Cold War would still be raging." She was surprised: "Why do you say that?" So I said: "Where were you in 1976? Where was Lech Wałęsa? Where was Václav Havel? Where was John Paul II? And where was Mikhail Gorbachev? None of you were in power. None of you! If my dad gets elected in 1976, at best, if he were reelected, he goes out in 1984. Mikhail Gorbachev does not come into play until 1985. So the Cold War would still go on. Lady Margaret, I am one of those people who believes that God chooses his moments. My father was not supposed to win in 1976. He was supposed to win in 1980 because then all of you were coming into place or were in place. And you needed that one leader from the United States who could bring everybody together and who ultimately could bring down the Berlin Wall and bring freedom to so much of the world." She looks at me and says: "I never thought of that." And I say: "Well, now you have."

What did your father appreciate about John Paul II the most?

My father really believed in Divine Providence. William Clark — known as the Judge — served my father as counsel, and was a close advisor and friend. Bill Clark opened the door to the Vatican. He also arrived in Rome ahead of my father to help lay the groundwork for the historic meeting between John Paul II and Ronald Reagan. He consulted with a number of Vatican officials as well as with the pontiff for a couple of hours. Both Clark and my father believed that Poland was the key to breaking the Soviet Empire. You have March 30, the date of the assassination attempt on my father. And soon after there is the assassination attempt on Pope John Paul II. I say it when I speak to groups: there are so many who recite the Lord's Prayer, but then you have to ask how many live the Lord's Prayer. Both of those men, Ronald Reagan and Pope John Paul II, lived the Lord's Prayer because both forgave their would-be assassins before they even went back to work: one to the White House and the other to the Vatican.

My father believed that he was saved for a purpose. What John Paul II was thinking, I do not know, but he must have been thinking somewhat the same. Not long after both attempts, my father and the pope meet for the first time in Rome. Look at the connection that they had. Look at what they are now able to talk about. Look at what they both had lived through. My father talked to me about that, and about meeting the pope. Both men lived and began a relationship that was really started with assassins' bullets in both cases.

Ronald Reagan, the political leader of the free world, and John Paul II, the spiritual leader of the Church, collaborated to defeat Communism in Poland and elsewhere. Was this Providence or coincidence?

Oh, I believe it was Providence. Ronald Reagan was fighting communism from the time he was in Hollywood. As President of the Screen Actors Guild, he was talking about communism and socialism. Also, my dad was a great reader of history. Simply by that he would have known about John Paul II and his fight for the freedom of the Polish people. Now you have both of them on the same page, both fighting communism and socialism. One was President of the United States, who did not want these to come to America; the other came from a part of the world that was under their control. The two men were able to work together because my father understood that the path to the Berlin Wall was through Poland. And Pope John Paul II knew the same thing: Poland was the key. You had to go through Poland to open up the Berlin Wall and bring freedom. If you did not free Poland, you could not free the rest of the Soviet Bloc.

My father had courage and faith. Think about the "Evil Empire" speech in 1983. Until my dad showed up, there was no world leader committed to fighting communism. Maggie Thatcher was there, but she was there for Britain. Her relationship with Reagan was strong; they had the same attitude. However, Pope John Paul II was the key. If the pope did not go to Poland, nothing was going to happen. Without John Paul II on the team, nothing ever would have happened. My father understood that. So did Margaret Thatcher. Until Ronald Reagan showed up on the steps of the White House, there was no leader in the United States willing to take on the Soviet Union. Before that, the word was, "just don't hurt Americans and we will leave you alone." My dad changed this. "We win, they lose." This was despite the media. People complain about the media today. The media was not that different back then. The only difference is that we did not have social media. But we did have NBC, ABC, CBS, the *New York Times*, and the *Washington Post*. They were absolutely against my father at every single turn. They only fell in love with him at his funeral. But my dad took on the press with a wink and a nod. He did what he felt he needed to do. His vision was to bring down the Berlin Wall and bring freedom to that part of the world. There had to be a way to do that. And that's why Pope John Paul and my dad spoke, I don't know, how many times a week? They were on the phone all the time with each other.

How can we rediscover the legacy of courage, hope, and freedom left to us by two extraordinary leaders?

I tell you, we have to follow their lead. When Protestant and Catholic got together, they figured out a way to bring freedom to the world. Ronald Reagan and John Paul II agreed on faith, albeit one from a Protestant position and one from the Catholic. But the bottom line is that Jesus was central in both cases. So they did not let religion get in the way of working together. They understood that they would upset people.

They both got shot, so they understood that. But they also understood that the end result was worth all that they were going through to bring freedom to Poland and, ultimately, to tear down the Berlin Wall. Pope John Paul II was willing to fight because of his experience in Poland before he became pope. He did not decide, well, I am pope now so I cannot fight for Poland. He did not stop fighting for Poland. He was happy to have a comrade-in-arms at the White House who supported him. The rest is history.

John Paul II and Ronald Reagan were both men of the theater. How did their theatrical experience help them understand the human condition?

They were both men of the theatre. They believed in the power of the spoken word — the word that finally helped them to change the lives of people from all around the world. The fact that they were actors helped them not only in terms of communication skills and keeping contact with crowds; it also shaped how both of them looked at being human. In their own ways, they used the power of the word to confront evil. They both asked the question: How do we bring communism to its knees? That's why 1980 was such an important election. I think John Paul II and Ronald Reagan really could see the future. They had a shared vision of what it could be.

Did your father's faith and spiritual life help him better understand John Paul II?

Oh, absolutely. My dad was a great reader. He actually read, and often re-read, all the books in his library. He really became very knowledgeable. He had a photographic memory — at least to a certain extent. When I speak to Young America's Foundation kids at Rancho del Cielo, I tell them: "If you only listen to one thing I say, remember this: readers are leaders." John Paul II and Ronald Reagan were both readers. And therefore they were leaders. Too many people now do not read. They turn on that 60-inch peep hole to paradise and they think they know everything. And they end up knowing nothing.

Donald Trump does not read anything. He listens to talk radio and watches Fox News. Then, based upon this, he tweets. He [ran] his presidency accordingly. And you can tell. Readers are leaders. Ronald Reagan and John Paul II were readers and leaders. Both knew about each other before they met for the first time. And it does not hurt to have someone like Bill Clark in your corner. Paul Kengor would not write this in his book on Bill Clark because Bill did not want him to say that, but Bill Clark was the conscience of Ronald Reagan. This was your guy. Ronald Reagan would go to a million people in Washington, D.C., to get an answer, but at the end of the day he would go to Bill Clark; he knew he would not get the political answer but he would get the right answer.

Why did your father decide to help John Paul II and Poland?
He understood the political dynamic. First of all, now he's got a friend at the Vatican. Before that time, what ally would the United States have had in trying to help Solidarity and bring freedom to Poland? There was not even a U.S. ambassador to the Holy See. Ronald Reagan opened up that door with the help of Bill Clark. He recognized Rome as a crucial force. He saw John Paul II as a crucial ally, as the pope did Reagan. You had a working dynamic. Reagan had been fighting communism forever—since the 1940s. Now he was elected President of the United States. Now he had the pope as an ally. Talking about the perfect storm! Thatcher was there too.

Would communism have collapsed without John Paul II and Ronald Reagan?
Of course it would have collapsed at some point in time. But who knows when? It might have not after all. It would have depended on world leadership. Would Pope Francis do the same thing as Pope John Paul II? Would he take the same step? I do not think so. But he did, being from Poland; not so much Francis, who is from Argentina. It was a perfect storm for both of these men: Reagan and Wojtyła. There was the Polish pope who wanted to bring freedom to his home country, Poland. And there was an American president who wanted to bring freedom to the world. They needed a door to go through. They both agreed that the door was Poland.

What do you think of John Paul II's first visit to the United States?
Anytime the pope comes to the U.S. it is a big deal. There are many Catholics here. At that time, because of the sexual assault stuff that happened to me in the 1970s, I had left the Church and all religion. I walked away from God and everybody else. I was only finding my way back after 1984. I told my dad about it for the first time and then wrote a book addressing those issues. I was always enamored of John Paul II.

When I was in school, Pius [XII] was pope. My Catholic mother taught me love and respect for pontiffs. I absolutely loved Karol Wojtyła. When John Paul II came to L.A. and made his appearance, it was great for Los Angeles. Then he went to Florida, where he met with my dad. I have that little statue that you sent me of my dad and John Paul II together. No other religion had this kind of a world leader. Same goes for the President of the United States. There were no more powerful people than the Polish Pope and Ronald Reagan.

What did John Paul II mean to you personally?

He was probably one of the major reasons I returned to Catholicism. I had so much respect for him, maybe because of his work with my father and what he was able to accomplish. It was also amazing to go to his canonization. Chris Ruddy organized a group; he took us to Rome. It was phenomenal. We had dinner with Lech Wałęsa before the ceremony. It was tremendous for my daughter Ashly to be there. She is a Catholic. She teaches at a Catholic school. My wife became a Catholic. My son is Catholic. My daughter-in-law is now Catholic. The grandbabies are baptized. Someone asked me, "Why would you go all the way to Rome for the canonization of John Paul II?" I responded: "Because I do not want to go to hell. I do not want to die today and get up to the Pearly Gates, where John Paul II will be, and not be able to answer why I did not make the canonization." It was incredible to be at the canonization of John Paul II also because Pope John XXIII was canonized at the same time. Further, there were two popes presiding over the ceremonies: Pope Emeritus Benedict and Pope Francis. So we had four popes! That'll probably never happen again. It is also important to me because I never met John Paul II in person. I never had gone to Rome before.

What lesson did you learn from John Paul II?

The lesson I learned was to look forward. Too many people look behind. My wife says to me: "Don't let somebody else's bad attitude influence the rest of the day." My dad and John Paul II never allowed anyone's bad attitude to determine their attitude for the remainder of the day. They kept their focus. Like Ronald Reagan, the pope made lemonade out of lemons. He believed he could change the world he lived in to make it a better place for everyone. Reagan felt the same way. Both of them looked at the positive.

What would they do today in our world of chaos?

I think they'd be leaders. Right now we lack leaders. The leaders are in China and Russia. Where are our leaders? We allow social media to destroy the underpinnings of America. I get it: the media have been against Donald Trump since day one. But it is about how you handle it. Ronald Reagan knew how to do it. He used humor. We don't have that today.

Why, despite the presence of Zbigniew Brzezinski, did John Paul II and Jimmy Carter not click?

Jimmy Carter had Brzezinski but Carter did not want to stand up to communism. Brzezinski alone could do nothing because the president was not on board. Ronald Reagan did it. And Carter did not have Bill Clark.

How did your father meet Bill Clark?

They were both members of the Rancheros, a riding group out of Solvang, California. Every year they met to ride for seven days. Bill Clark got my dad into the Rancheros. Most members were captains of industry or otherwise prominent businessmen. In turn, my dad brought him later into his gubernatorial administration in Sacramento. Bill became his chief of staff.

How do we build a civilization of love?

Don't watch the news; turn off TV; and spend time with the people you love and not the television set. Really. I love football but the most important thing to me is my relationship with my wife. We have been together for 47 years and just had our 45th wedding anniversary. So often, we'll get home, pour a glass of wine, and spend at least an hour sitting in front of the fireplace just talking about how our day was. It is just us.

I must admit that the whole experience of the theatre left a deep impression on me, even though at a certain point I came to realize that this was not my real vocation.

John Paul II

And so, before I leave you...
I beg you
—never lose your trust, do not be defeated, do not be discouraged;
—do not on your own *cut* yourselves off from the roots from which we had our origins.

I beg you
— have trust, and notwithstanding all your weakness, always *seek* spiritual power from Him from whom countless generations of our fathers and mothers have found it.
—*never detach yourselves* from Him.
—*never lose your spiritual freedom,* with which "He makes a human being free."
—*never disdain charity,* which is "the greatest of these" and which shows itself through the Cross. Without it human life has no roots and no meaning.

John Paul II

GRZEGORZ GAŁĄZKA

Papal photographer who took the official image for the beatification and canonization of John Paul II

How did your journey with Italy start?
I had always dreamed of going to Italy. My grandfather fought there, at the battle of Monte Cassino in 1944, under General Władysław Anders. Once Karol Wojtyła became pope, I wanted to be near him. I needed an accreditation to become a papal photographer. I remember that Archbishop Bronisław Dąbrowski helped me to get the accreditation and the Primate of Poland Józef Glemp provided me with a letter confirming that I worked for the Polish episcopate. I took my first photo of John Paul II on December 8, 1985, at the papal basilica of Santa Maria Maggiore in Rome.

Where did you take the photograph that was chosen as the official image for the beatification and canonization of John Paul II?
This is the photo of a lifetime. It was taken when the pope visited a Roman parish on February 19, 1989, one of his many visits to Roman parishes.

How did this photo get singled out?
I have been collaborating with the magazine *Totus Tuus*, affiliated with the Roman vicariate. I regularly gave them photos of John Paul II. Therefore, they knew my art there very well. They chose this photo for the beatification and canonization process, only changing the background.

How did you feel when you saw your photo displayed on May 1, 2011, at St. Peter's Square?
I was honored and deeply touched. I cannot find the words to describe my emotions. It was the culmination of my career, a result of my hard work, determination, and perseverance. It was a dream come true. It was also my thank-you and token of appreciation to John Paul II for his service.

What do you remember most about John Paul II?
His prayers. The pope prayed everywhere. There was no place where he would not pray. He was incredibly focused on prayer. His face was very expressive; you could tell that he was in a relationship with someone when he prayed.

Did John Paul II have any favorite places?

I believe that one of John Paul II's favorite places was his private papal chapel at Castel Gandolfo. He spent a lot of time there. The icon from the chapel of the Black Madonna of Częstochowa, which he kept a copy of there, reminded him of Poland.

What do we need to build a civilization of love?

Prayer. And to love one another as God has loved us.

I invite you to carefully study the social doctrine of the Church so that its principles may inspire and guide your action in the world. May the Holy Spirit make you creative in charity, persevering in your commitments, and brave in your initiatives, so that you will be able to offer your contribution to the building up of the "civilization of love." The horizon of love is truly boundless: it is the whole world!

Pope Benedict XVI

EDWIN MEESE III

American attorney and law professor. He served in official capacities within the Reagan administration, and as the 75th United States Attorney General. He is Ronald Reagan Distinguished Fellow Emeritus, Meese Center for Legal and Judicial Studies, at the Heritage Foundation.

Mr. Meese, once you said: "I walked into this meeting as a Lutheran with great appreciation for the head of the Catholic Church." What were the circumstances of your meeting with St. John Paul II?

I was the Attorney General at that time. I went to Rome on other business, and the U.S. Ambassador to the Vatican — Frank Shakespeare — invited me to meet with John Paul II. I met the pope in February 1988 and was very happy to see him. It was a great privilege for me. I had great respect for the pope. I had a roughly 15-minute audience with him. We spoke about a number of things, such as the state of morality in the United States. We talked about the pope's appreciation of the United States, his support for our people and President Reagan, who admired him for his strong moral stand as the leader of the Catholic Church.

What inspired you most about the Polish Pope?

He was a man of great presence and a man of great faith. I remember the assassination attempt and his appropriate and Christian reaction to that. Let's just look into the way he handled this difficult moment by himself as Ronald Reagan did. Both of them were victims of assassination attempts. I admired the Holy Father's wisdom, intelligence, and outspoken dedication to moral teachings, moral values, and moral actions. I was also impressed by his great sense of humor.

What are your thoughts about natural law in light of John Paul II's teachings? Are they aligned with yours?

Yes, they are. I think the pope was able to clearly express natural law in a very commonsense way. He acknowledged that man is a unique and special creature of God because of his dignity and free will. His free will gives him reason and opportunity to understand things and decide — as part of his free nature; but it also gives man the right to choose to align his actions with the natural law. Human beings have responsibility for their own actions. Freedom is a natural state of man.

Can we speak of a friendship between Reagan and John Paul II?

They were friends in the sense that they had similar ideas, particularly in terms of the Soviet Union. There was a friendly spirit between them, even though they didn't have an opportunity to be together very often. They also had very similar views of humanity, and an appreciation for each other as leaders. Ronald Reagan's faith helped him to better understand this pope. Reagan admired John Paul II as the leader of his Church.

In With Reagan: The Inside Story *you wrote: "A vivid example of the Reagan strategy in action was the liberation of Poland. Reagan conducted this effort in concert with Pope John Paul II, himself a native of Poland, whom the President greatly admired." Were there any particular reasons that Ronald Reagan wanted to help Poland or was it just part of his grand strategy to defeat the Soviets?*

President Reagan was impressed by John Paul II. He greatly admired him. The president was very dedicated to the cause of freedom in the world and he desired to remove Poland from the oppression of the Soviet Union. It was a part of the overall grand strategy to defeat the Soviets. Reagan's strategy had three parts: (1) to engage the Soviet Union on a moral plane; that's why he called the USSR an "Evil Empire," something on which he and the pope definitely agreed; (2) his desire to stop the aggression of the Soviet Union, which was trying to undermine free countries and to extend Marxism into those countries; (3) support for freedom movements throughout the world. Both the president and the pope sought to bring freedom to Poland. Poland at that time was the leading country behind the Iron Curtain and it provided serious resistance to the Soviet Union. Reagan trusted that Poland, with its strong Church and unique commitment to God, would defeat the communist regime. In 1978 Poland received that chance from God when Karol Wojtyła became pope.

How would you explain the phenomenon of collaboration between the Protestant president and the head of the Catholic Church? How far did the President's faith impact his relation with the pontiff?

I think they came from the same basic premises as far as faith is concerned, even though they came from different kinds of Christianity. They believed in the Bible and believed in God. They both believed that

God affects the course of human events. They both had a similar vision of the role that religion plays in life. President Reagan had an encyclopedic knowledge of the Bible, and religion was an important part of his daily life. The reason one did not see much about it in the news is that he never wanted anyone to think that he was using his religion for political purposes or he that was showing off how religious he was.

What did Ronald Reagan most appreciate in John Paul II?

The things I remember the most are related to the assassination attempt and Reagan's appreciation of the pope's bravery and his gracefulness. The pope was a man of great moral principles and a great example of strong Christian leadership. He was also very knowledgeable and intelligent. He was a very good man. Reagan knew about this and he admired him a lot.

Once Richard Allen said: "This was one of the great secret alliances of all times." Did Reagan and John Paul II have a secret alliance or simply an aligned foreign policy strategy that helped to end the Cold War?

It was not an alliance in a formal sense. It was two people working toward the same goal, each in his own way, one from the religious standpoint and the other from a political standpoint. They did have a great deal of informal communication during that period. Reagan communicated through his National Security Advisor Bill Clark, who worked closely with Pio Cardinal Laghi, an Apostolic Delegate of John Paul II and later a Pro-Nuncio to the United States.

Do you think that communism would have collapsed without Reagan and John Paul II?

I think that communism was destined to collapse at some point in time. There is no question that collaboration between the president and the pope definitely hastened it, and caused the end of the Cold War with the free nations winning.

Could both leaders have done anything better or differently?

In my opinion they did very well. I cannot think of anything particularly that they could have done better. This was a very delicate type of relationship. On the one hand, they didn't want to do anything that would unduly provoke and enrage the Soviet Union and Marxist leaders, to make them more oppressive. At the same time, they wanted to provide hope and motivation to the people who were working for freedom in Poland and elsewhere in the world. I think they handled it extremely well.

What should the younger generation know about both leaders and their work bringing freedom to the world?

The first thing would be the importance of religion, faith, and God as a foundation for people working together to maintain freedom. Our young generations have to learn a sense of freedom and a sense of responsibility. They have to know about history and what freedom is all about. That knowledge will help them understand what happened during the Cold War and why it was so important to free Poland and other nations. But it is also important to learn how people of good will can cooperate and support each other in fighting for freedom around the world. Speaking about President Reagan and Pope John Paul II, we are also taking about their responsibility to provide moral leadership to the people they were serving and leading. Their moral clarity and moral leadership were a part of their success against the Soviet Union, against communism and Marxism. Blessed with optimism, Ronald Reagan and John Paul II proved that freedom works, not only for the people of Poland, but also for those who suffered elsewhere from the excessive power of government. As the president himself put it: "We came to change the nation, and we changed the world!"

Did John Paul II change your life? What did you learn from him?

I admired his personality, and his strong standing for moral principles. He showed his love and respect for other people. He was a great leader of the Catholic Church who stood for the freedom of the human person. He defended the dignity and rights of all people.

How did this man from Wadowice who lived through the Second World War, lost his family, and fought against Communism become the head of the Catholic Church? How did it happen?

I think that God was instrumental in putting people in the right place at the right time. I think it applies to President Reagan and to Pope John Paul II as well. They both exercised leadership when it was needed to bring peace and the elimination of oppression in the world.

What do we need to build a civilization of love?

I think this represents the basic principle of respect for others, even those who are opposed to us politically. We need to have good will toward others. If you have respect for others and act in a civil manner, with genuine love and concern, it gives you a framework to emphasize those things where people agree, rather than focus on areas of disagreement.

PETER ROBINSON

Spent six years in the White House, serving from 1982 to 1983 as chief speechwriter to Vice President George Bush and from 1983 to 1988 as special assistant and speechwriter to President Ronald Reagan. He wrote the historic Berlin Wall address in which President Reagan called on Mikhail Gorbachev to "tear down this wall!" He is the Murdoch Distinguished Policy Fellow at the Hoover Institution, where he writes about business and politics, edits Hoover's quarterly journal, the Hoover Digest, *and hosts Hoover's video series program,* Uncommon Knowledge.

Who or what inspired you to convert to Catholicism?

The process began when I started studying history at college, finding, to my astonishment, that only a single institution went all the way back to the beginnings of western civilization: the Church of Rome. Assuming the Protestant Reformation had made all kinds of unanswerable arguments of which I was simply unaware, I took a course in that very topic. But the Protestant founders often seemed tendentious and frequently mistaken. When Luther was right, I decided, he was unoriginal, often presenting an insight from Augustine as his own, and where he was original — so it seemed to me — he was mistaken. The day before I graduated, an English professor, Jeffrey Hart, a convert himself, made a remark that lodged itself in my mind: "The Catholic church is the Church. Everything else is footnotes and criticism." After college, working in the Reagan White House, I received instruction from the late Msgr. Lorenzo Albacete, finally converting in 1984. Over all this, though, the figure of John Paul II loomed: titanic, holy, appealing, both challenging and reassuring. I joined the Church because I decided that what it claimed was true — but also because of the pope. I wanted to be on that guy's side.

Why is faith important in your life?

An arresting question, and one I scarcely know how to answer. It's like asking why air is important in my life. As a practical matter, which I suppose is what the question is getting at, I'd have to admit that I find quite a lot of life really very difficult. Providing a stable home for children? Trying to stitch together a career, such as it may be, from the oddments that my experiences and talents provide? How? And if I were somehow to manage all that, what about losing parents, then friends? What about illness? What about—death? I grope about as best I can, trusting, again, as best I can, that God is fitting the events of my life—and of my wife's, and my children's, and my friends' and colleagues'—into a loving plan. That is the *only* way I can proceed. In some ways the central passage of the Gospel for me—the one that seems to speak to me directly—is the one in which Our Lord calls Peter to walk across the water to him. When Peter removes his gaze from Jesus, he sinks. When he fixes his gaze upon Jesus instead, he can do as he is bidden.

Peter, you had just turned 30 years old when you were tasked with drafting one of Reagan's most famous and important presidential speeches: "Mr. Gorbachev, tear down this wall." How did this influence Poland's predicament, which was a great concern to John Paul II?

I believe that speech gave dissidents throughout Eastern Europe an important sense of encouragement, reminding them that they weren't alone. Joachim Gauck would go on to become president of a reunited Germany, but at the time of the speech he was a Lutheran pastor, a position in which he agitated for human rights, in the East German town of Rostock. Gauck said at a dinner at which I was present not long ago, "Ronald Reagan said exactly the right thing in exactly the right place at exactly the right time."

How did you get the idea for "tear down this wall"? What was your inspiration for this speech?

From Ingeborg Elz, a woman in West Berlin. "If Gorbachev is serious about this talk of glasnost and perestroika," she said to me, "he can prove it. He can come here and get rid of the wall."

How did you gather all the material for the speech?

I visited West Berlin to research the speech. I went to the site where the president would deliver the address—he was to stand immediately in front of the Berlin Wall. I spoke with diplomats in West Berlin. I was given a ride in a U.S. Army helicopter over the perimeter of West Berlin, our flight following the wall itself. And I spent an evening with West Berliners—it was at this event that I met Ingeborg Elz.

Peter Robinson

Were there any speeches on your mind when you were drafting the speech?

Only one: I wanted to *avoid* any comparisons between John Kennedy's *Ich bin ein Berliner* address and anything President Reagan would say. The times were too different.

The speech was putting Gorbachev on the spot in Moscow itself. Did you get any opposition from Reagan's administration regarding the speech?

The State Department and the National Security Council both fought the speech — bitterly. President Reagan himself had to overrule them to deliver it.

What did you feel when you heard President Reagan reading out your words? Did it feel like you made a difference in the world?

To tell you the truth, the fight over that speech had been so intense — the State Department and the National Security Council had tried to suppress it — that when the president delivered it I felt only one thing: relief. It didn't occur to me — or, as far as I can tell, to anyone else — that the speech was in any way historic until 28 months later, when the Berlin Wall (to my astonishment) came down.

What else in Reagan's speech is worth remembering today?

At the very end of the speech, the president ad-libbed a remark. Speaking of the protesters who had tried to interrupt him with chants and shouts, he said this: "I wonder if they have ever asked themselves, that if they should have the kind of government they apparently seek, no one would ever be able to do what they're doing again." A perfect — and unanswerable — observation.

What did Ronald Reagan, a Protestant from the Midwest, appreciate in John Paul II?

Start by recalling that Reagan's father was a Catholic — and that his older brother, "Moon," became a Catholic himself (although the one time I heard Reagan comment on that, it was to say that his brother had converted "to marry a Catholic girl"). What this meant was that Reagan had none of the anti-Catholic sentiment that was common among Protestants of his generation. Add to that that John Paul II was a man's man, the kind of strong figure Reagan admired: the pope understood how to perform in public, how to move audiences, how to get things done. And of course Reagan saw in the pope a fellow anti-communist.

Most important, though, I always felt, was that Reagan recognized that the pope was not simply a fellow head of state but, like Reagan himself, a man of faith.

Did Ronald Reagan and John Paul II have a secret alliance or simply an aligned foreign policy strategy that helped to end the Cold War?

My feeling is that "an aligned policy" comes closer to capturing what took place. The term "secret alliance" conjures up images of Cold War movies, hotlines, and so on. On the other hand, there's no doubt that the relationship between the Reagan White House and the Vatican was very close.

What did John Paul's death mean for you?

Watching the last few weeks felt like watching a martyrdom—the obvious weakness and pain, the insistence, even so, on offering up all that he was experiencing. A life—and death—that enlarged my sense of the kind of life—and, again, death—that is possible.

What does the new generation need to believe in to build the civilization of love?

Prayer.

> Yet, as Genesis has it, all men and women are entrusted with the task of crafting their own life: in a certain sense, they are to make of it a work of art, a masterpiece.
>
> *John Paul II*

NEWT GINGRICH

American politician and author who served as the 50th speaker of the United States House of Representatives. He is well known as the architect of the "Contract with America." Mr. Gingrich is Chairman of Gingrich 360, a multimedia production and consulting company. He is a Fox News contributor, podcast host, and syndicated columnist. Mr. Gingrich and his wife Callista produced a documentary about John Paul II: Nine Days That Changed the World.

What did you think when the Polish cardinal Wojtyła was elected pope?

I thought it was an enormous help in undermining the Soviet Empire. I was very involved in developing strategy to defeat the Soviet Union and we were close to the Reagan people. I thought that the moral impact and nationalist impact of John Paul II were extraordinary and could become a major factor in dissolving the Empire and Eastern Europe.

What did the election of a pope from behind the Iron Curtain mean for America and the American people?

Well, first of all, I think there was a pretty large Polish-American population and they were of course totally thrilled. I think that Catholics in general were attracted to him because he was young at that point and dynamic. He was very successful; he drew very large crowds. At one point, his staff was worried about coming to America, and he insisted doing his thing with the crowd, which was enormous, and I think it vindicated his approach. So from the very beginning he was kind of a rock star, going to Mexico, then to the US — and his extraordinary trip to Poland in 1979. Callista and I made a movie about that.

Do you remember your first meeting with St. John Paul II?

I met him one-on-one when I was Speaker of the House in the 1990s. I think I underestimated how important he was and how much force he had in his personality. As I look back to that time, I was not very clever in that meeting. Only later did I begin to realize his profound impact. All of us were aware that he had been shot, and it was very strange that Reagan was shot almost at the same time; later that event became a bond between them, a sign that God must have saved them for some reason.

How does human dignity, defended by John Paul II through his entire life, connect to natural law?

What is most powerful about John Paul II's witness is that he doesn't say, "have courage," but instead, "be not afraid." I think that was central to who he was because as a young person he had to deal with the Nazis, and during his entire time as a seminarian, he faced the death penalty if he was caught. Yet he calmly and steadily persevered—and then the Nazis were replaced almost immediately by the Soviets. So his entire formative experience was under anti-religious dictatorships. I think that a part of his strength was an almost mystical belief in God that transcended any human pressure. I also think that the mystical component of his faith is very hard for Westerners to fully grasp. Faith transcends reason. And I think that in that sense he was truly remarkable.

I also thought it remarkable that he and Reagan had been actors. Both of them understood how to play their roles: Reagan played the role of president and Wojtyła that of the pope, and both of them were playing the roles of world leaders setting out to change things. John Paul II's great achievement was reawakening Eastern Europe and sustaining its Christians in the face of the Soviet Empire's secularism.

John Paul II began warning us in the early 1990s that commercialism would be a greater threat to Christianity than communism. What we don't know is whether we could have had John Paul II, given the force of his personality and his intellect, focusing on creating a modern understanding of Christianity in contrast to the secular commercialism, and what his total impact might have been. By the time he began shifting to that he had already spent most of his energies first in Poland surviving under Communism, and even thriving, and then as pope methodically helping to take on the Soviet Empire. I think he was in his seventies by the time he was able to shift gears. I think he had a strange combination of Francis's personal appeal and Benedict's intellect. It made him maybe the greatest pope in the last three or four hundred years because he combined these characteristics in a way that was really, truly extraordinary and that changed history more than any pope in modern history that I know of.

Have you ever considered the mystical dimension of his pontificate?

I think the degree to which John Paul II was committed to a faith-based understanding of reality rather than a rational one is insufficiently appreciated. He saw reality as transcending the grasp of a rational mind. He also had a unique capacity for looking into people and understanding them and inspiring the best in them. There are many stories of him interacting with people in a way that was transformative. I think this was partly because he was looking for your soul and not just your rational surface. And he was always trying to help you find a larger meaning in your life and a larger cause to dedicate yourself to; something that gets you closer to God. I think in that sense he had an enormous impact upon almost everybody he dealt with.

How compatible are the principles of John Paul II with political pursuits?

I think that his long-term impact will be a rediscovery of the central role of faith and the notion that if you truly believe in God you do not have to have courage because you can simply relax in the shadow of God's love, and God provides the courage. The Trump administration's efforts to fight for religious liberty everywhere are a direct consequence of John Paul II's sermons, speeches, and encyclicals. There is greater awareness today of the importance of religious liberty than there would have been in 1977 or 1978, and I think that is a direct reflection on John Paul II.

Why did Reagan need Poland to destroy Communism? Was it a matter of convenience because the Poles rebelled? Was it just a tactical move?

I do not think he chose Poland. I think Poland chose him. I was in my second term in Congress. I won in 1978 and then in 1980, when Reagan won. So I was a very junior congressman, but I was very active on national security issues with the Reagan team. Remember that this was the period of Solidarity. It was a period when we were actively fighting against the Soviet gas pipeline into Europe. We were actively collaborating with both the Church and Solidarity to, for example, smuggle printing presses into the country. Poland has always seen itself as a Catholic bulwark against the East. It is also true that the Poles were probably more devoutly Christian than anybody else in Eastern Europe. That is partly how they survived the Swedish Lutheran "Deluge" in the 17th century, how they survived the long wars against the Cossacks, long fights with the Russians. So I think you have to look at the depth of Polish readiness to rebel and fight.

Of course, we had Polish freedom fighters coming to the U.S. during the Revolutionary War; one of them — Thaddeus Kościuszko — has a statue across from the White House. We had other Polish fighters come in the 19th century. So the hunger of the Polish people for their identity, the fact that their state disappeared, dismembered by their neighbors, makes it poetic that John Paul II was born when Poland reappeared after over 120 years of absence from the map of Europe. Suddenly Poland once again existed, and the Polish army, with the help of French advisors, defeated the Soviet army in 1920. We saw Poland ultimately as a big country, bigger than Czechia or Hungary; and I think its identity is much more religious than that of any other in the region. I think there was a deep sense of guilt in the United States that we betrayed Poland and all of Eastern Europe at Yalta in 1945. These nations had fought on our side. There are Polish military cemeteries in Italy. There were Poles who died in Belgium and Holland. Polish aviators flew in the Battle of Britain. So the Polish people earned a level of affection and a level of sympathy with us. There was a fairly large émigré community in the U.S. and, on the political side, Reagan had ties to that community; he drew advice from it. So all of that came together and made the struggle in Poland one of the pivots of the fight against the Soviets.

Afghanistan was on the other side of this. We provided them with weapons and money to bleed the Soviet Empire. But in Poland we had a chance to confront it directly. With John Paul II the Vatican abandoned Ostpolitik, which was an appeasement strategy, for challenge and confrontation. However, minding his people under communism, John Paul II was very careful about how far he would push in Poland. Because he had lived there, he understood that the communists would just kill you. So he was constantly saying: walk to the edge, but do not walk over the edge. Sometimes people forget that that there were a lot of different things going on simultaneously there. In my mind at least, John Paul II, Thatcher, and Reagan were the trio that decisively defeated the Soviet Empire.

You and your wife produced the documentary Nine Days That Changed the World. *What did you learn about John Paul II in the process?*

A lot of things! We had done a movie on Ronald Reagan called *Rendez-vous with Destiny*. We were in Eastern Europe, interviewing Lech Wałęsa in Gdańsk and Václav Havel in Prague. In both cases we asked them what they considered the decisive turning point. With Lech Wałęsa you could have guessed what he would have said. He was a devout Catholic, wearing a Black Madonna pin, all his life. But

Havel was not Catholic and did not live in Poland. And they both gave exactly the same answer. They said that when the pope came to Warsaw in 1979, it reverberated all through Eastern Europe and not just Poland. It sent a signal that freedom was possible. As somebody says in our movie, when there were three million people in Victory Square in Warsaw for the Mass on the first day of his visit, they looked around and realized that there were a lot more of them than of the security forces. And that rippled all across Eastern Europe. During the Soviet period people had cabins in the mountains, so you'd go up to the cabin and you were able to walk across the mountains to see your friends in Poland or Czechoslovakia. When John Paul II came for his visit, it just sent a signal to all those people. Because Callista is half-Polish and 100% Catholic, when she heard Havel talking, she turned to me and said: "We've got to make the movie about the pope." I smiled, and she continued: "No, no. We have to make the movie." So in a sense it is a tribute to both Polish nationalism and Catholicism.

When we set out to make the movie, to be fair, the real driving force was George Weigel, who had written a brilliant chapter on the 1979 Warsaw visit in his biography of the pope. When you read the chapter you really see where we got the core structure of the movie. Weigel is just a remarkably brilliant and energetic guy. He also found out that the bishops distrusted the Soviet media and so they had given out home movie cameras, and there were thousands of hours of footage of the visit that no one had ever seen. So we sent Vince Haley over to negotiate with the bishops to get permission to use this. Of course they did not trust anybody, especially lawyers. They did not particularly want to do it. Vince was about to get married, but we told him: "You cannot come home until you get this contract." So he wrapped it up. And when you look at the movie there are scenes in there entirely taken by the local people. It will give you the intimacy about the speeches, riding through town, levels of joy and excitement. *Nine Days* was really well received. Cardinal Timothy M. Dolan told us that he uses it in his catechism classes. I think it is one of the best things that Callista and I have done.

What do we need now to build the civilization of love today?

I have just read a novel about St. Paul and the Corinthians. The author is writing about the centrality of charity: without charity, nothing matters. And he is trying to get across to them that we have to individually communicate our love to each other. That is not something that you legislate; it is something you live. If enough people do that, then in fact you change the world. And that's what early Christians did. And, in a sense, that's what John Paul II did. And every generation has to do it. You can't say that, oh, they did that in the last generation, so now we get to relax. Every generation has to reestablish a culture of love and faith and hope.

PAUL KENGOR

Senior Director and Chief Academic Fellow for the Institute for Faith & Freedom; Professor of Political Science at Grove City College; author of over a dozen books, including A Pope and a President: John Paul II, Ronald Reagan, and the Extraordinary Untold Story of the 20th Century.

Tell us how your journey with St. John Paul II started.

I became interested in John Paul II through my study of the end of the Cold War. I knew that this man had played a major role in the defeat of atheistic Soviet communism. I found him bold, brilliant, and inspiring. He had real courage, telling us to "be not afraid." As I studied him closer, I also began reading his encyclicals, particularly *Evangelium vitae*, *Veritatis splendor*, and *Fides et ratio*. Those particular studies drew me to the Catholic Church. I came into the Roman Catholic Church in April 2005, precisely when John Paul II died. That was no coincidence.

Why did you choose the Polish Pope as the protagonist for your book?

I had included John Paul II as a figure in other books on the end of the Cold War, including *The Crusader: Ronald Reagan and the Fall of Communism* (2006). Including him was, of course, quite natural — given his role in the fall of communism. I came to see that he and Ronald Reagan had a remarkably historic partnership. I knew that very little had been written on that partnership. The more that I learned about that partnership, the more I realized that I needed to write a book on how John Paul II and Ronald Reagan worked together to defeat atheistic Soviet communism.

Are there any words that particularly strike you from John Paul II's speeches?

Probably the most conspicuous is "be not afraid," which, of course, is a very common exhortation throughout Scripture, from the Angel Gabriel speaking to Mary at the Annunciation to the many occasions where Jesus Christ urged his followers to have no fear. Another signature phrase of John Paul II that stands out is "culture of life." That phrase has profoundly influenced the entirety of the pro-life movement (Catholic and non-Catholic) worldwide. Another significant phrase is "theology of the body," which refers to his work on sexual ethics.

In the last will and testament of the Holy Father John Paul II, we read: "In life and in death [I am] Totus Tuus through Mary Immaculate." Could you comment on his devotion to the Virgin Mary.

It's one of the most moving things about him. After the death of his earthly mother, the Blessed Virgin became his mother even more so. His father told him, "This is now your mother."

In his book Memory and Identity, *John Paul II said: "patriotism is a love for everything to do with our native land: its history, its tradition, its language, its natural features." What should we take from his concept of nation, culture, history, and freedom?*

I appreciate his phrase "memory and identity." You have observed that John Paul II saw how Polish identity was preserved and kept alive through the memory of history and poetry and theatre and literature. That's a very valuable lesson. It shows that political powers might be able to erase a nation's boundaries, but they cannot erase the memory and identity of that nation and its people.

You begin your book A Pope and a President *with a quote from John Paul II: "Every human being [is] unique and unrepeatable," and then from Ronald Reagan: "There is purpose and worth to each and every life." How did you come to choose these quotes?*

I've long known that quote from John Paul II, and loved it. I noticed the second quote etched on Ronald Reagan's tombstone at the Reagan Library in Simi Valley, California. I was there that summer researching my book on Reagan and John Paul II. It immediately struck me how similar it was to John Paul II's statement.

How would you explain the role of divine providence in John Paul II's life and work?

There are so many ways, but the one that I've given special attention to is how John Paul II and Ronald Reagan came together at the Vatican in June 1982 and said to one another that they believed that God had spared their lives from assassination attempts in March and May 1981 for a larger purpose, a divine purpose. They had come together, they believed, as part of a divine plan — the doing of divine providence. That plan, they hoped, was for them to work together to defeat atheistic Soviet communism. And that's exactly what happened.

What impact did communism have on Karol Wojtyła, especially during his young formative years?

He learned early on, in the 1940s, that atheistic communism was stifling and repressive — that it was not only economically destructive but spiritually destructive. It was, above all, anti-God. Like his Church, John Paul II realized that the battle against communism was first and foremost a spiritual battle.

What were the pope's religious and political strategies to defeat Communism?

Well, I wrote a 700-page book on the subject. So, this is the hardest question to answer among all those you've asked me. For the pope, the religious strategy was to boldly proclaim the truth of the Gospel, unafraid — speak truth to power. From a political perspective, it was — as he said in his first visit to his Polish homeland in June 1979, speaking at Warsaw's Victory Square — his call for an "independent Poland" on the map of Europe. He and Ronald Reagan would work together to save and sustain the Solidarity movement as the crucial organization that could help drive a wedge into the Communist Bloc.

How would you describe the friendship between John Paul II and Ronald Reagan? How might history have been different without their alliance?

It was a special relationship and partnership, and both men respected and liked one another. As to how history might have been different, let me put it this way: If these two men had bled to death after the assassination attempts made against them in March and May 1981, you and I would not be doing this interview right now. The Berlin Wall would not have fallen in November 1989, and the USSR would not have fallen apart in 1991.

What's your reflection on the moral clarity and moral leadership by John Paul II and Ronald Reagan?

Neither man was afraid to call evil "evil." As Reagan said in the Evil Empire speech in March 1983: "For too long our leaders were unable to describe the Soviet Union as it actually was. I've always believed, however, that it's important to define differences.... The Soviet system over the years has purposely starved, murdered, and brutalized its own people. Millions were killed; it's all right there in the history books. It put other citizens it disagreed with into psychiatric hospitals, sometimes drugging them into oblivion. Is the system that allowed this not evil? Then why shouldn't we say so?" Reagan said such candor was needed to "philosophically and intellectually take on the principles of Marxism-Leninism." He noted: "Marxist-Leninist thought is an empty cupboard. Everyone knew it by the 1980s, but no one was saying it." Ronald Reagan knew that such moral clarity was important, as did John Paul II.

What lesson of John Paul II would you convey to the younger generation today?

Be not afraid. Speak truth to power. Have courage and moral clarity. And above all, as both John Paul and Ronald Reagan showed, speak with kindness, love, charity.

What do we need to build a civilization of love today?

Don't be afraid to speak the truth, but do so with kindness.

JOHN O'SULLIVAN

President of the Danube Institute in Budapest; editor, columnist, and senior fellow at the National Review Institute in Washington. Mr. O'Sullivan is a senior fellow at the Hudson Institute, a Commander of the Order of the British Empire, and former special adviser to Lady Margaret Thatcher. He is the author of The President, the Pope, and the Prime Minister.

Mr. O'Sullivan, what did you appreciate the most about St. John Paul II?

My first, immediate, and completely justified reaction to John Paul II was a political observation. In the 1970s, the Soviet Union seemed to be riding high. Brezhnev had said that no major decision could be taken or real politics be conducted without the consent of the Soviet Union. Suddenly, you have a man who became pope with an extremely good reputation — as a man of great political courage and faculty. He humbled the communist government very effectively, providing with Zbigniew Brzezinski a canopy under which intellectuals of all religions, not simply Catholics, could keep opened and honest discussion about the most delicate topics. And my second reaction was a religious observation. The Church would be more orthodox. It would be more confident in its mission and doctrine. And this confidence would be presented by the human faith of this man.

You attended an audience with John Paul II but you didn't have a chance to meet him in person. However, you have said, "I have a pretty good insight into him, I think." What's your insight about the Polish Pope?

I expected at first that he would be a powerful figure on the one hand in resisting political tyranny of communism, and on the other that he would strengthen the self-confidence of the Catholic Church, which was still hurting from the divisions and schisms of the 1970s and from the emergence, which began in the 1960s, of the unorthodox liberation theology, which seemed to substitute Marxist revolution for the Catholic faith on the one hand and the destiny of man on the other. That was my response to him and I think it was largely correct.

You were a senior policymaker and speechwriter at 10 Downing Street for Margaret Thatcher when she was British Prime Minister. What can you say about the relationship between John Paul II and Margaret Thatcher? How would you describe Mrs. Thatcher's attitude towards the pope?

The relationship was one of mutual respect, I think. Yet it was not a natural relationship or warm one. I think that the pope was not quite understood. The first thing to say is that the relationship between the two of them existed because they both worked very closely with Ronald Reagan. He was a pivotal figure. They both had an immense trust in him and respect for him. And secondly, Mrs. Thatcher's firm opposition to communism was a point of common ground. Mrs. Thatcher was the most outspoken critic of the Soviet Union's activities in Poland. She even began urging every Western statesman visiting Poland to begin his sojourn by visiting the grave of the priest [Fr. Jerzy Popiełuszko] who had been murdered by the communist secret police. It was an extremely powerful rebuke to communism, a symbolic act. Margaret Thatcher was also very friendly to Catholicism, or at least to Catholics. We talked sometimes about religion; I am a Catholic. She seemed open to the Catholic religion. She did go to see the pope at one point. I would have loved to be present at the meeting between them when she was her combative and confident self. I have complete conviction that if they knew each other, they would have really liked each other.

Did you ever hear Mrs. Thatcher say anything about John Paul II?

Yes. She was deeply grateful. This conversation took place two or three years after the pope's visit to Ireland. I remember when he spoke at the cathedral. She was very impressed by his speech.

How did Margaret Thatcher and the pope get along?

First of all, they never did meet. There was a great opportunity which was missed for a good reason. It was 1982, when the pope visited Ireland. England was in a war, an undeclared war with Argentina for possession of the Falkland Islands. They declared limited hostilities over the islands. That war caused the pope to cancel a visit to England. I think there was a feeling in the Vatican diplomatic world that the pontiff could not visit a country which was engaged in hostilities with a Catholic country like Argentina. Our government didn't want to cancel the visit because it didn't want Catholics in England to be disappointed. For the visit to go ahead, Mrs. Thatcher and her ministers all agreed that no ministers, including the Prime Minister, would meet with the pope during his visit. I personally deeply regret that the meeting didn't happen. Each would have discovered in the other more shared political, economic, and organizational ideas than they would probably have expected.

Why did Margaret Thatcher decide to join forces with John Paul II and Ronald Reagan to defeat the evil of communism? How did she contribute to this mission?

She was against communism. She believed in freedom, historic national traditions, and the Christian faith of Europe. When she took office, within a very short time she made a plan that she felt was necessary for rebuilding the defenses of the West. It was the first thing she thought she had to do. Poland became the focus of the conflict once Wojtyła was elected pope. Both she and Reagan reached out in various ways to Solidarity and helped, through both official and unofficial channels, to keep ties between the West and Poland alive. And the pope knew that. There was a great cooperation between the pope and Reagan. They and Mrs. Thatcher were all of the same mind in this. At some point, the pope and Mrs. Thatcher influenced Reagan in his policies. And Reagan influenced the pope. The pope, who was generally very friendly to American policy, saw in Reagan a good man, who stood for freedom, democracy, and peace.

Would communism have collapsed without John Paul II, Ronald Reagan, or Margaret Thatcher?

I think that communism would have collapsed eventually no matter what. It collapsed more quickly because of the moral influence of three leaders and particularly because of the pope, and we cannot forget about Reagan of course. It was important, I thought, that people in Poland, Hungary, and elsewhere felt they had friends who did everything to help them. Reagan took note of John Paul II's first papal visit to Poland. He had a sense that religion could help to defeat communism. Finally, all three recognized the importance of having a positive view opposed to communism, proposing a remedy, and putting pressure to force communism to reform—but communism, it turned out, was not reformable.

John Paul II, Ronald Reagan, and Margaret Thatcher each suffered an assassination attempt. Please explain Margaret Thatcher's Methodist view of the providential character of her survival.

Both Reagan and the pope felt that their lives were due to a providential intervention. In my book, I made the point that God's providence intervenes in history through human agency and through national events. Reagan felt himself a Catholic inside. The pope and Reagan had a similar sense of destiny. Mrs. Thatcher, as a Methodist, felt by contrast that Christianity was primarily about moral duty for the good of society.

How did you get the idea to write a book about Ronald Reagan, John Paul II, and Margaret Thatcher? Which of these three was the biggest challenge for you and why?

I got this idea from Mr. [Tom] Philips, who was running Regnery Publishing. He asked me to do it the day after the pope died. I had done research about Mrs. Thatcher already and I knew her quite well. I found Reagan also easy. He was a political figure and I was a political journalist. I was following his career. I really needed to spend the most time researching the pope because I didn't speak Polish, and I didn't have enough knowledge of Polish history. I had general knowledge about Catholicism and its history. And I had always been interested in Cardinal József Mindszenty, feeling that the Church in the early seventies had treated him a bit shabbily; it led me to think that Vatican diplomacy was fundamentally not as strong as it should have been, too willing to yield to the practical if not theoretical claims of communism. I could see that this was not true of the Polish church, and it proved not true of the church of John Paul II.

In your book, you describe "Reagan as too American, meaning too optimistic, Thatcher as too conservative, the Pope as too Catholic." What really brought all these great personalities to power?

They all had courage, of course. They were representatives of important truths, not exactly the same truths but overlapping truths. They all had conviction. All three had a moral sense that whether they won or lost, they still had an obligation to defend the truth, and they defended the truth very aggressively.

RYSZARD LEGUTKO

Polish philosopher, politician, speaker, and author. He is a professor of philosophy at the Jagiellonian University. He co-founded the Centre for Political Thought and is currently member of the European Parliament, where he sits on the Foreign Affairs Committee, heads the Polish Law and Justice Delegation to the European Parliament, and is Co-Chairman of the Conservatives and Reformists parliamentary group.

What are your thoughts on Karol Wojtyła and Kraków?

John Paul II experienced war and occupation as my generation, born in the People's Republic of Poland, never did. We knew that the Church in Kraków suffered a lot, but it never gave up, even in the most difficult times. We looked up to the Kraków Curia with confidence as our spiritual guardians who endowed us with a certain sense of security and continuity. As a little boy, I grew up in an atmosphere of great reverence towards Cardinal Adam Sapieha, the Metropolitan of Kraków, who was perceived as a kind of prince. We perceived Karol Wojtyła as continuation of Cardinal Sapieha. We also saw in him a prince, a monarch, informal and uncrowned, but fulfilling a similar role, at least in our hearts. For Kraków, which was still quite traditional at that time, much more than today, such monarchical associations were quite popular.

People of my generation raised in a patriotic tradition also needed someone who would express an alternative to communism, not only privately but also institutionally and doctrinally. Wojtyła was someone like that in Kraków, just like Wyszyński in Poland at large. They were both a symbol of the fact that Poland existed as a nation, but also as a certain spiritual entity. It was quite natural when Wojtyła became pope; we treated it as a triumph for Poland, which "has not yet perished," as the Polish anthem has it. And when the national liberation movement and Solidarity were established, it was natural that John Paul II was treated as their patron, protector, and spiritual guide. It was also natural that when Solidarity was banned, the pope was asked for spiritual as well as political support.

What did the pontificate of John Paul II give to the world and to the Catholic Church?

There are people who are much more competent than I to assess what the pontificate of John Paul II gave to the world and the Church. I can only present my opinion, and it is a partial one. In my view, Catholicism found itself in a crisis after the Second Vatican Council. The Council was supposed to keep the world close to the Church; the fathers and supporters of the Council emphasized this message and were proud of it, while the reality was a bit different. Secularization was progressing, especially in Western European countries, and the Church's message, instead of being widely adopted, was quite brutally rejected. In my view, post-conciliar Catholicism found itself in crisis. After Pope John Paul II was elected, the Church began to appear — thanks to his charismatic personality — as bursting with spiritual energy, and its message found a wide response. Millions of Catholics woke up suddenly and proudly manifested their faith, but also organized themselves and turned to action. There were conversions; the Church was seen as an institution and community to which everyone wanted to belong.

Before John Paul II the Catholic Church in Western Europe had received a frosty, and sometimes even hostile reception that slightly abated only when the Church yielded under the pressure of liberal forces. Now the Church began to be viewed with sympathy during the new pontificate, respected as a unique conservative institution of integrity. The message of the pope, as head of the Church, was undiluted, not adapted to the circumstances or the economic situation, not fitted to current fashions and tendencies. And that's why it sounded sincere and had such an impact. Commentators knew that the pope, who had spent his childhood and youth under the German occupation and later communism, was not inclined to yield to new ideologies. He was respected for his sincerity and for his numerous "divisions," referring to Stalin's contemptuous sneer about the number of troops the pope fielded. John Paul II had millions of them, and wherever he appeared, he awakened hearts and souls.

Was John Paul II a politician?

John Paul II was a politician, because every pope as the head of a state and a great international organization must also be a politician. Of course, it is difficult to consider him a politician compared to the president of the United States or the chancellor of Germany, whose primary focus is on politics, but he could not totally separate himself from such a role. While traveling around the world, the Polish Pope met various leaders and was responsible for Vatican diplomacy. The important thing is that when he engaged with political leaders, even those with whom he disagreed, he never lost his focus. His pilgrimages to Poland were a great example: he was welcomed by communist dignitaries and still delivered invariably strong and unambiguous messages to the Polish people, but never in an aggressive way that would exclude future visits.

I was amazed by the way he observed all political and diplomatic rules, and his kindness, which always made some people defensive, uncomfortable, and awkward in his presence. That left the communist leaders and heads of other oppressive regimes helpless before his influence on their societies. This was the case with Wojtyła's first unforgettable papal pilgrimage to Poland, and in the 1980s, when he asked the people for both solidarity and Solidarity. It is worth remembering that those were the times when some members of the Polish episcopate, including the primate himself, consigned Solidarity to the ash heap of history and did not even mention its name. When the pope promoted it in Poland, he again poured encouragement into the souls of Poles. There was a well-known incident in Nicaragua where the pope reprimanded one of the leaders of the national regime, who was a priest. As a politician, John Paul II is most appreciated for his pressure on the USSR to avoid a possible military intervention in Poland in December 1980. Yet there were other such cases. The role of John Paul II in overthrowing the communist system has been emphasized many times and it cannot be denied. The most famous study on this issue is John O'Sullivan's *The President, the Pope and the Prime Minister*, depicting the influence of Ronald Reagan, John Paul II, and Margaret Thatcher on the collapse of communism in Eastern Europe.

What is the importance of freedom in Karol Wojtyła's thought?

John Paul II spoke about freedom many times, which was understandable given his background. However, his views diverged from what was considered popular and mainstream at the time. Simplifying a bit, it can be said that the world was dominated by a negative approach to freedom, defining it as a space in which man is not forced to act. Such freedom is the avoidance of violence: I am free as long as no one interferes with what I do or think. The pope, on the other hand, believed that in order to understand freedom, man should understand the human condition and its nature. Freedom is not only free space but also a free man who recognizes the moral and spiritual order. If we stick to the liberal definition, we will quickly become enslaved — by succumbing to temptations which, as we know, quickly overwhelm us and make us passive in the face of emerging desires. Slavery also comes through the mechanisms of propaganda, advertising, ideology, mass culture, and overwhelming consumerism, which further make man passive and subject to external control.

The pope's thoughts about a free man who recognizes his moral and spiritual condition have their roots in Greek antiquity, and they have also accompanied Christianity from the very beginning. No wonder that the liberals and people influenced by them criticized the pope. When John Paul II said that "obedience to the truth about God and man is the first condition of freedom," Milton Friedman protested: "Whose 'truth'? Decided by whom? Echoes of the Spanish Inquisition?" This was a rather silly response, but a symptomatic one that indirectly confirms John Paul II's view of liberty. It shows that the advocates of negative freedom treat the basic categories that define a human being — such as truth — as a threat. But it's not just the truth that they don't like — also good, beauty, all classical metaphysics, a well-defined conception of man, and so on. But again, it should be clear for everyone that if we take away these concepts from a man or discredit them in his eyes, we will not give him freedom at all, but make him defenseless against the world and incapable of being responsible for himself. One final note: if I were to point out a philosophical thought of John Paul II that influenced me the most, it would be his reflections on freedom.

What was John Paul II's vision for Europe?

The pope was a European in a classic, noble sense. His intellectual formation was drawn from the European culture that he knew well as a philosopher, artist, and theologian. But the pope also looked favorably on the European integration project, which he saw as an opportunity to revive the European spirit. This is most evident in his speech given at the European Parliament in 1988 — before the fall of communism and before the European Union was established under the Maastricht Treaty. The pope looked to the future Union, which would be established in 1992, with sympathy, but he preferred the term "free association of nations"; he did not want a European superstate. For the pope, in the term "European integration" the adjective European referred to the Europe that formed him, that is, Europe as a cultural and spiritual entity. This is evidenced by his statement that he would like integrated Europe to be defined not so much by geography as by history. His entire speech was devoted to the coexistence of two spheres—"divine" and "imperial." The pope argued that both are necessary and both served as building blocks for Europe. The "divine" sphere must exist as something that places human authority within healthy limits, determined by conscience, ultimate destinies, the highest sense of existence, openness to the absolute, striving for goals that are never fully attainable, that stimulate efforts and prompt it to make the right choices.

Could Europe exist without this divine, transcendent dimension? John Paul II affirmed that this dimension rests in the heart of the European character and its absence must lead to the worst forms of tyranny. His speech contains other narratives that I will omit. From today's perspective, we see that the European Union did not follow the path indicated by the pope but chose the opposite. It is completely imperial and rejects all divine limits to its power. The Europe Union is a Europe that has a geographical dimension but has no history and no culture. It is a completely political and ideological construction. Even the economic sphere is subordinated to politics and ideology. I imagine—as an experiment—the papal speech of 1988 given in today's European Parliament. It would be met with hostility, and after some time, the deputies would start leaving the plenary chamber in protest.

What is the place of culture, nation, and homeland in the teachings of John Paul II?

These three words—"culture," "nation," "homeland"—often appeared in John Paul II's speeches. This is understandable if we remember the pope's concept of man. It was a version of the classical image of man as a being with several dimensions: transcendent, social, and historical. Who we are and how we are depends on how we define our relationship with God, how we define ourselves through participation in the community, and how history has shaped us. A man deprived of all these three dimensions is a kind of cripple. Therefore, the pope, who knew the history of his nation, knew that in totalitarian systems these three dimensions are sometimes cut off, by violence and ideology severing man from God, as well as from culture, nation, and homeland, replacing them with a brave new world created in opposition to what is real and familiar.

When the pope spoke about culture, he was taking about a different concept from the one we know today. Currently, the word has a sociological meaning and describes all kinds of regular human behaviors — beach culture, prison culture, etc. John Paul II associated culture with artistic creativity and spirituality. Thus, on the one hand, culture is a script of human experience endeavoring to endow our existence with some sense. On the other, culture is a striving for the best: God, good, beauty, truth, and virtue. In his speech at UNESCO, as well as in his *Letter to Artists*, the Polish Pontiff emphasized this understanding of artistic and intellectual creativity. Quoting St. Thomas Aquinas — *Genus humanum arte et ratione vivit* ("Man lives by art and reason") — the pope pointed out that culture understood in this way also plays an educational role and it does so in a fundamental sense: it allows us to realize our humanity.

If we do not live *arte et ratione*, that means part of our humanity is damaged. Our natural cultural environment is the nation, its history, art, customs, identity, and everything else that the word "homeland" conveys. The pope knew Polish culture and history thoroughly and, above all, he knew Polish literature. The latter shaped him to a large extent. At this point, I would like to highlight two of his thoughts. The first one he revealed during his memorable homily at Victory Square in Warsaw on June 2, 1979: "Without Christ it is impossible to understand and appreciate the contribution of the Polish nation to the development of man and his humanity in the past and its contemporary contributions." We were shocked by his words — both those people who were awakened by them and those who were frightened by them for they sensed that it would be the beginning of the end of their power. The second thought appears in several different places, including *Memory and Identity*: love of the motherland teaches us about the attitude called *pietas*, by which we express our respect and devotion to our parents. The love of the homeland, its heritage and spirit, its nature, landscape, and language, is the school of love. Thus we learn how to love that which is more durable, broad, and expansive than we are. Just as by loving our parents and children we transcend our individual existence, so by loving the homeland we become part of it and continue a great heritage. This is not love forced by duty but love which allows us to comprehend our duty.

EDWARD PENTIN

Edward Pentin began reporting on the pope and the Vatican with Vatican Radio before moving on to become the Rome correspondent for EWTN's National Catholic Register. He has also reported on the Holy See and the Catholic Church for a number of other publications including Newsweek, Newsmax, Zenit, The Catholic Herald, and The Holy Land Review, a Franciscan publication specializing in the Church and the Middle East. Edward is the author of The Next Pope: The Leading Cardinal Candidates *(Sophia Institute Press, 2020) and* The Rigging of a Vatican Synod? An Investigation into Alleged Manipulation at the Extraordinary Synod on the Family *(Ignatius Press, 2015).*

How did your journey with John Paul II start? Did you ever meet him?

I first became aware of Pope St. John Paul II when I heard of the assassination attempt on May 13, 1981. I was just 10 at the time and I remember my mother telling me, very soon after the attack, that the pope had forgiven his assailant. I was deeply impressed that he'd forgiven Mehmet Ali Ağca, and it seemed to me then to be something heroic, almost otherworldly, and one had no doubt that he meant it. From that moment on, John Paul always stood out to me as a great and principled leader, and he had a considerable influence on my becoming Catholic 17 years later. In 1982, I would see him in the flesh when he made a historic visit to my hometown of Canterbury in England and prayed at the site of St. Thomas Becket's martyrdom in Canterbury Cathedral. I never met John Paul personally.

As a Vatican correspondent, you have witnessed three popes: John Paul II, Benedict XVI, and Francis. How has the Catholic Church changed between 1978 and 2021?

John Paul II devoted himself to engaging directly with the world, consistent with the goals of the Second Vatican Council, and you saw that in his many travels and general outlook. Benedict continued that line, but the crises began to mount as he took on the mantle of reform. He also had to contend with largely hidden enemies within who wanted a more liberal Church and, ultimately, a pope who would further such an agenda. Benedict did not conform with their wishes. With Francis, the liberals' favored successor whom they maneuvered into position, the Church has actually become less about evangelization and more about liberal reform. Despite Francis's wish, stated early in his pontificate, for a Catholic Church more missionary, less self-referential, and more willing to listen, she has become considerably less outward-looking over the past nine years, and instead been preoccupied with internal division between those safeguarding tradition and orthodoxy and others, close to Francis, determined to adopt more of the world's thinking and reform along those lines. This division simmered under the last three previous pontificates but with Francis it has boiled over and revealed to all with eyes to see.

Each pope brings his own style to the Church. What was the style of John Paul II? Was he a pope for his time, or was he anachronistic?

To me, John Paul II's style was heroically evangelical. He wanted to open wide the doors for Christ, as he said on the day of his election, and do it without compromise. He truly desired a Church in mission that would bring the Gospel to all people, and especially to his homeland of Poland oppressed by communism. Only the message of Christ, he believed, would free nations from the shackles of Soviet communism, and he was proven right. But his ability to evangelize an increasingly secularist West, especially the continent of Europe, was undercut by an expanding relativism (some would argue apostasy) that had crept into the Church after the Second Vatican Council, one that would look to the truths and "positive aspects" of all religions, ideologies, and people, even those opposed to Church teaching. This would ultimately weaken the Church's witness and coherence despite John Paul's heroic defense of moral doctrine — so much so that John Paul would occasionally express his frustrations to Cardinal Joseph Ratzinger that the Church's moral teaching wasn't being widely followed in spite of his impassioned defense of it in speeches and encyclicals.

What were the continuities and discontinuities between John Paul II and Benedict XVI?

Pope Benedict XVI brought quite a different approach to the Vatican. Although he carried forward the great prophetic teaching pontificate of John Paul, he also brought the beginnings of structural reform, regarding the sexual abuse crisis, Vatican finances, and the Roman Curia. His pontificate was also stricken by crisis after crisis, connected with these three reform areas, partly because Benedict was touching on truths which others didn't want revealed or dealt with. The most obvious area of discontinuity was in style, Benedict's much more low-key, academic approach.

What's the major difference between John Paul II and Pope Francis? Do they have anything in common?

The major difference is in the area of the Church's moral teaching and theology in general. John Paul was a philosopher whose personalism sought to make the faith more accessible and relatable to the individual without compromising it. Pope Francis cares little for philosophy or theology, and instead plays fast and loose with doctrine, molding it according to what he believes is best applicable to today's world — what some have argued is the kind of situational ethics that John Paul condemned. Francis has taken quite radical steps to distance himself from John Paul II's moral teachings, so much so that he has undone much of John Paul's work in that area, conspicuously ignoring the latter's encyclicals on the Church's moral teaching such as *Veritatis splendor*, and effectively gutting the Pontifical John Paul II Institute on Marriage and the Family so that its work bears few marks of John Paul's thought. What they have in common is a common touch with people and a willingness to bring the Church to the world, with Francis emphasizing more the marginalized and excluded.

Can the legacy of John Paul II, a man who struggled against Nazis and Communists, defend the Catholic Church from the "culture of death" and evil of our times?

John Paul's legacy, especially in his battles against communism, is so rich that it could certainly help today's world, which is in danger of again surrendering to the atheist tyranny of communism, but this time dressed up as globalism or Chinese-style communism. John Paul's understanding of individual freedom, his championing of non-negotiable values, and his vigorous defense of all human life — all in the context of proclaiming the resurrected Christ and the Church — provide just the kind of message the world needs today. He would also warn against extremes on the political left and right — a divide that has widened considerably in the nearly seventeen years since his death.

What do you think about the attacks on John Paul II? Why is he opposed by the forces of evil?

Shortly before he became pope, Cardinal Karol Wojtyła gave his famous speech asserting that the world was facing "the final confrontation between the Church and the anti-Church, of the Gospel versus the anti-Gospel." He was naturally perceptive in recognizing the spiritual battle underway and vigorously defended the true Gospel in the face of this struggle being played out in the flesh. This of course drew out those aligned with the devil who attacked him mercilessly yet unsuccessfully, and as far as his lasting teaching legacy is concerned, still attack him to this day.

What do we need to build a civilization of love today?

John Paul taught us that without Christ and the underlying truth that man is created in the image and likeness of God, there can be no love in society. This has been clearly witnessed as nations and individuals have turned from Christ and his true Church. Authentic charity has been lost, together with faith and reason. For John Paul II, a "civilization of love" was the foundation of a humane world at a time when societies were becoming ever more cultures of death realized through, for example, legalized abortion, euthanasia, and legitimization of same-sex unions. To build a civilization of love, John Paul II believed, societies must therefore first and foremost turn back to Christ, something implicit in his 1994 *Letter to Families*. Only with strong families, John Paul II believed, could such a civilization be (re)created.

GIAN FRANCO SVIDERCOSCHI

Journalist sent by the Agenzia Nazionale Stampa Associata to Vatican II. He has since served as deputy director of L'Osservatore Romano *and is the official biographer of John Paul II, with whom he collaborated on the book* Gift and Mystery.

How did your journey with John Paul II start?

I met Karol Wojtyła during the Second Vatican Council; he was one of the many Polish bishops. Later, I met him at a conference. That's all. My main point of reference could only be Cardinal Stefan Wyszyński. In January 1977, I went to Poland to investigate, to understand, what was behind the events in Radom and Ursus in June 1976, when the workers rebelled against the communists. And I was the only Western journalist who discovered — by coincidence — that the workers' protest was different from the previous ones; this time around, there was also the solidarity of other social groups, intellectuals, universities, peasants: it was a kind of pre-Solidarity. For this reason, I also spoke about the Polish Church in my articles. And it was Karol Wojtyła, Cardinal Archbishop of Kraków, who wanted to meet me in Rome after reading my articles. He told me he wanted to publish a congratulatory letter to the workers in my newspaper (*Il Tempo*, center-right), but I advised him not to as it would have been too risky and it would have been used by the communist regime in Poland against him. He did not listen to me, and, being the brave man that he was, he wrote the letter, which I decided not to publish because of my fear. In that letter — which I am quoting here for the first time — he spoke of the radical "contradictions" in his country: Marxism in power on the one hand, and, on the other, "Christianity deeply rooted in national tradition." At the end, thanking me for my articles, he wrote: "I must confess that what foreigners write about us is a vindication; it gives further credibility to us and how we see ourselves." The letter was dated April 12, 1977. The following year, he became pope.

I eventually met him in Ireland in 1979. One morning I had written an article expressing my worry about the threats to this pope who had started traveling so often. He saw me on the plane and teased me a bit about that article. He began to interview me: "Listen to Svidercoschi — do you really think that this pope is in danger? Tell me, tell me." From there, our story began, and our friendship.

As a journalist, you accompanied the Holy Father on his travels for many years and got a close look at him. What aspect of his spirituality was particularly important for you?

He was a mystic in the true sense of the word. A man of faith and prayer who knew how to immerse himself completely in God. He had a relationship with the Invisible that was incredible. It was enough to see him praying: deeply and with complete detachment from the world. He prayed everywhere, not only in his private chapel but while traveling by plane, in his closet, or passing by a Via Crucis in the corridor of a nunciature. He prepared for meetings through prayer. For example, he once said: "I have to talk to the American President by phone," and he left the table and guests to go and pray in the chapel. There was nothing conventional or routine in his spiritual life. There was no pride when he fasted and abstained from meat. He was an extraordinarily mystical man who was able to reach a perfect synthesis between contemplative life and active life and between prayer and action. He made decisions in the constant intimacy with God.

He always asked himself and his collaborators: "What would Jesus do in this circumstance?," or, "The Gospel, what would be the answer from the Gospel?" I remember his trip to the island of Gorée, where the black slaves had been loaded on boats for the New World. He was standing there with his arms crossed, praying. He looked at that sea, imagined the martyrdom of thousands of men, women, and children torn from their houses, and he began to cry. He prayed and cried. That dramatic experience brought one of the most passionate appeals of John Paul II in favor of Africa, of the Third World. Like the prophets in the Old Testament, Wojtyła had an extraordinary ability to interpret the signs of God's presence in history. And, like the ancient prophets, he felt it was his fundamental obligation to proclaim the truth of God, invoking his right of intervention against the cruelty of men. This he did in Sicily, in Agrigento, in the Valley of the Temples, when he came out with that great invective against the mafia.

John Paul II received much media attention. Once, Cardinal Dziwisz said that journalists called him "the Great Communicator."

He had been an actor. He had been familiar with large gatherings, especially of young people. He knew several foreign languages, so he was able to communicate with many people. He was a "great communicator," a pope who immediately started using the word "I" instead of the plural form to refer to himself, and who wanted to set his pontificate on a missionary path, to bring the announcement of the Gospel to all continents. For that reason, without any difficulty, he accepted the rules of the media system. After each trip, he would come to the booth where the journalists were staying and answer all their questions. I also have to emphasize that John Paul II never let himself be influenced by the media, never attenuated the message he wanted to announce for fear of being exploited or manipulated. In short, while constantly making use of the media, he was never a prisoner of it. I remember in particular one episode, a year after the assassination attempt, he went to Fátima to thank the Blessed Mother for saving his life from Ali Ağca's deadly bullets, one of which he wanted to be set in the diadem of the Madonna.

Arriving there in front of the statue, he remained in prayer, then in silence, for at least twenty minutes. He wanted to pray. He wanted to tell the Virgin Mary everything he felt in his heart. For all those twenty minutes, television cameras throughout the world recorded nothing but silence, a scene without movement, and a man dressed in white, kneeling, completely absorbed in his prayer. The pope had not imposed anything, forced anyone. At that moment, he did what he felt spiritually proper to do: pray. But I would like to mention also another episode. John Paul II made his first papal visit to France in the spring of 1980. An exasperated secularism reigned then, and *Charlie Hebdo* mocked him with a headline: "The biggest opium dealer of the peoples arrested in Paris." At the end of the trip, Eugène Ionesco, who also did not have great Catholic sympathies, wrote: "For a long time no one spoke about God or love; it was thought, on the contrary, that this would make people grin. But this time the crowd came to listen and didn't laugh. I believe that many of those who went to hear the pope heard for the first time a man addressing them on faith and not politics. Good politics and true justice spring from faith, which, before being justice, is charity."

Which of the books about John Paul II you have published is most dear to your heart and why?

Definitely *Letter to a Jewish Friend*. It is the story of two friends, a Catholic and a Jew, who found themselves alive twenty-six years after the Second World War had separated them. That book and its story were intended to support the Catholic-Jewish dialogue after the Second Vatican Council. And that book was also, implicitly but clearly, a very harsh attack on anti-Semitism: an anti-Semitism that was being reborn, more and more violent, more and more intolerant.

It was November 1965; the Council was ending. Archbishop Wojtyła unexpectedly received a phone call from Jerzy Kluger, a Jew and one of his closest friends, with whom he had attended school in Wadowice. Jerzy was deported by the Soviets to Siberia, and then he fought against the Germans at Monte Cassino in the army of General Anders. However, after the war, he no longer wanted to return to Poland. How to go back to the place where his mother, sister, and grandmother were taken away by the Nazis to be killed in the gas chambers of Belsen and Auschwitz? Indeed, Kluger returned there only fifty years later. He came to Wadowice, where he was born, for the inauguration of a commemorative plaque in honor of the Jews living in the region who were exterminated by the Nazis. To give him encouragement, to overcome the anguish that he carried inside, John Paul II wrote him: "I remember the synagogue of Wadowice very well." How could Jerzy Kluger refuse his Catholic friend, who was the first pope in history to enter a synagogue and left a note at the Wailing Wall in Jerusalem asking the "elder brothers" to forgive the wrongs done by the Church of Rome?

You cooperated on the book Gift and Mystery *with John Paul II. What were the circumstances of this project?*

Fifty years after his ordination as a priest, John Paul II was asked to tell about the path he had followed in making a decisive choice in his life. And then, I was also called to cooperate on the project. "You," the pope told me, "will be the narrator and I will try to remember, as a witness, even with simple flashes." But then, some of the Secretariat of State monsignors decided — not the person directly concerned! — that there would be only the testimony of John Paul II. No questions asked. Nothing happened with the "script" that I developed to help Karol Wojtyła remember and arrange his story. A beautiful autobiographical portrait was nonetheless created.

But to tell you the truth, I would prefer — and I know the pope would have too — the original approach for this project. For example, the book begins with a question: "The history of my priestly vocation?" I, on the other hand, would start with a strong, precise picture to make sense of the decision that this young Pole was about to make. And that is why I would start from October 1942. Karol worked all night at the compulsory labor assignment. When he left work in the morning, he didn't even change: he was wearing a worn shirt, gray pants, and clogs on his feet (a detail the pope did not remember). It was evident that this young man was in a great hurry; but, as always, he entered the church to attend Mass. Afterward, instead of returning home, he headed for the center of Kraków, with German soldiers who, lost in thought, paid no attention to this worker walking with his head bowed. This went on until Karol arrived at the chancery and applied to the rector of the (then-secret) seminary and asked to be accepted as a candidate for the priesthood. This is where the pope's testimony could begin: "The history of my priestly vocation? ... "

In your opinion, were all the years spent by Karol Wojtyła in Poland fundamental for his formation and preparation for his mission as head of the Church?

On November 2, 1939, two months after the outbreak of World War II, Karol Wojtyła wrote to his friend the theater director Kotlarczyk: "I believe that our liberation must be the gate of Christ." These are almost literally the same words from his inaugural speech as Pope John Paul II on October 22, 1978. There was also a memory of his often dramatic personal experience: of one who first survived Nazism (in fact, he escaped with his father, walking over a hundred miles), persecution under the German occupation (with the attendant risk of landing in a concentration camp or worse), then communism (an escalating clash with the Marxist regime, especially during the celebrations of the millennium of Christian Poland), and the terrifying tragedy of the Holocaust (with many friends who disappeared in the extermination camps). Therefore, it is precisely his past that helps us understand the profound meaning of the pontificate of John Paul II.

In *Gift and Mystery*, in fact, he first remembers having been able to know, from the inside, the two totalitarian systems that marked the twentieth century. And he observes: "It is therefore easy to understand my sensitivity to the dignity of every human person and respect for their rights, starting with the right to life...." And I believe his entire experience, all his Polish years, significantly affected his pontificate. The deep love of freedom. Participation in the Second Vatican Council. *Mea culpa*. Attention to young people and to families. The conviction that the Catholic Church, at the end of the second millennium, had to carry out a profound purification, which would lead to the great Jubilee of 2000.

John Paul II was the first foreign-born pontiff in 455 years. What really happened during the conclave?

John Paul I died suddenly at age 65, 33 days into his pontificate. It was a time of great suffering and great confusion for the Church. A successor had to be found quickly. But the conclave proceeded slowly. There was the dispute over the two leading Italian contenders: Siri and Benelli. Well, their dispute caused a deep division of the electoral body. One after another, the votes led nowhere. And then, on the afternoon of October 15, someone started looking outside of Italy. It was the Austrian Franz König. Authoritative. Reliable. Convincing. He had a specific name to propose: Karol Wojtyła, Archbishop of Kraków. Young — 58 years old — but with extensive experience, and respected. The next day, on the seventh ballot, Wojtyła collected more than half of the votes, but he was ill at ease. The Polish Primate Cardinal Stefan Wyszyński went to talk to him. "If they elect you, please don't refuse! You must accompany the Church to the third millennium." He also asked him to take the same name as Pope Luciani, out of respect for Italian people who already loved him so much. Wyszyński was worried about how people would welcome a non-Italian pope. The Primate of Poland also said to me later: "Please, you write for a newspaper in Rome, help him, help him!" But Karol Wojtyła, at least at that moment, did not need any help: he obtained 99 votes out of 111. The Italian monopoly on the papacy ended.

You once wrote: "Karol Wojtyła showed us the face of God. God's human visage, if you will. He displayed the features of God incarnate. He thus became an interpreter and instrument of God's Fatherhood, a man who narrowed the gap between heaven and earth, transcendence and immanence. And in so doing, he laid the groundwork for a new spirituality and a new way of living the faith in modern society."

Of course, the first step is to take into account the time that has passed since the death of Pope Wojtyła. In fact, there is an objective danger that with the passage of time — and above all in such a time as ours, with such rapid rhythms and cycles — the personality and work of John Paul II will fade from people's memories. Or, even worse, that collective memory gradually turns into something purely sentimental, nostalgic, emotional, entrusted simply to hundreds of kindergartens, streets, squares, hospitals, oratories, and football tournaments named after Karol Wojtyła. Professor Andrea Riccardi, historian and founder of the Community of Sant'Egidio, also shared his concerns: "Our time of forgetfulness risks forgetting this great figure. It is the reality of the world, not only sensitive and capricious, but finally afraid of the great witnesses, those who have nurtured and proposed a vision. There is an instinctive and widespread revisionism that tends to distance and shrink the great figures." So more than forgotten, more than removed, I have the impression — to put it brutally — that John Paul II is "terrible." I recently wrote a book with my friend Giacomo Galeazzi: *Who's Afraid of John Paul?* And the answer to this question is probably hidden in those who — outside the Catholic world, but within the centers of power, and certainly not the people of God — are afraid and therefore reject the heritage of this pope who changed the history of the Church and the world. But who — this is a reason for fear, rejection — at the same time paved the way for an even deeper, more radical change, both in the Church and in the world.

You had a unique opportunity to observe the "Wojtyła revolution" from within the inner circle of the pope. Is the memory of John Paul II more forgotten or suppressed today?

There are people who still say that John Paul II wanted to diminish the Second Vatican Council, or at least to dampen its prescriptions. This is a falsehood. Karol Wojtyła, son of the Second Vatican Council, was the pope who perhaps most translated the council into ecclesial reality, which means passing from the most beautiful documents to concrete initiatives. Just think, for example, about one of the great themes of the constitution *Gaudium et spes*: family, culture, justice, war, and peace. For each of these, Pope Wojtyła reflected on the new needs of the Church, the new human condition, and the new situations in the world. Another thing: religious freedom. The council wrote revolutionary words in this regard, but again it was Wojtyła who combined the respect for religious freedom with respect for human rights. And again: relations with Judaism. At the Second Vatican Council, the Catholic Church under Pope Paul VI issued the declaration *Nostra Aetate* that repudiated Jewish guilt for the crucifixion of Jesus and recalled the inextricable spiritual ties between Christians and their "elder brothers." But all of these, in some respects, remained written on paper only, in the words of a conciliar document. It was John Paul II who made this historic gesture — the first pope ever to enter the synagogue — who brought to fruition what the council had written.

What do you miss the most about John Paul II today?

His gaze. Maybe I will seem a bit stuck-up to say that, but we talked with our eyes.

What do we need to build a civilization of love and truth today?

We need a less bureaucratic Church and, at least in a sense, a more synodal Church. It should be less clerical, with a greater space for lay Christians, and in particular (despite the still widespread misogyny) for the female "genius." A Church must be less dominated by moralism, that is, by a Christian life reduced to the moral question. A moral proposal is taking shape based on the plan of salvation of God the Father — a demanding and at the same time merciful Father — and it tends to the maturation of the conscience of the believer. We need a Church incarnated in history, freed from any ideological and political connivance. Thus, today, one can take the field and credibly fight the "battle" in defense of human rights, starting with respect for life and the rights of people. And probably right here, in the strenuous defense that John Paul II made of Poland's Solidarity but also of the other countries held prisoner in the Soviet empire, the "origins" of the attack on the pope should be traced. In conclusion, we need a Church that is a more transparent and convincing image of God's love, of his mercy. A Church closer to men and to the problems of men, more courageously committed to building peace, justice, and an authentic "family" of peoples and nations.

WŁODZIMIERZ RĘDZIOCH

Polish journalist who worked for more than thirty years for L'Osservatore Romano. *He has also been a regular contributor to the magazine* Inside the Vatican *and to various Vatican news agencies. Currently he is correspondent for the Vatican and Italy for the Polish Catholic weekly* Niedziela. *He is the author of several books about the Vatican. In 2006, Pope Benedict XVI awarded him the title Commander of the Equestrian Order of St. Sylvester, Pope and Martyr.*

You were in Paris when Cardinal Karol Wojtyła became pope on October 16, 1978. How did you react to the election of the Archbishop of Kraków to the See of Peter?

After studying engineering at the Częstochowa University of Technology and African studies at the University of Warsaw, I left for Paris to continue my studies. The election of the Archbishop of Kraków as Bishop of Rome seemed unbelievable, but it became a reality. The son of Poland, *"semper fidelis,"* sat in the See of Peter. I did not realize how much the Slavic Pope would change the course of history not only for the Church and Poland, but also for the whole world. Until 1978, I knew of Cardinal Karol Wojtyła from his articles published in *Tygodnik Powszechny*, a Polish Catholic weekly. Then, I discovered him, just like millions of people around the world, as pope. I could not predict that this would change my life so radically, but it did.

You lived the entire pontificate close to John Paul II. What did John Paul II mean for you?

In March 1980, I started working at the Corda Cordi center for Polish pilgrims in Rome. I led pilgrims to the audiences with John Paul II. Then, I worked in the office of *L'Osservatore Romano* for over 30 years, so the pope became my "employer"; I was one of over 2,000 people working in the Vatican and supporting his mission. John Paul II was my spiritual father, a point of reference on the paths of my life, and his teaching formed me as a believer and a man. His unwavering faith strengthened my faith. His life of prayer in communion with God was a stimulus to my faith and spiritual life. His missionary zeal reminded me that I should also proclaim the Good News with my life. I felt a special bond with John Paul II when he gave blessings, whether after the Angelus or during the solemn celebrations of the Lord's Resurrection or at Christmas (these were special blessings called *Urbi et orbi*, to the city and the world). I perceived him to be the Vicar of Christ. Providence let me spend 25 years next to John Paul II.

How did the Italians perceive John Paul II? Did they consider him "their" pope? Did they also perceive him as a pope from a distant country?

After a moment of consternation — for the first time in modern history, a foreign pope was elected! — Italians immediately took to John Paul II. The "Pope from Poland" conquered their hearts with his directness and spontaneity. He broke the rigid framework of the Vatican protocol in order to be with people, and people truly appreciated it. Thousands, even tens of thousands of people came out for papal audiences and Masses. The Italians were interested in this energetic man — "God's athlete," they called him — who had worked as a laborer in a quarry in the past, written poetry and drama, was an actor, went skiing, kayaking, and hiking in the mountains. That particularly fascinated young people, for whom he became a point of reference in their personal and religious lives. Millions of Italians, whom John Paul II accompanied for 27 years, said of him: "He is my pope."

I would also like to emphasize the special relationship of John Paul II with Rome. Wojtyła's love for the Eternal City began in his student days. He studied at the Angelicum in 1946–48. From the moment he was elected pope, he felt responsible for the city of which he was bishop and for its inhabitants in a special way. The Romans often equate the Church with the hierarchical Church, and the pope wanted the Church in the city to be understood as God's flock. His contact with Rome and the Romans was an important element of his ministry. He often went to meetings in the city, and the most important were visits to Roman parishes. He had visited over three hundred parishes by February 2002. Later, when he had no more energy for pastoral visits, he received delegations from most of the city's other parishes in the Vatican. There are only few people who know that every evening, before going to bed, the pope would stand in his bedroom window and bless the city. It was a sincere gesture of concern for Rome and the Romans, who treated John Paul II as their own.

In an interview given for your book, Benedict XVI said: "It was becoming more and more obvious to me that John Paul II was a saint." What is your reaction to these words?

Benedict XVI, speaking about the sanctity of John Paul II, stresses "his deep relationship with God, his abiding in close communion with the Lord." Having had the opportunity to participate in Masses celebrated by the pope, I was struck by the way he prayed. It was a deep conversation with God; I would say it was an immersion in God. John Paul II was a mystic who experienced God's presence and union with Him, which did not isolate him from reality. On the contrary, it was the communion with God that "was the source of his joy, which he radiated in his most painful hardships, and the courage with which he carried out his task in a really difficult time," as Benedict said.

John Paul II lived in a mystical relationship not only with God but also with the Mother of God. I found out about that from Cardinal Andrzej Maria Deskur, a friend of the pope. In 1997, at the pope's request, the cardinal went to Coimbra, Portugal, to meet Sister Lucia, one of the three seers of Fatima; he was to ask whether the act of consecrating humanity to the Immaculate Heart of Mary by the pope in communion with all the bishops of the world had been done the way the Madonna wanted. When Sister Lucia assured him that the consecration had taken place in the right manner, the cardinal asked the nun if she could "convey some message to the Holy Father from the Mother of God," to which Sister Lucy replied: "No need, because the Madonna speaks to him directly." This is another proof of the mystical life of John Paul II. It is hard to find a better proof of the sanctity of John Paul II.

For 27 years, this Peter of our time strengthened the faith of his brethren and led his people to meet Christ. It was thanks to his great faith that millions of people did not lose their faith, and millions of people discovered faith at a time when a wave of secularization was sweeping through the world. The words of an Italian journalist who criticized the pontificate of John Paul II for many years became etched in my memory. Before the journalist's death, he asked a friend, also a Vaticanist, to convey a message to the pope: "Let him know that I thank him for the help he has given me to believe. I had so many doubts and so much difficulty in believing. The strength of his faith helped me a lot. Seeing that he believed so strongly gave me a little strength too." It was his monumental faith and boundless trust in God that convinced John Paul II, despite the drama and turmoil of history, of the final victory of good over evil, and he poured this Christian hope into people's hearts.

You observed the pontificate of John Paul II closely, as a man and as a journalist. What should we know to better understand Wojtyła?

It seems to me that hardly anyone speaks of John Paul II as a Franciscan. Although, as pope, he did not take the name of Francis, Karol Wojtyła was fascinated by the figure of St. Francis of Assisi and lived in a Franciscan manner, i.e., in poverty. He was completely detached from earthly goods; he kept only such few things as were necessary for his daily life. As a rule, others took care of these things out of love for him. Even as pope, he was not attached to material possessions and left very few things behind. In his last will and testament, he wrote: "I do not leave behind me any property that needs to be disposed of.... Everyday items that I have used, please distribute as you wish." The pope combined this inborn love of simplicity and poverty with an attitude of openness to the needs of others and a willingness to help the poor.

Wojtyła's second Franciscan trait was the great importance he attached to the role of the cross in the priest's life. And his fascination with the figure of St. Francis resulted from the fact that the Poor Man of Assisi wore the signs of the Passion of the Lord on his body — the sign of the Cross. Few know that the Archbishop of Kraków wanted to celebrate Holy Mass on the anniversary of his priestly ordination in the place where, on September 14, 1224 — the Feast of the Exaltation of the Cross — the Poor Man of Assisi received the stigmata, on the rock of La Verna. He always recalled November 1, 1946, when he was ordained a priest by the Metropolitan of Kraków, Cardinal Sapieha, in the private chapel of the residence of the Archbishop of Kraków. As pope, he wrote about this special moment in his book *Gift and Mystery*, writing, *inter alia*: "In lying prostrate on the floor in the form of a cross before one's ordination, in accepting in one's own life — like Peter — the cross of Christ and becoming with the Apostle a 'floor for our brothers and sisters,' one finds the ultimate meaning of all priestly spirituality." John Paul II was convinced that every priestly vocation is a mystery and a gift.

On September 17, 1993, John Paul II became the first pope in history to climb La Verna. This shows how much importance he attached to the message of St. Francis of Assisi, who preached with his life and continues to proclaim the saving word of the Gospel today. I had the opportunity to talk to the former guardian of the Sanctuary of the Stigmata, Fr. Eugenio Barelli, who revealed to me the words of the Polish Pope in the refectory during a meeting with the Franciscan community: "In this privileged place not only was Franciscanism born, but Christianity was born anew." I do not remember any papal biographers citing such a significant statement. It is worth adding that the first papal visit of John Paul II to Italy (not taking into account the short trip to the sanctuary in Mentorelli) was his pilgrimage to Assisi, to the tomb of St. Francis, on November 5, 1978. Afterwards John Paul II would return to Assisi five times. I believe that this Franciscan aspect of John Paul II's personality remains unknown, which is a pity.

How did John Paul II evangelize through the media?

John Paul II was extremely expressive; he fascinated journalists just as he fascinated other people. That is why the media was drawn to him. The number of Vaticanists and journalists dealing with the pope increased enormously during his pontificate. Of course, the pope wanted the media not to focus on his person, but to convey his ideas and thoughts. The pope preached the eternal Gospel message, but he did it in a new, attractive, convincing, and competent way, because he was familiar with the cultural, social, and political conditions of the contemporary world. Navarro Valls, director of the Holy See's press office, told me that John Paul II wanted through the media to reach every modern man living in uncertainty, oscillating between arrogance and confusion, with the message of Christ. To this day, the media repeat the words of the pope from a homily of his first papal Mass: "Open the door to Christ." Only Christ allows every human being to understand himself and his relationship with God.

EUGENIUSZ MRÓZ

Lived in Wadowice in the same tenement house as Wojtyła's family. He attended high school with Karol Wojtyła. The two remained friends for 70 years.

Please tell us about the Wojtyła household.

From the front porch, you entered the kitchen, where you could find a cupboard and a wood- and coal-burning stove. From there, you entered into a small room and then into a large room. So it was a one-bedroom apartment. The floors were made out of wooden planks, and the apartment was filled with books, devotional art, and family photos. In the place of honor was a photo of Wojtyła senior in a military uniform. At the entrance to the kitchen, there was a small porcelain font with holy water. The Wojtyłas always made the sign of the cross when leaving or returning to the apartment.

You were a classmate of the future pope...

I was also Karol's classmate from the fifth grade until our baccalaureate and high school final exams in May 1938. Karol—we called him Lolek—grew up in holiness from early childhood. He received a proper upbringing from his parents. They began and ended each day with a family prayer. They prayed before and after every meal. Lolek's father, Karol Senior, a retired military officer, read from the Bible each evening. Lolek's mother, Emilia, was in poor health and did not work outside, but took care of the household. Lolek served as an altar boy. The Wojtyła family was characterized by deep, authentic faith.

What was Karol Wojtyła's relationship with his father like?

Father and son were inseparable friends. At the time of the death of his mother, Emilia Wojtyłowa, Karol was nine years old. From then on, Karol's father took care of his son and the household. He really took the place of his son's mother: he was a caring protector, a wonderful educator, and a faithful companion for walks and vacations. They agreed on most everything and understood each other perfectly. However, the father, with his full dedication and care, did not pamper his son but required order from him, and instilled in him a sense of duty and orderly intellectual habits. I believe that his father played a huge role in shaping the righteous character of Lolek, his great personality, strong moral sense, and academic achievements. That man gave his son all his strength. The attitude of this modest and brave father was a model of nobility and duty, a role model for us—his son's friends.

When I visited them in the neighborhood, I often found Karol's father busy with household chores. He cleaned the apartment himself, did the laundry, altered his uniforms into pants, and cooked. The Wojtyłas ate breakfast and supper at home, while they went out for lunch to the diner run by Maria and Alojzy Banaś, across the street from their building. Their favorite dishes were sour rye soup with sausage and potatoes, Ruthenian dumplings, and cheesecake. They also liked tripe soup, a typical Wadowice dish. They started their day singing these words: "Let our lips praise the Holy Virgin,/ heralding her incomprehensible glory," or another song, "When the auroras dawn in the morning." Lolek had a wonderful voice, powerful and resonant, just like his father.

Did you spend a lot of time with Karol Wojtyła?

Sometimes we did our homework together, with other friends. Karol would leave us for a few minutes and go to pray in a small room where there was a statue of the Mother of God, a kind of home altar, with a kneeler in front of the image. Right after his prayers, Lolek would return to finish his homework. After school, we usually played soccer; we swam in the waters of the Skawa River on warm days, and played ping-pong during winter. I saw the father and son almost every day taking walks, and sometimes I even joined them, proceeding towards the bridge on the Skawa River, or to the park in Zaskawa.

What kind of a student was Karol Wojtyła?

He impressed us with his simplicity, directness, and great joy of life, despite the fact that his childhood was overshadowed by orphanhood. He was a top student throughout high school. We felt great nobility emanating from him, warmth imbued with the charisma of deep and authentic religious devotion, a sensitivity to poverty and the suffering of others. He was always a cordial, cheerful friend, who rushed to help us with homework. We shared Lolek's passions for theater, travel, and sports.

He distinguished himself in high school with great erudition, broad interests, and a phenomenal memory. His main focus was on the humanities. Karol stood out among us with a great intellect and a strong, noble personality. He was always very well prepared for each lesson and exam.

However, he was not a teacher's pet, always cramming away. In fact, because of his great abilities, he did not have to spend much time studying. Yet he read a lot. He ensconced himself in challenging books, well beyond his age: the classics, as well as Polish and foreign poets. In the seventh and eighth grades, he read German poets and philosophers in their own language: Schiller, Goethe, Kant, and Schopenhauer. He gave brilliant dramatic recitals of the *Iliad* and the *Odyssey* of Homer and excerpts from the works of Cicero, Virgil, Horace and Ovid. We couldn't keep up with him, for he made giant steps of spirit, heart, and mind.

What about Karol Wojtyła and sports?

Indeed, Karol was fond of sports. Soccer played an important role in his life. We played wherever we could. In winter, we played hockey and went sledding and skiing. His father taught him to swim, and Karol junior swam perfectly. Together with Lolek's father, we hiked in the Beskid, Gorce, Pieniny, and Tatra Mountains. We loved the Tatras above all others, so we visited them often. It seemed very natural that after John Paul II rode up in a ski lift to the Kasprowy Wierch in 1997 he listed from memory the names of the Tatra peaks one by one from the observation deck.

Wojtyła was also a great actor. How did his theatrical adventures start?

We had our own theater in the high school; it was established in 1935. We mainly performed plays from the classical [Polish] repertoire: Słowacki, Fredro, and Wyspiański. Wojtyła later became fascinated by the poetry of Cyprian Kamil Norwid. Karol played leading roles in all these plays. He had perfect diction, gracefulness, a sonorous voice, and total identification with the character. He was interested in theater not only from the practical but also from the theoretical side.

As a high school student, Lolek met Mieczysław Kotlarczyk. He taught Lolek about the power of art to shape society and develop it spiritually and morally. He also presented the actor as a "priest of art" responsible for the fate of the nation. Lolek played in productions directed by Kotlarczyk. Everyone predicted a splendid career for him. He thought of acting as his way of life, and therefore he chose to go to college.

What were Karol Wojtyła's relationships with women like?

I never saw Karol on a date with a girl. He respected women very much, but he viewed them platonically, as friends. He treated them with great kindness and courtesy, like a real gentleman. He was not afraid of girls. He did not avoid them, but he did not seek any deeper intimate involvement.

Please reflect on the high school reunions you attended with Karol Wojtyła.

Our first high school reunion took place in July 1948 in Wadowice. Lolek had just returned from his studies in Rome and joined us. I think we postponed the event for him. It was our first meeting with Karol Wojtyła as a clergyman and we felt a bit intimidated by this, but he was very direct with us so we also treated him as before, during our school years. We met again in Wadowice on September 14, 1958, where we celebrated the 20th anniversary of our final exam. As a bishop and later as a cardinal, he invited us to his place in Krakow. He hosted us in the archepiscopal palace in Kraków. We met on several occasions later as well. We were planning the 40th anniversary of our high school graduation in December 1978 in Kraków. Karol invited us to come with our wives; all our reunions so far had been attended by men only. However, in October of that year, he went to Rome for the conclave and remained there as pope. So he missed the 40th reunion.

Under what circumstances did you find out that Karol Wojtyła had become pope?

I was at my son's house on October 16, 1978, in the afternoon. I was working in the garden and listening to the radio. And then I heard the news that the conclave had elected Cardinal Karol Wojtyła as pope! Tears came to my eyes. I stopped working and went home to share this amazing piece of news with my family. And Wojtyła did not forget about his high school friends from Wadowice as pope. He wrote to us, visited us in Wadowice, and brought us to Rome, the Vatican, and Castel Gandolfo.

When was your first meeting with Karol Wojtyła as pope?

During his first pilgrimage to Poland in June 1979. We met with a group of friends in Wadowice. We were a bit stressed, but Karol was very direct and everything turned out normal, as during our school times. We gave him a bouquet of white and red roses. He hugged each of us — we cried, and tears flashed in his eyes too. He invited us to his new rectory in the Vatican. He said: "Come to me; I shall provide you with food and accommodation." Then he added: "Boys, we are getting old." And we visited him in the Vatican and at Castel

Gandolfo. During all the pilgrimages of John Paul II to his native country, despite his very busy schedule, he always found time for us, his friends from Wadowice.

I remember our 50th anniversary reunion in 1988. For that occasion, the Holy Father invited us to the Vatican. As during our previous meetings, we reminisced about our teachers, sang songs, and recited Homer's *Iliad*. In August and September 1994, we spent pleasant moments with friends in Castel Gandolfo. The first Mass celebrated by our classmate in the chapel there acquired a special dimension for us. The words of his homily impressed me deeply:

> My dear friends, high school classmates from Wadowice! We meet again 56 years after graduation. Thank you joining me here at the Castel Gandolfo chapel. This chapel has a special meaning for us Poles. It was established by Pius IX, who during the Polish-Bolshevik War's Miracle on the Vistula had served as the papal nuncio in Warsaw and loved Poland very much. The decor of this chapel tells us about it. There is a painting showing the defense of Warsaw on one wall. A young priest, Fr. Ignacy Skorupka, with a cross in his hand, leads the host of defenders and encourages them to fight the enemy. That happened near Warsaw in 1920. It is also the year of our birth, the year when our life began. The history of independent Poland began with this generation. Our childhood and adolescence passed in it. Today's reading calls us to be grateful. Various gifts have come to us from God, from parents, and from educators.
>
> Our meeting is also about gratitude. The character of this chapel, which refers to the events of 1920, obligates me to remember and be grateful. Here, we should also mention those who paid the debt of gratitude with the sacrifice of their lives. Among them were those who took part in the Warsaw Uprising about 50 years ago.... This chapel tells us that our human life is related to the work of salvation. This is the most beautiful gift a person can receive. God's Son is the basis of our salvation. We all participate in it, including the students from the Wadowice high school and those whom we remember. Among them, there was Prince [Cardinal] Adam Sapieha, who visited the high school in Wadowice just before our graduation. Today I recall all this, an entire stage of our life, its events, the people who went before us to meet the Lord, so we also may gaze at his face and find each other in eternity. Thank you, dear friends, for your presence here, so that we can pray together for our parents and our deceased friends and classmates, and that our paths may cross again at the Father's house.

Do you remember your last meeting with John Paul II?

It was on August 18, 2002, at the archepiscopal palace in Kraków. The pope was already in a wheelchair. We did not sing our favorite scout songs as before, and I did not play the harmonica. We realized, with a great sadness, that our friend Lolek—John Paul II, the Pope of Hope—was slowly passing into eternity.

Did you participate in the funeral of John Paul II?

On the day of the funeral, I went to the sanctuary on Mount St. Anna, where I lit a candle and placed flowers at the monument of John Paul II. I sang the *Pater noster*. As in old times, I played the harmonica and sang a verse that I composed especially for him: "Pray, John Paul, for the well-being of the world. May your intercession bring all people together. Let us sing and play for him all the way from the Vistula River to the Vatican." That was my farewell.

AMBASSADOR JANUSZ KOTAŃSKI

Polish historian, journalist, and poet, serving as an ambassador to the Holy See and Order of Malta from 2016 to 2022.

What personal qualities of John Paul II determined the global success of his ministry "ad Petri Sedem"?

Karol Wojtyła's 27-year pontificate permanently changed the world, the Church, and millions of people's lives. Yet the term "success" sounds a bit commercial. I am aware that in assessing Saint John Paul II it takes discipline not to fall into empty verbosity. Why? Because he was an absolutely extraordinary man, a spiritual giant, a prophet and a mystic. He was a true witness of Christ. For me personally, the important thing in studying the life and teaching of Karol Wojtyła — Saint John Paul II — is that delving into his entire legacy always becomes a great spiritual and intellectual experience and challenge. Moreover, it is impossible to delineate the end of the horizons of his thoughts. While serving in the Holy See, John Paul II showed a remarkable ability to reconcile divine and human matters, and to operate in the perspective of the Gospel and, simultaneously, in a purely existential perspective.

Undoubtedly, of enormous importance were his spiritual formation and background, and thus his education, exceptional intellectual vivacity, great curiosity about the world and man, and artistic experience. But also there were his personal experiences and experiences of his Polish nation. All this constituted a great asset, which he used fruitfully in Rome for the benefit of us all. I am convinced that what helped him to open the whole world to the Good News was — apart from his personal charisma — a kind and natural openness to other nations, traditions, and cultures. John Paul II stood "face to face" with immediate problems and challenges and at the same time undertook long-term activities, such as his preparations for the Great Jubilee of the Year 2000. He had a clear vision of how the office of Peter should be executed, as his first programmatic encyclical *Redemptor hominis* shows.

Above all, I think it should be constantly recalled that as the head of the Church and of the Vatican, he always showed great responsibility and concern for the whole world in both the spiritual and political spheres.

How did the diplomatic relations between communist Poland ("People's Republic of Poland") and the Holy See change after the election of Cardinal Karol Wojtyła as successor of St. Peter in 1978?

The history of Poland's diplomatic relations with the Holy See is long and rich. Let me remind you that one of the oldest nunciatures in the world was originally established in Poland in 1519. When Poland regained its independence after the partitions in 1918, it established diplomatic relations with the Holy See. The Second Republic and Rome signed a concordat in 1925. In 1945, it was broken by the communists.

Obviously, the election of the Archbishop of Kraków to the See of Peter fundamentally changed the relations. We are talking about a pontificate that ran from 1978 to 2005, so we are talking about Poland under a communist regime and then a free Poland. During this period, Solidarity emerged, martial law crushed it, Poland regained its independence after 1989, and, finally, Warsaw shaped its sovereignty. As stipulated by the mission of his office, John Paul II was interested in the Church universal and the world. However, it is understandable that the matters of his native homeland remained dear to his heart. Therefore we heard from him many directives regarding fundamental matters. We witnessed his actions and telling gestures supporting our aspirations for freedom, as well as the *Santa Sede*'s full commitment to backing constructive approaches to Polish affairs. The Holy See consistently supported our entry into NATO and the European Union. John Paul II's impact on our path to freedom cannot be overestimated, nor can his impact on diplomatic relations between Poland and the Vatican. These were tedious, consistent, and delicate steps, time-consuming and often torpedoed by the communists. John Paul II raised the issue of establishing full diplomatic relations between Poland and the Holy See during his first pilgrimage to his homeland in 1979, in a meeting with the First Secretary of the Communist party, Edward Gierek.

As the Bishop of Rome, he took seriously his responsibility to the local churches, so he strove to have a representative of the Holy See in Poland again. Ultimately, full diplomatic relations resumed only in July 1989 with the first "Solidarity" government. Finally, in 1998, on the threshold of the third millennium, the Concordat was ratified. The Holy Father knew the communist system inside-out. For the communists — both Soviet and Polish — he was an extremely difficult and unpredictable rival, whose strength was forged "in battle," when he served as the metropolitan of Kraków.

Under John Paul II, the Vatican "Ostpolitik" changed. It was previously limited to ensuring relative freedom to protect religious life in countries enslaved by the USSR, including Poland, and waiting for a change of power on the international scene in an undefined future. The Polish Pope pursued not an open confrontation but a dialogue, a path of the Gospel and, as George Weigel put it, a new "personalistic Christian alternative to the false communist humanism." He was prudent, consistent, and responsible. And it needs to be emphasized that his political vision encompassed not only his homeland, but all of eastern Europe. He often talked about the two lungs of Europe. It was clear that the pope did not agree with the *Diktat* of Yalta.

The pilgrimages of John Paul II to his homeland were of great importance, and they should be considered in terms of bilateral relations. After all, these were encounters not only with the faithful, but also with the representatives of the highest state authorities, which gave the pope an opportunity to present the position of the Holy See on the most important issues: freedom of conscience and religion and human rights. Each of the eight papal visits had its own specific religious and spiritual overtone, and formed a step in developing relations between Poland and the Vatican. In difficult and painful moments, we were aware that our fellow countryman was in Rome, and that we were not left alone. We knew that his voice—which the world took into account—would always ring clearly and unambiguously, as at the introduction and persistence of martial law in Poland in 1981 and after. As the nation fought for its rights, we were likewise aware of Ronald Reagan's support, also *via* the Vatican, and John Paul II's close relationship with the American president.

This topic you are asking about is extremely broad. After all, it is not only specific documents, agreements and contracts, words and gestures, and *ad hoc* interventions that count. It is also about long-term diplomatic efforts behind the scenes that brought tangible results.

Does the Polish Embassy to the Holy See continue today the mission of John Paul II?

Let me clarify: The Embassy of the Republic of Poland to the Holy See pursues the goals of Polish foreign policy and works to deepen and strengthen diplomatic relations. It does not pursue its own policies. The pope is both the head of the Catholic Church and the head of the Vatican. Each pontificate leaves an imprint on the Church and the world; it writes another page in our common history. I would like to recall a fragment of Karol Wojtyła's speech in Wawel Cathedral in 1964:

> If you want to call it a program, you can. There is nothing original about this program; it is simple and eternal. The matters of eternity, the affairs of God, are the simplest and deepest; there is no need to create new programs; it is only necessary to enter into this eternal program, the eternal program of God, the program of Christ, in a new way, with a new zeal and new readiness, and to fulfill it according to the standards of our time.

Let us translate these words into our reality: we have to work honestly, reliably, with full dedication, carrying out the tasks entrusted to us, caring for the public welfare, for the homeland. Indeed, Saint John Paul II can inspire us on many different levels because the range of his activities was enormous. He preached the word of God, but he was also a leader on a global scale. For diplomats, his approach in solving conflicts, problems, and challenges — not only of a political nature — should be extremely instructive.

So, first of all, there was the culture of encounter and genuine dialogue: respect and willingness to understand the other's arguments. There was searching for solutions but also resolute defense of one's own view. There was knowledge and understanding of the topics covered; an ability to present your arguments. And what is especially important, there was efficient dealing with current issues, that is, the "program for today," which was always combined with the vision for the future.

How did the representatives of the diplomatic corps in the Santa Sede perceive John Paul II? What did they appreciate most about him?

I will answer this question with great pleasure. I frequently heard words of the highest appreciation for the Polish Pope's extraordinary knowledge of the problems of a country he had just visited. He was perfectly prepared to meet the faithful, clergy, and politicians of each place. These were not courtesy visits, but national events and cleansing spiritual retreats. John Paul II was not afraid of any challenges, or confrontations with the most difficult matters for the local churches and their societies. Moreover, the example of our great fellow countryman encourages diplomats to visit Poland. They want to get familiar with the country of the Holy Father, and personally feel the atmosphere of his native land, while looking for the sources of the phenomenon of this extraordinary man. So John Paul II continues to play the role of the Polish ambassador to the world.

Let me give you one example: a former South Korean ambassador — a zealous Catholic — came to Poland to join a pilgrimage on foot to Jasna Góra from Warsaw. There is a widespread belief in our diplomatic corps that John Paul II was an outstanding statesman, not only a religious leader. Diplomats accredited to the *Santa Sede* remember the role he played in the peaceful transformations in Central and Eastern Europe as symbolized by the fall of the Berlin Wall. They further link him with the emergence of the Solidarity movement. I deeply regret that due to the pandemic, in May this year [2020], on the 100th anniversary of Karol Wojtyła's birth, Pope Francis could not celebrate Holy Mass in St. Peter's Square. While preparing well in advance for these celebrations that, alas, never would happen, I encountered enthusiastic reactions from foreign diplomats, with promises of mass participation by politicians of the highest level. We are grateful that Pope Francis remembers his predecessor, as evidenced by his celebration of Holy Mass at the tomb of Saint John Paul II.

On July 16, 2017, the Embassy of the Republic of Poland to the Holy See organized the Karol Wojtyła Rally in Rome. How did you choose its locations?

Our embassy organized two "editions" of the Karol Wojtyła Rally in Rome, retracing his steps there, in 2017 and 2018. Another event was planned to celebrate the 100th anniversary of his birth, but it did not take place because of the coronavirus pandemic. In October 1978, during the inauguration of his pontificate, John Paul II spoke the following memorable words:

> To the See of Peter in Rome there ascends today a bishop who is not a Roman. A bishop who is a son of Poland. But from this moment he too becomes a Roman. Yes — a Roman. He is a Roman also because he is the son of a nation whose history, from its first dawning, and whose thousand-year-old traditions are marked by a living, strong, unbroken and deeply felt link with the See of Peter, a nation which has ever remained faithful to this See of Rome.

Before Karol Wojtyła became the 264th pope, he had visited the Eternal City dozens of times. Undoubtedly, Rome, the heart of the Christian world, had a great influence on his life.

He studied there. As a Council Father, he participated in all sessions of the Second Vatican Council, and the Synods of Bishops later on. In 1967, he received a cardinal's hat in the Sistine Chapel, and his titular church of San Cesareo in Palatio. In 1976, he preached a retreat for Pope Paul VI in the Vatican. His Roman journey started at the Pontifical University of St. Thomas Aquinas, the "Angelicum," in 1946–48. It is difficult to count the places associated with the presence of Karol Wojtyła on the Tiber. Initially, he came to the capital of Italy as a young priest to continue his studies at the behest of Cardinal Sapieha. Young Wojtyła "studied Rome intensively" — as he himself wrote in *Gift and Mystery*, "the Rome of the catacombs, the Rome of the martyrs, the Rome of Peter and Paul, the Rome of the confessors of the faith." And he immediately added: "I often think back on those years with great emotion." Because, for him, Rome "strengthened [his] priesthood" and gave him a more profound "vision of the Church." One of the important and honorable tasks of our embassy is to preserve the legacy of Saint John Paul II and the memory of our holy countryman. We agreed that the rally was a great idea. There was no problem with selecting places; the concern was about mapping the routes to include points in different parts of the city within a reasonable amount of time.

Rome is a crowded city, full of tourists. There were about 100 participants in each rally — mainly Poles but also Italians and representatives of other nations, including diplomats. The first rally visited the Angelicum, the Pontifical Gregorian University, the Pontifical Polish Institute, Vatican Radio (Polish section), and the Polish church of St. Stanislaus, Bishop and Martyr. It concluded with a lecture by Prof. Stanisław Grygiel in the hall of St. John Paul II. We organized the second rally in 2018 on the 100th anniversary of Poland's independence and the 40th anniversary of Karol Wojtyła's election to the Holy See. It went from the church of Santa Maria in Trastevere, the titular church of the primates of Poland (Cardinal Stanisław Hozjusz, Cardinal Stefan Wyszyński, and Cardinal Józef Glemp) to the church of St. Bartholomew (formerly St. Adalbert) on Tiber Island. I would like to remind you that in the year 2000 John Paul II dedicated the latter to the memory of the martyrs of Christianity from the 20th century — mostly victims of Communism and National Socialism; for example, Saint Maximilian Maria Kolbe and blessed Jerzy Popiełuszko.

From St. Bartholomew's we proceeded to the Basilica of St. Sabina (St. Jacek Odrowąż Church) and then the Polish Pontifical College (where the bishop of Kraków used to stay during his visits to Rome, including for the conclave). The lecture concluding the rally was delivered by Fr. Dariusz Drążek, rector of the College.

Who was Saint John Paul II for you personally?

He was a spiritual giant, a prophet, and a mystic. He was a saint whom I was fortunate enough to meet. He was an exceptional priest and bishop whom Providence prepared for an absolutely exceptional pontificate.

It is amazing how much Karol Wojtyła allowed himself to be led by Providence. He is a symbol of trust and belief for me. Fr. Jan Twardowski wrote: "John Paul II knows that he is sent by God. He is aware that he is with God. This is the power of this extraordinary man of our time." I think of him as a man who was able to respond to a vocation despite having his own "life plan" — theater and the word. He searched for the Truth, found it, and remained faithful to it. He devoted himself completely to this most important service, just like St. Paul, who in the First Letter to the Corinthians wrote: "I have become all things to all people so that by all possible means I might save some. I do all this for the sake of the gospel, that I may share in its blessings." Yes, for me, Saint John Paul II is a true "successor of Peter, at the service of the whole Church," as he wrote in the *Letter concerning pilgrimage to the places linked to the history of salvation*.

What truly fascinates me about the personality and spirituality of Karol Wojtyła is the harmonious and natural connection of *Totus tuus* and Christocentrism, the past and the Third Millennium; *ratio et spes*, culture and faith, adoration of God and human affirmation, adherence to tradition and modernized communication with the faithful, mysticism and absolute openness to other people. Karol Wojtyła was an integral man. For me, he is also a model for combining pride in Polish tradition, history, and culture with an awareness of the importance of being a European. In his case, we are dealing with a great triad because our fellow countryman always emphasized that he was a Pole-Slav-European. He writes of himself in the encyclical *Slavorum apostoli* (1985): "Peter from Poland, and thus from the midst of the Slav nations."

As a historian, I greatly appreciate Saint John Paul II's fondness for the muse of Clio — he often referred to our history, especially to the Polish-Lithuanian Commonwealth as a symbol of religious tolerance, and he recalled eminent Polish saints. I remember, during martial law, when one of the so-called real politicians scowled at the so-called extremists, the pope responded: "Ah, our extremists: Kościuszko, Piłsudski..." And one more fundamental issue: Saint John Paul II's attachment to the arts! What especially touches me is his love for poetry, especially Juliusz Słowacki and Cyprian Kamil Norwid—because I also appreciate them. After all, Wojtyła was a poet himself. And I have the impression that his poetic and dramatic works are still not fully known or appreciated. Yes, I will always associate with our Holy Father his Norwidian approach to art as a "Jerusalem of the eternal rainbow" and beauty as "the shape of love." He began his unprecedented *Letter to Artists* with the following words: "None can sense more deeply than you artists, ingenious creators of beauty that you are, something of the *pathos* with which God at the dawn of creation looked upon the work of his hands" (1999).

You belong to the generation of John Paul II. You discovered Karol Wojtyła through meeting him, listening to him, reading his works, and following him on pilgrimages around Poland. What did you learn from the Holy Father?

It was my discovery of our pope, going out into the depths with him. Those were the lessons of faith, history, and patriotism. In those difficult times, John Paul II gave us hope and allowed us to survive as a nation. I was impressed by the Holy Father's discussion of events from the history of Poland and his very clear vision of our history. He inspired me to work on myself, to seek spiritual and intellectual renewal.

What image of Wojtyła as a man, pilgrim, and saint do you keep in your heart from your meetings with him?

There are plenty of these memories: they are words, pictures, and places that I will remember until the end of my life. There are scenes from the pilgrimages, an audience for pilgrims at St. Peter's Basilica 35 years ago, and then another private audience in Castel Gandolfo, or an amazingly prayerful Paris during World Youth Day in 1997. Finally, there is his voice—its extraordinary timbre when he talked about Solidarity on the Baltic coast. Our friends' daughter, hearing him, asked: "Is this God who speaks?"

What would you say to the world on the occasion of the centennial of John Paul II's birth [in 2020]?

First of all, I would say that his historic pontificate changed the Church and the world. By preaching the truth of the Gospel, the Polish

Pope was able to attract millions of people all over the world to God. His words reached non-believers and agnostics. The world must be reminded of his great courage and boldness. It was Saint John Paul II who brought young people to the Church by establishing World Youth Day. It was he who providentially prepared the Church for the third millennium. We were also able to celebrate the Great Jubilee of the Year 2000 with him. It was John Paul II who carried the *cultus* of the Divine Mercy into the world and canonized its apostle, Sister Faustina Kowalska.

He was the first Bishop of Rome to visit a Roman synagogue and a mosque. He paved the way to the ecumenical, interreligious meeting in Assisi. It was John Paul II who constantly reminded us about the call to holiness. He restored the memory of numerous martyrs from all continents and consistently enlarged the *Martyrologium Romanum*. On the occasion of the Marian Year 1988, John Paul II published the apostolic letter *Mulieris dignitatem*, devoted to "the dignity and vocation of women," a theme he had treated from the beginning of his pontificate.

Europe in particular should remember how much the Polish Pope cared for her fate. He knew a tremendous amount about the history and culture of Europe; he emphasized the value and potential of European civilization; he fought for its survival in a spirit of fidelity to its Christian roots. He struggled for her unity, to make her breathe with two lungs, Western and Eastern, to continue the tradition of a voluntary union, "from the Union of Lublin [1569] to the European Union!"

We should never forget his appeal from Compostela, especially the words: "I cry with love to you, old Europe.... You can still be a beacon of civilization." We cannot, we should never forget that, in particular us — his compatriots. Referring to the "definition" of the papal office by Cardinal Agostino Casaroli, Secretary of State of the Holy See, we can say with all our strength: yes, John Paul II "hovered with wings spread over the whole of the world," and his ministry was distinguished by "its loftiness, its history, its influence."

Why does the world need the teaching of the Polish Pope today?

Because the world is rushing at breakneck speed toward a catastrophe. All boundaries and barriers have been crossed. Fundamental rights and values are being questioned. Insane ideologies are promoted. Affirmation of extreme individualism does not bring a person happiness but, instead, very often deprives him of all restraint. Relativism denies the existence of objective truth. Nihilism destroys the social fabric and the joy of life.

We cannot allow our life to be deprived of the transcendent dimension, as John Paul II said. In 1975 he wrote: "Creation is constantly fulfilled on the level of nature when it comes to beings devoid of transcendence." We badly need his insights concerning the meaning of life and human vocation, such as here: "The land to which man embarks by following God's call does not solely belong to the earthly geography."

What do we need to build a civilization of love today?

It would seem that the answer is simple and obvious: We need good will and a desire for solidarity. Moreover, we need to become aware of the situation in which the world finds itself with all the political and ideological threats, fragility of systems, and helplessness in the face of cataclysms of various kind, such as epidemics.

In his drama *Our God's Brother*, Karol Wojtyła wrote: "Allow yourself to be shaped by love." He always advocated for the civilization of love, in which he saw salvation from the world-embracing civilization of death in all its manifestations, against freedom and human dignity. (That is why he defended life so firmly from conception to natural death.) He believed in the strength and power of love as an emanation from the Most High: "Have the courage to live for Love, God is Love."

Do we know a better signpost?

AMBASSADOR ANNA MARIA ANDERS

> *Having grown up as an exile in Great Britain, she now serves as Ambassador of the Republic of Poland to Italy and to San Marino. She is the daughter of General Władysław Anders, the Commander of the Polish Forces at the battle of Monte Cassino in World War II. She was awarded the Gold Cross of Merit for her service to Polish veterans in the UK and for writing about the exploits of the 2nd Polish Corps during World War II.*

Did you hear about Karol Wojtyła or Primate Wyszyński from your father, General Władysław Anders?

I heard a lot about Cardinal Stefan Wyszyński, the Polish Primate of the Millennium, how wonderful and brave he was under Communist rule in Poland. In the '60s, Karol Wojtyła was relatively unknown outside Poland.

You were a British subject when John Paul II was elected pope. What did that moment meant for the Anders family and for you personally?

My father died in 1970, so he did not see Karol Wojtyła become pope. The fact that I was a British national was irrelevant. My Polish roots was what counted. Of course my family, like all other Poles, was delighted and proud.

At his Inauguration Mass, Pope John Paul II laid out the central message of his pontificate: "Be not afraid. Open, I say open wide the doors for Christ." What does this mean for you personally, for Poland, and for the world? Why do we need the pope's words today?

I think we need the pope's words today not only regarding religion. We live in a world which is politically correct, and often people are afraid to be honest and speak their minds. From the religious point of view I would say that it gives one courage — the knowledge that if we open the doors for Christ, he will help us overcome our difficulties. We will not be alone.

Do you have a story about John Paul II you would like to share?

Yes, I was lucky enough to meet Pope John Paul II three times. The first was the most memorable, at the Polish cemetery at Monte Cassino in 1979, when he came up to my mother and me (we were in the front row) and said to my mother, "Witaj Pani Generałowo" [Hello Mrs. General — she was the wife of General Anders], as if he were greeting an old friend. It was amazing.

As the Republic of Poland's Ambassador to Italy and San Marino, living in Rome, you can see and observe more than outsiders; can you tell me what the Eternal City misses the most about John Paul II?

Everyone here misses the Polish Pope. The Italians adored him, and he was able to reunite everyone. At the moment there are many divisions and controversies in the Church. It would be wonderful to have him back. This perception is not restricted to the Eternal City.

John Paul II spoke a lot about nation, identity, culture, and freedom. What are your thoughts about patriotism? Did you learn about patriotism at home?

I was born and educated in the U.K. My education was all British but my home life was Polish, and naturally I studied Polish literature and culture. It is only when I visited Poland that I realized how familiar everything was to me. I think it is only since the fall of Communism that Poles in Poland can feel patriotic. Those who had fought in World War II were beyond patriotic — they were willing to die for their country. The danger today is that the EU would like us to be Europeans above all. Those who show themselves to be patriotic are often called nationalists or fascists.

What should we learn from the alliance between John Paul II and Ronald Reagan?

History matters. We must learn from history in order to avoid the mistakes of the past. We have to carefully examine those two people who made such a big difference in the world. Both had an incredible charisma. They were both actors, and they used the stage to address the most important challenges of their times. They both inspired people to act. John Paul II and President Reagan are no longer with us, but their legacies shine brighter now than ever before. Our need for moral clarity and moral leadership remains.

AMBASSADOR ALBERTO PIEDRA

Has served as Professor Emeritus at the Institute of World Politics, Director of the Latin American Institute at The Catholic University of America, President Reagan's Ambassador to the Organization of American States and Guatemala, and a special advisor to the General Assembly of the United Nations. He also held an appointment to the Human Rights Council in Geneva.

How did you first meet John Paul II?

I was in Rome while I was the ambassador to Guatemala in the early '80s. John Paul II invited me to one of his private Masses. I was blessed and honored by his invitation. It was a unique experience for me to watch him from so close while he celebrated the Mass. He prayed so passionately and so intensively. He was focused on his prayer.

Are there any words from him you especially cherish?

He always talked about sanctity in the middle of the world, and how the best way to reach that objective was through the love of Jesus Christ, his Holy Mother, and our neighbors. As he repeatedly said, love your neighbor as yourself.

Why did Cuba not experience an anti-communist uprising like Poland's, in spite of John Paul II's efforts?

Unfortunately, Cuba had been under the influence of socialism for many years, especially in the educational system and the armed forces.

What kind of hope did John Paul II bring to Cuba?

He brought Cuba a deep reminder that with God's help everything is possible, including the fall of regimes as harsh and monstrous as the one prevailing in Christian Russia during the Bolshevik revolution of 1917.

What do you miss the most about John Paul II?

His modesty, sincerity, and perfect understanding of the fundamental difference between right and wrong. For example, in the case of abortion, there are not a few Christians who accept abortion as something good when in reality it is intrinsically evil. This confusion is widespread, but John Paul II did not hesitate to declare that abortion is evil and cannot be accepted by the Catholic Church. Once again, I repeat that one of the biggest problems facing our society is a relativism that rejects absolute right and wrong.

What do we need to build a civilization of love?
We need the willingness to give ourselves to others and love them without violating the basic principles of natural law.

ANIKÓ LÉVAI-ORBÁN

Hungarian speaker, author, entrepreneur, and wife of Hungarian Prime Minister Viktor Orbán

What did St. John Paul II mean to you? Did you ever meet him?

Pope John Paul II always gave me strength and hope. I remember well his election as pope; I was in secondary school at the time. A Polish bishop! My father, who was a traditional peasant from the Great Hungarian Plain, commented on the news that we heard on the radio in the kitchen: "Maybe one day it will be over!" Even though I was a child I knew exactly what he meant: he was waiting for the end of communism. Many people like us felt the same way. Szolnok, the town where we lived, was called at that time little Moscow, and it was the citadel of Hungarian socialism; still, when the news came of the election, many farmers from the neighbouring town attended a holy Mass of thanksgiving. The elevation of a Polish pope brought hope for us. His credo: "Do not be afraid." In 1987, during the dictatorship of General Wojciech Jaruzelski, he visited many Polish cities, and we also joined the pilgrimage and marched with the pope from Kraków through Warsaw to Gdańsk.

We Christians of central-eastern Europe could feel for the first time that one of us was going to represent us among the major leaders of the world. There was someone who would not forget about us, who didn't seek to victimize central-eastern Europe. Someone who believed in us — and that is why we also believed in him.

Viktor and I met the pope in 1998 at Castel Gandolfo. I was so happy that I could take my children to him — at that time we had three children. He was already quite old and was not too healthy either; still, he dealt in a friendly manner not only with my husband, who had been elected Prime Minister for the first time, but with me and my children as well. My children also have cherished memories of this meeting.

What do we need to build a civilization of love and truth today?

Pope John Paul II was a distinctly modern thinker; he addressed not only Catholics but the whole world. He was a resolute man, but profoundly humane. For me, his teachings about women and for women are especially significant and encouraging. His letter to women in 1995, on the occasion of the Fourth World Congress of Women, is a particularly valuable statement of gratitude for the good women do in the world. This has now become very relevant again in the COVID pandemic because we can see how heavy a burden is placed on women who work, homeschool their children, cook, run the household, or nurse the sick. The pope's deep faith, his attention, love, and encouragement, can strengthen us in the conviction that our strenuous work has a goal and a meaning. Through his teachings we can find the way to the society of love and righteousness.

KRZYSZTOF ZANUSSI

Polish film and theatre director, producer, and screenwriter. He is a professor of European film at the European Graduate School in Switzerland and the recipient of the Golden Lion at the 1984 Venice Film Festival, the Jury Prize at the 1980 Cannes Film Festival, and grand prizes at the Gdynia Film Festival.

Under what circumstances did you meet John Paul II?

My first encounter with Karol Wojtyła was in 1958, his first year as auxiliary bishop of Kraków. I met him at the home of the Vetulanis in Kraków, where I studied together with Jan Vetulani, their son. The father, a canon lawyer, was a friend of Wojtyła. I noticed that Wojtyła was very attentive to those he spoke with. It was quite endearing and surprising for me at the same time. You could feel that he was asking you a question because he really wanted to hear your answer. And later I realized that this was a practical implementation of his personalism. He simply cared about every individual.

When else did you meet Karol Wojtyła?

I had business with him because I was shooting my graduation film at a monastery in Tyniec when some unexpected difficulties arose. At that time, I asked Bishop Wojtyła for some advice and help. He put me in touch with another monastery, where we finished the film. He said it would be the best practical solution. Thus we became reacquainted.

When he became pope, I thought with great regret that I had missed so many opportunities to see him in Kraków, and somehow I did not imagine that I would ever see him close-up as pope. It turned out that we would now see each other much more frequently than when we both lived in Kraków. This happened because of the movie I made, or rather that I agreed, very reluctantly, to shoot: a biographical film about John Paul II.

Please tell me about this film.

The film, *From a Far Country*, was an American-British-Italian co-production. Lew Grade, who produced Franco Zeffirelli's famous *Jesus of Nazareth*, was one of the producers. We gave the pope and the Vatican a script for review, written hastily by two of my colleagues: Jan

Józef Szczepański and Andrzej Kijowski. The Vatican had a few objections. To be honest, I harbored an unspoken hope that these would give me an excuse to withdraw from the project. Yet history compelled me to make this movie as a kind of "mission impossible" project. I could not make a film judging his life. This would have been dramatic but tactless. Therefore it had to be a movie about a witness of history, a daunting and unpleasant task from my perspective. I knew well that many people would be disappointed by the film for its lack of gossip or partiality.

I shared my concerns with Andrey Parkovskii, who urged me to emulate his film *Andrei Rublev*. The movie depicts the great iconographer Rublev as if he were completely unknown. He himself is only a witness in the film, but Parkowski could depict his deeds. I approach the film along these lines, and it reached theaters in 1981.

What was the pope's impression after watching the film?
The screening took place at Castel Gandolfo. The pope watched it attentively. He said he couldn't really comment on it, except that he got the impression that it would help him in his mission.

How did you react to the election of Karol Wojtyła to the See of Peter?
It was a surprise for everyone. I was in Mexico when I found out. I can recall landing in Yucatán, where a man was waiting for me. He said: "Oh, you are from Poland; a pope from Poland has just been elected." I don't speak Spanish very well, and I kept asking him from which city, who was it, and which cardinal was elected. I don't know why, but then he said that the pope was from Hungary. I though he must have been mistaken. I didn't bother any more about that until the evening, when Józef Klasa, the Polish ambassador to Mexico, told me that Karol Wojtyła had been elected pope. Again, obviously, it was shocking news. I was to have a press conference. The news arrived that a new pope was elected. I thought no one would ask me about films at the press conference, but only about the new pope. So I prepared a funny answer. And, indeed, someone asked me whether I knew the new pope. I responded that, yes, I did know John Paul I as the patriarch of Venice, Paul VI, and even John XXIII. However, Wojtyła was the first pope who knew me!

I would get to know the pope even better. I was invited to visit him quite often, and I know it was for a reason. The pope suffered a lot from living such an artificial life. He was isolated at the papal residence, and leaving the Vatican as a private person was practically impossible. When he spoke to me there, he wanted to hear real-life stories, which I told as a screenwriter but also as a man of the world. He was interested in my travels and encounters, about daily life.

What do you owe to John Paul II?

It's very hard to say. His activity was multifaceted, and I myself probably do not realize how much I owe him. When I look at how much the Church owes him, I think I owe him a deep and well-founded hope. He rejuvenated a Church which usually looks back to its old triumphs. He said that the Church was the future, not just tradition, and that the wisdom of the Church was useful in this new world that seemed so different but really was a continuation of the world we've been living in for 2,000 years and more. In the teaching of John Paul II, in his relation to culture and art, and in his way of ordering values, I found something close to myself and thus I became much more friendly towards the Church as an institution. He also stressed the relation of reason to faith, and this certainly will be a subject of further development.

*You drew my attention towards one of John Paul II's better-known encyclicals—*Fides et ratio. *Why did you become interested in this particular encyclical?*

I meant not the encyclical *Fides et ratio* itself but the whole concept of Faith and Reason. It was subjected to such misunderstandings, but it remains deeply relevant to the use of modern science in contemporary theology.

At the beginning of the aforementioned encyclical, the pope gives a beautiful image: "Faith and reason [fides et ratio] *are like two wings on which the human spirit rises to contemplate the truth." Do faith and reason contradict or complement each other?*

In my opinion, there is no contradiction. Faith and reason are not only compatible but necessary for each other. Faith is a kind of different reality, while reason is a tool. An intuition is also a tool, a legitimate tool, and it can lead a man to faith. In this sense, they are complementary. Faith without reason leads to superstition. Reason without faith, as John Paul II argues, leads to nihilism and relativism. Rational and mystical knowledge complement each other.

Can faith alone lead to the truth?

Of course, but as always we are imperfect and in this imperfection we must constantly protect ourselves from the stupidity and error that haunt us.

How would you apply the encyclical Fides et ratio *of John Paul II today?*

This is an encyclical that confirms the teachings of the Church since antiquity. It refers to a certain unity between reason and faith. People often contrast the two, and probably unnecessarily. It was the nineteenth century that created the illusion that these realities exclude each other.

In your opinion, is the encyclical Fidelis et ratio *a continuation of Wojtyła's earlier work in* Person and Act?

Wojtyła's entire intellectual output is coherent. He was both coherent and extremely versatile, and therein lies his genius; there had not been such a versatile pope for centuries. That does not mean that his pontificate was faultless—he made many mistakes, widely exposed and sometimes unfairly exaggerated. Yet the coherence of his thoughts and actions is an indisputable fact.

Why does John Paul II refer to the foundations of philosophy in diagnosing the spiritual predicament of modern man? How does philosophy help man to seek the meaning of faith, reason, and truth?

Because our civilization is built on reason and it led us to this extraordinary summit on which we found ourselves among the developed countries. It is from this summit that an illusion arises that we do not need God.

Why, in your opinion, are we running away from the Absolute today, the Absolute Truth, God Himself?

Because we live in a greenhouse world. This advanced humanity has such a weak existential experience, and looks at its existence so carelessly. The carelessness is due to infantilism and immaturity arising from material and social conditions. But this is opposed to our human dignity, and we should resist it.

Please reflect on Karol Wojtyła's great passion for the theater.

Indeed, theater was his great passion. He understood it as a mission—Promethean theatre. Remember that participation in the underground theater during the Second World War was risky, and you could have been sent to a concentration camp or even pay with your life for your involvement. Theatrical activities were strictly forbidden by the Germans. They knew very well that culture had to be destroyed in order to enslave a nation.

Wojtyła wanted theater to lift the spirit in times of freedom. It is certain that Wojtyła understood that the liturgical character of theatrical action offered the possibility of entering into a new dimension and an unexpected authenticity. There is little distance between the profession of the actor and that of the priest. During the liturgy, the worship of Christ's Passion is played out.

What was the essence of Wojtyła's acting?

John Paul II's method of communication was very striking. He knew how to control his breath. He took pauses flawlessly. He knew how to inflect his voice. He had the ability to express himself through body language and intonation. His sense of time and space was great.

You produced and directed a film based on Wojtyła's drama Our God's Brother. *What made you interested in the play?*

It is one of the few works in Polish literature with such a universal dimension.

Again, I had to be persuaded to work on this project. At the beginning, I was supposed to be the producer only, but I became the director as well. I appreciated the text despite many dramatic and literary imperfections. The use of Lenin as a character suggests a great contemporary dialogue. And the author shows the way, that place where the ways of a Christian and Christ diverge, and at that point he is extremely farsighted. I also produced Wojtyła's *Job* as a play in Italy.

How much did Karol Wojtyła change as pope?

In my opinion, Wojtyła was always the same man. There is no disappointment or surprise here. He was himself. He was an authentic man.

How did you, as a Catholic producer and director from Poland, a country behind the Iron Curtain, manage to work in a Catholic spirit under communism in Poland?

I did my job with great limitations. Of course, I was afraid of failure. I was afraid that I could be eliminated in this system where the authorities granted artists the right to speak, especially when the rights were limited and my artistic pursuits were costly. But, somehow, I managed to survive in this difficult world thanks to my diplomatic talents.

Please reflect on John Paul II's relationship to communism in Poland.

It was an extraordinary phenomenon, but let's be precise: Polish communism was different from the Soviet one. We always have to specify which communism we are talking about. The Stalinist variety, circa 1950, was extremely different from the later communism of Gomułka, Gierek, or Jaruzelski. Each time this communism was transformed and modified, the relationship with the Church also changed. Wojtyła was the man who could see it so totally.

What did Wojtyła draw from his relationship with Cardinal Stefan Wyszyński?

This relationship should not be idealized, because it was very difficult, from what I know and was able to see. They worked together well, but they needed to compromise to succeed in their endeavor. In the meantime, there was a very perfidious attempt by the communists to antagonize them and set them against each other, and even some Catholics — perhaps unwittingly — took part in this operation. It was an extremely dramatic and difficult relationship, and very beautiful at the same time.

Which words of John Paul II are especially important to you?

It is very hard to say. I remember his anecdotes the most, and jokes he shared with me. He had a highly developed sense of humor, in Polish *z cicha pęk* (a wry humor). He developed a great technique; he really mastered it completely, especially in regard to timing. He often purposefully missed an opportunity to respond at the time we all expected his reaction. He responded with delay, or added something to a discussion which had been already finished. I was also very touched by his ability to look into himself and other people objectively.

Today, the memory of John Paul II remains alive. He refreshed our Christianity. He refreshed our Church. I was always impressed by his intelligence and good manners. He never interrupted anyone or never answered immediately. Wojtyła — like a good playwright — knew how to interlace one thread with another and return to the first one again.

What is less remembered is that John Paul II was an artist. He had a great understanding of art and its place in the Church. His *Letter to*

Artists is an example of his reflection on the mystery, beauty, and practicalities of worship. He was also a poet himself.

What do we need to build a civilization of love today?

This is the essence of our Christianity, so we need love and truth. We have to cultivate them and seek them, because none of us is able to reach the whole truth and love perfectly as well. However, our desire for truth and love already brings us towards a better world. There is nothing new in speaking of a civilization of love and truth. This is the original Christian message and it is still valid today.

KAZIMIERZ BRAUN

Internationally recognized theatre director, author, lecturer, and professor at the University of Buffalo, and former student of Karol Wojtyła.

Professor Braun, how and when did you meet Karol Wojtyła for the first time?

Wojtyła was a founder and mentor of the *Święta Lipka* ("Holy Linden") group. I joined it soon after it was launched in 1958 during a summer retreat in the Święta Lipka monastery in Northern Poland. The core of the group consisted of students and young scholars of the Catholic University of Lublin (Katolicki Uniwersytet Lubelski). The group reflected Wojtyła's way of evangelizing and shaping the character of young people through prayer and study circles; they fostered communal life on retreats, excursions, vacations, meetings. My sister, Maria, was a student at KUL and she became a member of the Święta Lipka. I learned about this group from her.

I met Wojtyła in 1959 at a preparatory meeting for a summer camp/retreat of the Święta Lipka in Pobiedziska near Poznań, at a monastery and school of Sacré Cœur nuns — vacant during the holidays.

Then-Bishop Wojtyła, learning that I was studying to be a director, gave me a paper to write: "Responsibility of a theatre artist." At that time, he was preparing his book *Love and Responsibility* for publication and the subject of responsibility was especially interesting to him. I knew, of course, that he had been an actor. Perhaps, as a former actor, he somehow singled me out as a student of directing and wanted to guide me in my way to theatre. During the summer meeting in Pobiedziska we held seminars at the lake shore. I delivered my paper there. After a spirited discussion by the whole group, the professor-bishop accepted it.

What do you remember from your meetings with the future pope?

His personality was striking and captivating. He was absolutely and unequivocally focused on what he was doing — when he celebrated Mass, when he lectured, and when he played volleyball. He had a melodious voice and he loved singing. The usual repertoire included a variety of songs: religious, folk, military — especially from the Warsaw Uprising of 1944. His power of concentration was, perhaps, most evident when he was listening to somebody and when he was talking to somebody.

This concentration, this focus was not tense, though. It was rather a full openness, and willingness to help, to serve. He often smiled. During a meeting with a student, a visitor, any person, he would devote to that person his total attention and as much time as needed.

He taught prayer by example. He prayed in every free moment. Besides daily Mass and the Chaplet of Divine Mercy, he prayed the rosary — over and over again. He meditated and prayed before and after each Mass. When he was a professor at KUL, he used to go to the church located on campus during every break. On hiking, kayaking, or skiing excursions he would go every day alone for a walk — praying, usually in the afternoon. We used to say: "He went up a mountain" — like Jesus, who often went up a mountain alone to talk to his Father. (With his permission and encouragement we called him "Uncle" — so we would rather say: "Uncle went up a mountain.") He fulfilled St. Paul's command: "Pray without ceasing" (1 Thes 5:17). He was able to immerse himself in deep prayer amid the shouting crowds, dancing cameras, flickering lights.

How did you become a student of Karol Wojtyła? What did you learn from him?

I was not formally his student at a university. I was a member of the group Święta Lipka and as such, I participated in occasional seminars lead by him during the meetings of that group. Additionally, I read all his plays, books, and encyclicals; I listened to his homilies.

What did I learn from him? Persistence, a tireless exploring, researching, analyzing a topic, a subject, a question, a problem — until a problem is solved, until an answer is found, until a right means of expression is created during a theatre rehearsal.

Once you said that Bishop Wojtyła asked you: "How do you want to unite faith with art in your theatre work? In the time of trial, what would you choose — the world or God?"

I'd like to elaborate more on that — crucial and memorable for me — meeting with Bishop Wojtyła in Kraków in the winter of 1960. At that time, I was already a student at the Drama School in Warsaw. I was about to graduate. I directed a play in Kraków. I called upon Bishop Wojtyła, and I had a long conversation with him about my future work in professional theatre. At the end of this meeting, he — in his usual way — told me to write a paper about the problems which we would discuss later. I had to list and analyze the moral predicaments of a young director who is Catholic and works in the world of theatre, which is totally secular. I wrote the paper and submitted it to his office, and after some time he summoned me for another meeting. He discussed it with me thoroughly. At of the end of the meeting he gave me some fundamental questions not to answer immediately but rather to think over, and to ask myself again and again in the future. I repeated them many times: "How do you want to unite faith with art in your theatre work? In the time of trial, what would you choose — the world or God?"

But there were more questions:

> How would you connect in your productions the quest for the highest aesthetic values with the quest for expressing ethical values and stand by your faith? How are you going to connect the physicality of your actors and the characters they portray with their spirituality? How will you lead your spectators to the realm of the spirit through the material fabric and sensuality of theatre? And, again, when trials will come, and they certainly will come, what will you choose: your career or your conscience? The world or God?

After his death, these words remained for me his last will and testament.

How did John Paul II use theatre to show you the way to Christ? How did it impact your faith?

John Paul II gave four models, as it were, of an approach to theatre: his brief yet important experience as an actor; his playwriting; his theatre critiques published under the pen name Andrzej Jawień; his references to the great Polish poets and dramatists Adam Mickiewicz and Cyprian Kamil Norwid in his homilies and in his *Letter to Artists* (1999). In all these fields he stressed theatre's spiritual potential.

Say more about Karol Wojtyła as a man of the theatre.

I visited the Wojtyłas' apartment in Wadowice — next door to the church, virtually wall-to-wall with the parish church. Bells, singing, choral prayers were audible in the kitchen and the bedrooms. This would have been a valuable stimulus for a child's sensitivity and imagination, as well as his religious upbringing. The church was so close, so easily accessible. He often attended it with his parents: Mass, rosaries, devotions, processions. After his mother passed away he was always in the church with his father. Early he became an altar boy, taking an active role in the services, thus "performing" in public. Known for his piety, he was selected as "chairman" of the altar-boy association. He acted in high school. There are testimonies that he was an outstanding, very talented actor. He was the "leading man" at an amateur theatre in Wadowice and then in the Rhapsodic Theatre in Kraków.

He was handsome, with a strong and melodious voice and an ability to remain himself in public. In theatre terms, he had a very strong stage presence and sense of truth. All that was combined with his brilliant intelligence and a profound spiritual life that shone through when he was acting or reciting poetry. He had a great potential to become an outstanding actor, a star shining in the roles of great heroes, such as Orestes, Hamlet, El Cid, or Konrad in the Polish masterpiece of poetic drama, *The Forefathers' Eve* by Mickiewicz.

Nevertheless, he chose the priesthood. His theatrical career came to an end in the late fall of 1942, when he exchanged his underground theatre for an underground seminary. He abandoned but did not forget theatre. He left a legacy and an example for all theatre people — actors, directors, designers, dramatists, everybody: you can be a brilliant artist, a perfect professional, a master of your trade, and, at the same time, you can be a good, devout, practicing Catholic. Yes. You can. And you should!

Did Wojtyła's experience in the Rhapsodic Theatre later help him carry out his mission in the Vatican?

Indeed. After all, for years — as a priest, bishop, archbishop, and eventually pope — he was a public figure, and he was a performer. His strong stage presence and "sense of truth" as a young actor remained a solid foundation: his perfect diction; his skillful control of his voice; his nuanced delivery of text; his ability to communicate with crowds, steer people's emotions, and convey in a convincing and clear way the most difficult theological and philosophical points. All that had its roots in theatre rehearsals and public performances — first in Wadowice, then in Kraków — under the guidance of Mieczysław Kotlarczyk, his teacher, mentor, and director. We may presume that these early acting experiences helped him in the following years in the public eye.

In his book Gift and Mystery *John Paul II wrote: "I stayed in contact with the theatre of the living word which Mieczysław Kotlarczyk had founded and continued to direct in the underground." What would you say about Karol Wojtyła's involvement in the Theatre of the Word?*

Why is John Paul II talking about "theatre of the living word"? Why does he use the word "underground"? This must be explained. Let's consider first the "underground."

As we know (the young generation might not know...), World War II began with the attack of Germany on Poland, September 1, 1939, followed by the attack of the Soviet Union on September 17. At that time Wojtyła was living in Kraków, where a year earlier he had enrolled in the Jagiellonian University's Department of Polish Literature. In the fall of 1939, Poland was divided into three zones: Germany took parts of her western, northern, and southern territories; the Soviet Union took the east as well as part of the north; the central part, including Warsaw and Kraków, was occupied by Germany and designated as "General Government." All Polish cultural, educational, and artistic institutions, along with the economy, administration, and judiciary, were either closed down or taken over by the invaders — for example, Polish schools on all levels were shut down under German or Soviet rule, while in the German-occupied zone they could have only four grades. The Jagiellonian University was closed, along with all other Polish universities. The Polish government was exiled to Paris, then, after France's defeat, to London. It kept an underground division in the country, with a civil administration, army, judiciary, and other branches.

The theatrical scene, very lively before the war, died away. Theaters were destroyed, taken over by the invaders, or simply shut down. Acting companies were disbanded. In this situation, a wide variety of secret activities led to the formation of a whole vibrant underground network of theatrical life, including performances, actor training, and playwriting. The Clandestine Theatre Council was organized, supervising and supporting underground activities. All these endeavors were guided by the venerable Polish tradition of "theatre of service" — theatre practiced as a service to both the art and the nation. In predominantly Catholic Poland that meant also service to God through art.

It should be clearly understood that all clandestine theatrical productions and other activities were illegal from the point of view of the occupying authorities and strictly forbidden by them. Both actors and spectators risked punishment by imprisonment, deportation to concentration camps, or even death. The productions were given in private apartments and homes, in monasteries and mountain shelters. To prepare underground productions, to perform them, or to attend them required courage, determination, and an unquenchable thirst for freedom. It was motivated by patriotism and a belief that human, spiritual, and artistic values must be celebrated in a world which was so utterly inhuman.

Within this context we can speak about the "theatre of the living word." Mieczysław Kotlarczyk (1908–1978) founded the Rhapsodic Theatre in Kraków under German occupation. It was an underground operation in complete secrecy. Karol Wojtyła was a member of its company from the very beginning. The Rhapsodic was indeed a "theatre of the living word." Why? Because the basic means of expression was the recitation, or rather expressive delivery, of poetry or prose — with restrained, stylized acting, minimal stage accessories, and simple costumes. The primary, the most important, practically the only essential means of expression and the major mode of the actor's communication with the audience was the word, the spoken text. The whole complex, multidimensional life of a stage character had to be conveyed only by the word. In a way, the word had to live its own, full life. Hence, John Paul speaks about "the living word."

Wojtyła performed in the first production of the Rhapsodic Theater, *King Spirit* by Juliusz Słowacki, which opened on November 1, 1941. He then participated in subsequent productions based on the poetry of Słowacki, Jan Kasprowicz, Stanisław Wyspiański, Cyprian Kamil Norwid, and Adam Mickiewicz. He gained skillful command over his voice, speech, diction, and interpretation of text, as well as his movements and emotions. Rehearsing and performing in the underground productions involved both acting and character development. Very simply: the underground theatre work was mortally dangerous.

The underground Rhapsodic Theater of Mieczysław Kotlarczyk was associated with the underground Christian democratic organization Unia, which Wojtyła joined. Unia was led by your uncle Jerzy Braun. Tell us about Wojtyła's connection with Unia.

It was Jerzy Braun who encouraged Mieczysław Kotlarczyk to create the Rhapsodic Theatre. In a way, then, Unia gave birth to the Rhapsodic Theatre.

Unia was a vast organization. It was founded in spring 1940 from the merger of three underground patriotic groups and soon was joined by other organizations, their common goal to defend Polish tradition, culture, and national identity, as well as to support cultural, intellectual, academic, and artistic life under the circumstances of the war and occupation. From the outset Unia had also its military units. Unia had several chapters: Union of Culture, Union of Labor, Women's Union, Social Union, and Union of the Youth. In Kraków Unia had about 1,500 members. It also had cells all over Poland.

The whole organization was active in three major fields: culture, politics, and military. In terms of culture, Unia published two — of course, underground — journals, funded publication of books, organized lectures, discussions, and both scholarly and literary symposia, and supported all sorts of cultural and artistic events — hence the idea of creating an underground theater. The political activity of Unia included participation in the underground Polish state. Jerzy Braun, president of Unia, was in 1945 the head of the underground parliament, and later the head of the home branch of the Polish government in exile. (He had the rank of Deputy Prime Minister while the Prime Minister resided in London). The military branch of Unia consisted of several fighting units and a huge clandestine plant producing grenades. Unia counted scholars, writers, artists, politicians, theatre people, and military men among its members, as well as clergy, including two bishops. There were great stars of pre-war theatre: Juliusz Osterwa, Stefan Jaracz, Leopold Kielanowski, and others. Kotlarczyk, along with Wojtyła, joined Unia and they took the oath. (It was wartime. Unia had a very strict clandestine structure and observed stringent procedures.)

I think that Unia was for Wojtyła an important experience. He participated in the scholarly and literary discussions, interacting with prominent scholars and writers. He attended academic lectures. He could read Unia's publications, which represented a very high intellectual and philosophical level. He found himself in a milieu of people for whom lofty ideas and the highest values had absolute priority and who were unblemished patriots.

Karol Wojtyła was undoubtedly shaped by Polish Romanticism. While his early dramas reflect his interest in Słowacki, Mickiewicz, and Wyspiański, it was Cyprian Kamil Norwid who exercised the most profound influence on his poetry. Can you explain Norwid's impact on Wojtyła?

Karol Wojtyła discovered Cyprian Kamil Norwid very early in his life. His father gave him private lessons in Polish history and literature, illustrated by readings of major poets, including Norwid, who fascinated him. For a high school poetry competition in 1936, he chose to recite Norwid's *Promethidion*, a philosophical-poetic treatise, in which the author writes:

> Thus I see the future art in Poland:
> As a flag on the tower of human labor.
> Not as an amusement or a harangue,
> But as the highest apostolic trade,
> Or as the lowest prayer of an angel.

That seems to be the ideal of both Norwid and Wojtyła in their poetry: an indissoluble bond between human work, art, and prayer.

Norwid was a profoundly religious man. He penned several religious poems and frequently included religious utterances in his other works as well as in numerous public addresses and speeches. His faith was inseparably linked with art, while art, he believed, could not exist without faith. An attitude of a Catholic and a true son of the Church, along with a deep knowledge of the Bible, was the foundation of all his writings. His Catholicism was deep, intellectual, and philosophical. He was always infusing poetry with philosophy. He looked at the universe from the perspective of a believer. God was always present in his vision of human existence and earthly reality. He was a staunch defender of both Christian and national tradition. At the same time he was a bold experimenter. His writings abound with linguistic inventiveness, powerful metaphors, and surprising imagery.

All these characteristics of Norwid's literary palette seem to resonate in Wojtyła's poetry. Wojtyła drew several other major artistic, ethical, and theological problems directly or indirectly from the thought of Norwid: the reality and the power of the word; human labor; the essence of humanity; the rapport between an individual, the nation, and the human race; the relationship between the human individual and the whole of humanity on one hand, and the Church — the universal, Catholic Church — on the other.

I presume that Norwid influenced also Wojtyła's vision of theatre. It was Norwid who penned this succinct definition of theatre: "Theater is the *atrium* of heaven" — the *atrium* in a Roman house was the central part of the whole building, without a roof, open to the heavens. John Paul II saw theatre as such a structure: with solid walls and many rooms housing many people; and with a living room which has no roof—it allows us to see heaven, the temple of God; it allows direct access to heaven. Theatre was for him also a vehicle which could and should uplift spectators—inspired by playwrights, guided by directors, led by actors—and transport them into a celestial realm.

This vision and model of theater—an *atrium* of heaven—formulated by Norwid, presented by Wojtyła in his own writings, recalled by John Paul II—had a significant effect on me. I studied Norwid, wrote about him, and directed several of his plays. That Wojtyła, and then John Paul II, followed Norwid in his understanding of theater was for me a confirmation that I was on the right track in my way through the world of theatre.

We find the most complete reading of Norwid by Wojtyła in his address to Polish pilgrims to the Vatican on the 180th anniversary of Norwid's birth in 2001. In this text John Paul II highlights fundamental characteristics of Norwid's writing: "The power of Norwid's authority derives from the cross"; and later: "Prayer allowed the poet to always discover God under the wrap of earthly matters." These statements can also refer to John Paul II himself. In the same address the pope approvingly quotes Norwid: "Humanity without God—betrays itself."

Which of Wojtyła's own plays is closest to your heart and why?

The Jeweler's Shop. Written in 1960, it stands close to his *Love and Responsibility*. The former is a poetic drama. The latter—a moral, philosophical, psychological, and also medical, study. They somehow complement each other. I first read *Love and Responsibility*. Actually, my then-fiancée, Zofia Reklewska, and I read this book almost as a manual. It helped us to prepare for marriage—sixty years ago. Later on I read *The Jeweler's Shop*. It is a profoundly psychological play and can also be treated as an artistic catechesis for people planning for marriage and seeking to live it honestly. It offers rich and complex material for actors and also for fashion designers and composers—in fact, two musicals have already been based on it. For a director *The Jeweler's Shop* is both a special challenge and a reservoir of opportunities.

This is the most frequently produced of Karol Wojtyła's plays. The world premiere was prepared by the great Polish director Leopold Kielanowski at the Teatr Polski in London in 1979, in Polish. More than twenty productions in professional theaters in Poland followed, first at the Teatr Dramatyczny in Wałbrzych in 1981. It was directed by Andrzej Maria Marczewski, who would later mount *The Jeweler's Shop* eight times on different stages. An excellent Italian movie based on it came out in 1988, directed by Michael Anderson, with Burt Lancaster as the Jeweler. I worked on *The Jeweler's Shop* in 1994, at the Teatr Polski in New York, consulting the production directed by Ireneusz Wykurz. (This production was performed in English.)

Once you said: "John Paul the Great has enabled people to put fear behind them. He has raised and made whole our hope like a broken reed. He has fanned the sparks of faith and courage into a flame. Above all, he has embraced all in unconditional love."

You are so kind to quote me. I can quote myself again to expand on this.

At the end of my novel on John Paul II, *Day of Witness*, his former student Father Andrzej (a fictional character) finds himself in great danger. He doesn't know what to do. But…

> He recalled the words of the pope. That great, simple catch-phrase which he announced at the start of his pontificate, and repeated so many times: "Be not afraid!" It was a summons to the old and young, spouses and children, the lost and the doubter, the disparaging, the fearful, and the dying—indeed to all humanity. A prophetic call drawn from depth of Isaiah: *Be not afraid, for I am with you.* Christ's admonishment and encouragement directed to the Apostles: *Do not be afraid, little flock*—and transported to our time.
>
> "Be not afraid!"
>
> Do not be afraid—thought Father Andrzej—for you are redeemed. Do not be afraid since the Blessed Mother is with you, and she did not fear. Do not be afraid since the apostles, martyrs, and saints did not fear. Do not be afraid since the light shines in the darkness and no darkness can quench it. Be not afraid since the power of Christ's cross and his resurrection is greater than any evil.
>
> "Be not afraid!"
>
> The Spirit of God gave these words to the man called to be pope from a distant land. They were to serve him as a sword and a buckler, as a torch and seed for sowing. And even when he is no longer able to voice them, these words will continue to sound in our hearts.
>
> "Be Not Afraid!"

What do we need to build a civilization of love?

A very difficult question... But the answer seems to be simple: We, everybody, the whole human race, should return to the Decalogue.

And an even more simple answer: We have to return to this first and greatest commandment: Love the Lord your God, with all your heart, and with all your soul, and with all your strength. And love your neighbor as yourself.

MARTA BURGHARDT

Scholar, speaker, editor, and author of books and articles about St. John Paul II. She belongs to the Theological and Philosophical Committee and the Literature Committee for the Critical Edition of the Works of Karol Wojtyła at John Paul II Cross-Cultural Dialogue Institute in Kraków. She studied at the University of Rome.

How did your journey with Karol Wojtyła start?

I should reply with the words of the Gospel: "You did not choose me, but I chose you." My journey with John Paul II has lasted continuously for 25 years. It started when I was studying in Italy and my friends wanted to get to know the poetry of the Polish Pope better. I translated for them very difficult poetry of Karol Wojtyła from Polish to Italian. Together we discussed it and looked for hidden meanings. In this poetry, each word has its own weight. According to the Italian students, my Polish roots virtually imposed on me the obligation to know every detail of the author's life. I did not want to disappoint them, so I tried to learn as much as possible about the Holy Father. I wrote my master's thesis on "Theories of literary translation based on the poetry of Karol Wojtyła." While writing my doctoral dissertation, I found out that the poetry he wrote in his youth had never been translated into any foreign languages, so I challenged myself and translated 17 "Sonnets" into the Italian. My university, Libera Università Maria Santissima Assunta in Rome, granted me a literary award that gave me an opportunity to publish my translation. I submitted all of his youth poetry in Polish with a parallel Italian translation, extensive critical annotations, and editorial explanations of more difficult terms. I also prefaced every single poem.

Please explain the nature of your current work on Karol Wojtyła.

In 2015, Cardinal Stanisław Dziwisz, the long-time personal secretary of Karol Wojtyła, first as the Metropolitan of Kraków and then as Pope John Paul II, established the Scholarly Committee for the Critical Edition of the Literary Works of Karol Wojtyła/John Paul II. I became its secretary. We are reviewing all surviving versions of each work: manuscript, typescript, first edition, and subsequent editions. Then we endeavor to restore the most faithful version possible, the closest to the author's intention. The author's corrections and deletions, listed in different iterations of the text, show the evolution of Wojtyła's thought, while variations in the publications are often mere errors. There is a great interest in our work worldwide. First translations have appeared of poetry and dramas in foreign languages based on our work, which presents his complete poems in three volumes.

What has been your biggest challenge in translating Karol Wojtyła's juvenilia so far?

I worked on the Italian translation in Rome from 2001 to 2003. As for his juvenilia, the greatest challenge was the stylized language. There are also many archaisms and regionalisms. There were references to certain people I was unable to identify myself. There were difficulties with which no one could help me. Fortunately, I was able to address my concerns directly to the author. Thus, I worked with the pope.

Describe the literary language of Karol Wojtyła. What difficulties, in your view, does it pose to readers?

In the poetry of Karol Wojtyła, there are elements of theology, anthropology, history, and tradition; he refers often to the Holy Scriptures, but also to the culture of antiquity. Literary texts are great for meditation. A young person relates to them differently from someone who reads them at the end of his life. Indeed, this poetry is not easy to understand; you cannot read it cursorily, and it demands maturity. Moreover, it is not enough to read it once to get the proper meaning. Wojtyła's literary work is very demanding and very deep. The poet confessed in his youth that he deeply carried his thoughts for a long time inside before he transferred them to paper. And this is evident even in his later work.

Moreover, the themes of his poetry and drama often return in a different form, such as a philosophical treatise, and years later in papal teaching. For example, love and marriage were the subject of his lectures on moral theology at the Catholic University of Lublin in 1956–1958. The lectures drew on his play *The Jeweler's Shop* (1960) and the monograph *Love and Responsibility* (1960). It is worth adding in this context that in 1960 then-Bishop Wojtyła established the Family Institute. Moreover, at the beginning of his pontificate, the pope's Wednesday catechesis concerned the theology of the body and resulted in the publication of *Male and Female He Created Them*. We cannot separate the poet from the philosopher and theologian; Wojtyła's work is always multi-layered.

Cardinal Dziwisz gave you a valuable manuscript (and a typescript) of thirteen catecheses of Archbishop Karol Wojtyła. As you have mentioned, you work with the Holy Father's manuscripts. Please explain how your work on "Areopagus meditations" proceeded. What are your thoughts on Wojtyła's text?

The "Areopagus meditations" are a series of thirteen catecheses influenced by the Second Vatican Council. Archbishop Karol Wojtyła was very involved in drawing up *Gaudium et spes*, the Pastoral Constitution on the Church in the Modern World. The exchange of views with the council fathers, who came from all continents, a new openness to non-Christian religions, and the need to return to the roots of Christianity in turn stimulated his own thought.

It is worth recalling that the council was held from 1962 to 1965, when Poland was under the communist yoke. The authorities granted permission to travel only to some bishops. And those who got passports went not only to Rome but, at the request of the Holy Father, to the Holy Land, in December 1963. On their way, they stopped in Athens, where they visited the Acropolis and the Areopagus. The awareness of following in the footsteps of St. Paul, the Apostle of the Nations, must have had a profound influence on Archbishop Wojtyła, since he took the sermon of St. Paul at the Areopagus and made it the starting point for a series of thirteen catecheses. We do not know for whom he intended them; we do not know when he delivered them; we are not even sure if they were delivered. The fact that they have been preserved in the form of a manuscript of 39 loose pages suggests that they were probably written in Italy. I was very touched when Cardinal Stanisław Dziwisz asked me to transcribe and edit them during Lent 2018. This became the most beautiful retreat for me — alone with the catechesis of the Holy Father John Paul II. A book resulted, which was published in the United States as *Teaching for an Unbelieving World*.

How did Karol Wojtyła's youthful study of Polish literature, his knowledge of the great classics of Polish Romanticism, his studies at the Jagiellonian University in Cracow, and his theatrical experience with Mieczysław Kotlarczyk shape his later writings?

Karol Wojtyła graduated from high school with a thorough knowledge of Polish literature, Greek and Latin, and modern German. He cherished geography and history, and belonged to many different school clubs, valuing theater and acting the most: he was not only an actor but also a co-producer and co-director. With his excellent diction, beautiful voice, good projection, reliable memory, and versatility, he found himself in demand among amateur theaters. He studied Polish language and letters at the Jagiellonian University. During the Second World War, the German occupation authorities arrested the professors of the Jagiellonian University, and before Wojtyła's very eyes, German trucks transported Polish elites to extermination camps. Yet the young poet did not abandon his studies. He continued studying Polish literature by himself, drafted his first plays, and learned French and Spanish. He memorized the classics of Polish Romanticism, which he presented together with a group of other enthusiasts, at the risk of their lives, to an audience of his countrymen enslaved by the Nazis. During the war, he encountered some distinguished theater people. In particularly, he acquired much knowledge and artistry from Mieczysław Kotlarczyk, with whom he co-founded the Rhapsodic Theater. The whole experience informed all his subsequent writings.

How do you remember your last meeting with the Polish Pope? Who was he for you?

My last meeting with John Paul II took place in his private library on November 19, 2004. I was there to present the Italian translation of his early poetry. John Paul II spoke with great difficulty, so Cardinal Stanisław Dziwisz conveyed his words to us. I had an impression that the secretary was reading the pope's mind. The meeting was very warm, cordial; it seemed a bit like a "parent-teacher conference," because the Holy Father asked about me, and my supervisor, Professor Paolo Martino, and LUMSA's president, Giuseppe Della Torre, spared no kind words on my behalf.

Yet it was on Palm Sunday in 2005 when I saw the Holy Father that I felt that I was bidding him farewell forever. I was standing in St. Peter's Square, and his appearance touched me deeply; I wept. On April 1 and 2 I kept vigil outside the papal window. Suddenly it was announced that he had left for the Father's house. I still can hear the endless applause and the spontaneous *Te Deum*. I was present when the body of John Paul II was taken from the apostolic palace to St. Peter's Basilica. I waited all day in line to pay my last respects. And I came to his funeral. I felt like I lost someone close. My Italian and French friends called me, wondering whether they should express their condolences to me or rather their gratitude to Poland for this great pontiff. After living many years in Rome, I returned to Poland two days after the funeral because I felt that to stay in Rome without John Paul II made no sense. Who was John Paul II to me? He was my father, my support, and my supreme authority. When he looked at me, I knew that everything I was doing was important. Therefore, I think that it was not I who chose the direction of my life journey, but Karol Wojtyła who chose me to serve him.

What do you consider the three most important ideas in the teachings of John Paul II that refer to his literary legacy?

I would divide his poetry into three separate groups: mystical and pastoral; ethical and social; and, finally, about his homeland, Poland. As for his teachings as pope, I would consider the following areas: first, the civilization of love, peace in the world, respect for human dignity, and protection of life. Second, there is his social teaching. Third comes the theology of the body and the role of women in the modern world.

The beatification process of the parents of St. John Paul II has just started. There is no doubt that the spiritual attitude of the pope was formed and fostered in his family. How could Emilia and Karol Wojtyła, the parents of John Paul II, become a paradigm for contemporary families?

At home, Karol Wojtyła acquired an ardent faith, a knowledge of the Holy Scriptures, and a respect for people. He recalled his mother's hands that taught him to make the sign of the cross. He said that he learned about suffering from his mother because he mainly remembered her as a sick person seeking help from numerous doctors. Karol watched his father kneeling to pray. The elder Wojtyła remained immersed in prayer during sleepless nights, especially after the death of his wife. Three years later another tragedy struck. His firstborn son, Edmund, passed away at age 26. A great doctor, he gave his life tending patients in an infectious-disease ward, defenseless in the face of deadly afflictions for which there was no cure at that time. The father endured these trials with a bravery approximating that of Job. He neither broke down nor fell into depression but offered his suffering to God.

Today, Pope Francis speaks about saints living next door. None of us remembers times more challenging than the one we currently live in: humiliated by the pandemic, powerless and helpless, when all the achievements of science seem to be worth little in the face of an invisible enemy. I think that the parents of St. John Paul II were exactly "quiet saints from the neighborhood." The elevation of Emilia and Karol Wojtyła to the altars can make us all realize that the pursuit of holiness takes place here and now, and not only after death. I see Emilia Wojtyła as the patroness of mothers with an endangered pregnancy, or mothers who lost their children right after their birth. Karol Wojtyła senior, in my opinion, is a perfect model for a single father raising his children. I think both parents are a good example for us, and not too distant in time. They lived in similarly difficult conditions to our own, struggled with similar problems, and yet never strayed from their path on the way to holiness.

What do we need to build a civilization of love today?

In building a civilization of love, we need faith, the strength of prayer, empathy, and sensitivity to the plight of others. As the Holy Father said, we must build bridges, not walls. And we all should be involved in this project.

STANISŁAW DZIEDZIC

Professor, Polish literary historian, author, lecturer, former Director of the Department of Culture and National Heritage of the city of Cracow

Which of your meetings with John Paul II do you most vividly remember?

Every single meeting with John Paul II was a great honor for me and each played an important role in my life. I remember them all well. The first took place at the Apostolic Palace, in the private papal apartment, in spring 1994. The Holy Father had just confirmed his authorship of seventeen youthful sonnets and a hymn called *"Magnificat,"* whose manuscripts were preserved in the private collections of Zofia and Mieczysław Kotlarczyk, to whom he had sent them in November 1939 for evaluation. The texts survived despite the turmoil of war and dislocation. Thanks to the kindness of the daughter of the Kotlarczyks, with full confidentiality, I presented photocopies to John Paul II. I was hoping for permission to publish them. Incidentally, so far, only the *"Magnificat"* has been published, though in a slightly different version. I will return to this later. The author agreed to share the sonnets with the Polish composer Juliusz Łuciuk, who composed an orchestral setting for Sonnet IX.

Please explain the title of your book about Karol Wojtyła: God's Romantic.

Wojtyła's romanticism (inspired by Mickiewicz, Słowacki, Norwid, and the neo-Romantic Wyspiański) was focused on God. In the hymn *"Magnificat,"* a nineteen-year-old Karol Wojtyła addresses the One God. He embodied a romantically striving philosophical and aesthetic imagination. With this imagination anchored to a well-formed awareness of the supernatural, he became a model of the ideal mystic — God's Romantic.

How did John Paul II understand the interpenetration of the word of God and the word of man?

Karol Wojtyła was a master of the word from early high school. He always understood language as the fundamental aspect of a nation's culture. This way of thinking about theater and poetry — carrying with him the idea of the word, also in a sacred sense — gave rise to the Rhapsodic Theatre. Cardinal Franciszek Macharski aptly referred to John Paul II as himself the "Rhapsody of the Eternal Word."

Let us focus on the last literary work of John Paul II, *Roman Triptych*. As Michał Masłowski rightly pointed out, Wojtyła was perhaps the first pope in history to use poetry to express the truth of faith. Masłowski also quotes the words of the Nobel Prize laureate Czesław Miłosz from the *Treatise on Poetry* to the effect that "one clear stanza can take more weight than a whole wagon of elaborate prose." Miłosz claimed that John Paul II achieved his goal in the *Triptych* by combining poetry, metaphor, and argumentative precision. He has furthermore stated that even John Paul II's encyclicals are the work of the last Polish Romantic, on account of their style, content, and form.

How would you describe the literary work of Karol Wojtyła?

The literary work of Karol Wojtyła includes drama and poems. Among the lyrical works, there are literary juvenilia, including two volumes of poetry: *The Beskidy Tramps* and *The Psalter: A Slavic Book*, also referred to by the author as *The Renaissance Psalter*. Further, there are two dramas from the early years of the Second World War: *Job* and *Jeremiah*. His earliest play, *David* (1940), has not survived.

There are next *Our God's Brother* and the last two meditative plays: *The Jeweler's Shop* (1960) and *Radiation of Fatherhood* (1964). His literary output also includes works of a mystical nature (including "Song of the Hidden God"). Among the poems, there is "Stanisław," completed a few minutes before he set off for the conclave on October 15, 1978. It is worth mentioning that his Kraków output includes thoughtful reviews and essays on theatre, especially the performances of the Rhapsodic Theater.

Why did Wojtyła choose to study Polish literature at Jagiellonian University in Kraków?

Most people in Wadowice who went to college did so in Kraków, with its Jagiellonian University, the Academy of Fine Arts, and the Mining and Metallurgical Academy. The Jagiellonian had the best professors of Polish studies. John Paul II repeatedly emphasized how much he owed them.

In his junior and senior years of high school, he showed interest in both theatre and literature. He performed on the Wadowice stages with success. There were many people who influenced him, most prominently his teacher Kazimierz Foryś and the founder of the Powszechny Theater, Dr. Mieczysław Kotlarczyk. They appreciated his outstanding acting talent and knowledge of theatre. At that time, he wrote quite frequently. He composed poems. It was in high school that he most likely wrote his first volume of poetry: *The Beskidy Tramps*.

His decision to study Polish literature — language and letters — was determined by an inclination towards *belles lettres*. Soon, he found himself attracted to the study of the language itself. This opened up completely new horizons for Wojtyła; it introduced him to the mystery of language itself. At that time, there was no professional theatrical school in Kraków, but he joined Juliusz Kydryński's "Theatrical Confraternity." After the German invasion it took to calling itself Studio 39. Together with Kotlarczyk, the group edited and published a clandestine literary journal. The theatre left a deep impression on Wojtyła.

How did Wojtyła's experience with the Rhapsodic Theatre prepare him for his papal ministry?

Mieczysław Kotlarczyk, who was twelve years older than Wojtyła, founded and ran the Amateur Powszechny Theater in Wadowice, specializing in staging the classics. Young Wojtyła, passionate about theater and fine literature, was a regular guest in the Kotlarczyk family apartment. In the summer of 1941, Mieczysław Kotlarczyk and his wife Sophia made their way from Wadowice to Kraków, where they lived with Karol Wojtyła. Sharing the same modest basement apartment, they were able to continue their conversations about theatre, but also to attempt to stage performances. Wojtyła became a co-creator of the Rhapsodic Theatre.

He had an incredible stage presence, as many outstanding artists acknowledge. He was endowed with excellent diction and a strong voice. He didn't indulge in cheap sentimentality. He tackled scripts intellectually, based on a deep knowledge of the subject matter. At the time when Hitler intended Poland to disappear and one of the main tasks of the Resistance was to save and transmit the Polish language and culture, Mieczysław Kotlarczyk organized clandestine meetings of the Rhapsodic Theatre in Kraków. Wojtyła, who was its pillar, left it in the fall of 1942 to embrace a higher vocation: the priesthood. Unlike his theatrical performances, the rhapsodic Eternal Word allowed him to gather millions of people for God.

You edited Karol Wojtyła's first poems written as a young person and received the Holy Father's consent to publish them. How did that happen?

When, during my personal conversation with the Holy Father, I finally obtained his permission to publish his seventeen sonnets and the hymn "*Magnificat*," while holding a photocopy of the manuscripts from 1939 in my hands, I asked him to consider allowing me to publish his early poetry. After some hesitation, he gave me permission and allowed the inclusion of photographs of saints by the folk sculptor Jędrzej Wowra.

Which of John Paul II's texts are particularly close to your heart?

Among the early works of Karol Wojtyła, from the period of the Second World War, is a mystical poem of extraordinary beauty, "Song of the Hidden God," published in 1946. A beautiful and profound text, I think it is one of the greatest mystical works in Polish literature. This work, so rich theologically and philosophically, and exquisitely crafted, came from the pen of a man in his early twenties. "Song of the Glow of Water" (1950) was a formal and spiritual continuation.

I also treasure Wojtyła's poem "Stanisław," short in length but rich in content, which brings a deep reflection about Poland as the "land of hard-won unity." He started writing it while preparing for the 900th anniversary of the death of Saint Stanislaus and completed it a day before he was elected pope. On January 6, 1979, the manuscript was received by Fr. Franciszek Macharski—the successor of Archbishop Karol Wojtyła in Kraków.

In his work, Karol Wojtyła drew from both the Bible and Polish Romanticism. What did he especially love about the great classics of Polish Romanticism and in particular Cyprian Kamil Norwid?

The Bible was Karol Wojtyła's basic point of reference: cultural, literary, and, of course, religious. Biblical threads, archetypes, and even extensive pericopes and stories have their deep literary references in many of his works: from youthful sonnets to the *Roman Triptych*. From the letters of the early German occupation period to Mieczysław Kotlarczyk, who at that time still lived in Wadowice, we learn how much the future pope took from "the songs of the bards, the Wyspiański Theater, Kasprowicz's books, and Norwid's philosophy." John Paul II expressed this sentiment years later in his famous *Letter to Artists* (1999). There is much to be said about the sources of these interests and his frequent reference to the works of the Romantic masters. In an interview with Tad Szulc, John Paul II simply confessed: "Norwid means a lot, a lot to me and I read him constantly."

What's your favorite memory of Saint John Paul II?

I met Cardinal Karol Wojtyła during my university studies in 1976; he would receive students in the episcopal palace at Christmastime. Being asked by the Cardinal where I came from and what I was studying, I replied that I was studying Polish literature and journalism at the Jagiellonian University and I lived in the "Żaczek" dormitory. The Cardinal replied that his study of Polish literature, very important in his life, was interrupted by the outbreak of the Second World War, and that he also lived in the Oleandry neighborhood for a short time, at the same place but under a different name at the time: the Jagiellonian University's Second Student House.

What do we need to build a civilization of love?

John Paul II proclaimed the idea of a civilization of love for all people, regardless of beliefs, religion, or race. In proclaiming and helping to implement it, he wanted to reach everyone, to help them strive against limitations and adversities, as well as against stereotypes. He loved people, whom he always saw as images of a loving God. Let us fill this world of hatred and twisted values with merciful love instead of nihilism.

FR. JOSÉ GRANADOS

Superior General of the Disciples of the Hearts of Jesus and Mary

Father, what was your first memory of St. John Paul II?

I was very young (eight years old) when John Paul II was elected pope. I remember especially his presence during my youth, at the World Youth Days in Santiago de Compostela and Częstochowa. Together with my friends I was anxious to see him but especially to hear his words, so encouraging and full of clarity and the assurance of faith, inviting us to beauty and greatness. I have also the memory of meeting him personally in Rome in 1998. When my mother was sick with cancer I wrote to him, and in a very short period of time I received an answer from his secretariat inviting us to join him during the Holy Mass. It was a consolation to receive his blessing at this moment of trial. I remember also the eagerness with which I received and read his encyclicals (many of them came out while I was studying theology), which opened up new views to my understanding of the dignity of the human person in the light of a call to communion and to the gift of self.

What do you appreciate the most about John Paul II?

I think it was his ability to put Christ at the center of human life and of society, his great passion for Christ as the fulfillment of all we yearn for. His focus on the importance of love, his theology of the body, his affirmation of the dignity of each human life — all this came from the confession of faith in Christ, who reveals man to himself, as he liked to repeat, quoting Vatican II (*Gaudium et spes* 22).

How could John Paul II have developed his "theology of the body" from his own experience?

John Paul II explains, in *Love and Responsibility*, how he was able to talk about matters of family life and sexuality even though he was not married. He pointed out his experience with young couples, the help he gave them in their marriages, counseling them and hearing their confessions. Human experience is not isolated, which means that we can share in the experience of others and learn from them. This capacity for empathy is at the root of the theology of the body, for the body is a place of contact and communion with others. Moreover, the vocation to consecrated virginity is not wholly alien to the vocation to marriage, for it is also a spousal vocation, inasmuch as it consists of the total gift of self to another, to Christ and to the Church. It is the whole person, with his masculinity or her femininity, that is consecrated to the Lord in religious life.

You have written that "the body speaks a language.... [T]he body's language echoes the voice of transcendence inviting us to venture out of ourselves in response to the call of love.... [T]he body is a significant and beautiful pattern that gives our love shape and structure...." Can you please briefly explain this?

John Paul II insisted that the body speaks a language that we ourselves have not created, and that we need to learn to re-read the language of the body in truth. The first thing the body tells us with its language is that we have not given life to ourselves. This is very concrete: our body recalls to us that we have been born from our mother and father, that we were formed in our mother's womb. This is a language of receptivity, which reminds us that the primordial task in human life is to learn how to receive ourselves from another, that is, to understand that we ourselves are gifts. Ultimately, the body teaches us that we are a gift from God himself, our ultimate origin. Once we have learned what we can call the "filial meaning of the body" (Benedict XVI) we understand that in the body we can give ourselves to other persons, in the conjugal union, and thus generate life. These are the unitive and generative meanings of the language of the body. The language of the body contains, in a sense, a grammar with which we can speak (freely and creatively) the language of love.

How would you explain "the meaning of human life" according to John Paul II's teachings?

I would say that the human person is called to love, which means that he is called to receive himself from another and, in his turn, to give himself in a generative way. One could summarize John Paul II's vision of life in this way: the human being is a son or a daughter, called to become a spouse (in marriage or in consecrated virginity), and in this way to be fruitful (fatherhood and motherhood). Life is fulfilled when we realize these dimensions: when we learn to receive life from another (as children), when we learn to live for another (as spouses), when we learn to generate life for another (as parents).

Why is St. John Paul II's theology of the body more important now than ever? What does it teach us?

Our culture shows a great interest in the body and even views it as a place of transcendence. This is why there is an eagerness to transform the body, to find new ways of experiencing with the body, of expressing oneself in the body (think for example of tattoos). Yet we have reduced the body to the projection of our own desires and in this way we have lost an essential part of its language. We have forgotten that the body, before being a tool to transform the world and to express ourselves, is a place that has been given to us by another, a place we are called to receive with gratitude. Sure, the body contains a language with which we can talk and be creative, but this language, like every language, has to be learned from another, or it remains a private language unable to communicate. The Theology of the Body teaches us the original language of the body, the language of the original gift of God, of the call to love between man and woman, of the destiny of the body in the glory of God. By talking about the body this theology is a theology of love, of the truth of love, so that love becomes more than just an emotion and can last and sustain our whole life even beyond death. There is, then, a transcendence in the body, there is a word (*logos*) of God in the body, and so we can speak of a theo-logy of the body. The foundation of this theology of the body is the fact that the Word of God himself has assumed a body.

"Man cannot live without love," John Paul II wrote in his first encyclical, Redemptor hominis. *How did John Paul II define love?*

John Paul II distinguished between three ways of talking about love. There is a love that is rooted in sensuality, a desire for physical pleasure with the other. There is a love rooted in sentiments, a desire for the intimacy that allows us to feel well together with the other. These two dimensions of love are good, but they cannot be made an absolute, for then they would not allow us to go out of ourselves (we remain in our pleasure and in our feeling) and would no longer be love. Both dimensions need to be integrated into what John Paul II called betrothed love, which entails the affirmation of the other person for what he or she is. To love someone means, then, to say, not only: "you are good because you are useful to me," or "you are good because I like being with you," but: "you are good just because you are," which is to say:

"you are beautiful." If we can say this, this is because we see something eternal in the other person, that is, because we understand that God loves the other person for him or herself. True love, in the end, needs to refer to God, the source of all love. True love means to receive the other person as a gift from God and to seek the good of the other person for him or herself, walking together with the beloved towards communion with God.

Let's take The Jeweler's Shop, *which Wojtyła published in 1960. What does Wojtyła probe in its story of three different couples?*

In *The Jeweler's Shop*, marriage is to love one another in such a way that this love opens up a way together towards God. Marriage is a mutual communication made possible because there is an original communication of the Creator (the Jeweler, in the play) to the spouses, who are entrusted to each other. In fact, husband and wife become one flesh in the very place where both of them were generated by God. In this way the spouses are called to understand the absolute dimensions of love, and not to remain on the surface of its current. When this happens they can mediate this meaning to their children, so that the children can get married in the dimension of the Absolute. It is Christ who has reminded us of this absolute dimension of love. He is the Spouse who comes to fulfill our vocation by revealing us the source of all love in the Father. In his light, marriage is also (this is the meaning of the second act) the place where the miracle of forgiveness is possible.

In the spirit of John Paul II, what would be your advice to a young couple getting married?

That they be open to marriage as a path together towards God. That they fulfill the promise they have made by exercising forgiveness each day of their life. That their love be open to transmitting life and educating their children for eternal life, for in this way they will preserve the freshness of their relationship. That they understand that they are not alone and that they need the accompaniment of the Church, for they are a sign of Christ's love for her; that their family be always open to receive other people, especially other couples, and to help them towards a common destiny.

How do the indissolubility and fruitfulness of marriage fulfill and crown the dynamism of love?

We can give ourselves entirely to the person we love only if we give our entire future. Otherwise we reserve something to ourselves. What this means is, again, that to love is to enter into a dimension that is greater than ourselves, a dimension that allows us to put our entire future in the hands of another (something we cannot do by ourselves). To say yes for the rest of our life is only possible if we trust in God, the Lord of the future. It is this presence of God that allows us to forgive, which is to renew the promise. When we forgive we say: the promise we made to each other is greater than this offense and betrayal. In addition, true love goes beyond the self, which means that it is fruitful. If love is not fruitful in some way, helping the person we love and by making us grow together, then it is not true love. The most telling sign of this fruitfulness is the begetting of a child.

What is the family's greatest challenge today?

First of all, there is a challenge to the very being of the family, inasmuch as our society proposes alternative views of the family that are not rooted in the sexual difference. This could invite the family to understand itself just as a personal preference of the spouses, who could have formed a different kind of family. In this way it is easy to lose grasp of something essential for the family: that the family is not a private project, but the foundation of society. The family — the union of a man and a woman for their entire life, open to the transmission of life — reminds us that we are called to foster receptivity and openness to an original gift that has been entrusted to us. This challenge implies a further challenge: how to educate our children into the vocation to love, at a time when children are seen just as the expression of the desires of their parents.

Can you see any weak points in the theology of the body?

I would say that there are many points that need to be further developed. John Paul II focused on several aspects of the theology of the body, especially sexuality. In different works he reflected also on other dimensions: the theology of the suffering body (*Salvifici doloris*), the theology of the working body (*Laborem exercens*)... I think the idea of the "filial body" and the importance of being a son or a daughter is very present in his work, but is not as clearly expressed as we find it in Benedict XVI (Discourse to the John Paul II Institute, May 13, 2011). Another aspect that needs further development is how Christ brings to fulfillment the language of the body.

What do we need to build a civilization of love?

John Paul II's teaching possesses a crucial social dimension. For in talking about love, he also talked about the foundation of our being together, of our social life. It is crucial to his whole vision that the family is the cornerstone of society. It is in the family that we learn the dignity of the other person, that we learn that it is good to be together with others, that we learn the importance of the common good. Thus, the civilization of love means that the love of the family is called to go beyond the family, it means that the family lives its vocation only when it lives beyond itself, when it is able to expand its love to the rest of our human relations. It means to build a family of families that gives meaning to our world and to our history.

You young people are the ones who embody this youth: you are the youth of the nations and societies, the youth of every family and of all humanity; you are also the youth of the Church. We are all looking to you, for all of us, thanks to you, in a certain sense continually become young again. So your youth is not just your own property, your personal property or the property of a generation: it belongs to the whole of that space that every man traverses in his life's journey, and at the same time it is a special possession belonging to everyone. It is a possession of humanity itself.

In you there is hope, for you belong to the future, just as the future belongs to you. For hope is always linked to the future; it is the expectation of "future good things."

> You are the future of the world;
> You are the hope of the Church.
> You are my hope…
>
> *John Paul II*

PAOLO FUCILI

Italian journalist based in Rome, where he covers the Vatican for the Italian TV channel TV2000. He is a contributor to many newspapers, books, and magazines and the author of several books and essays on various religious topics.

What did John Paul mean to you?

I was born in 1971, so for me John Paul II has been "the pope" — up to now — for more than half of my life. My memories about him start with watching his election on TV and then going on a pilgrimage to Rome as a boy scout in the Extraordinary Jubilee of 1983–84. I couldn't imagine then that the Vatican would become the place of my work as a journalist. But the milestone was certainly the Jubilee Year 2000, when I started working in Rome for TV2000, the Italian Bishops' Conference TV channel. Little by little, day by day, I became more and more certain that I was dealing with a saint, endowed with exceptional charisma, a giant in the history of the Church, which became evident to everyone at the latest on April 2, 2005, the day of his death. Besides growing up in a Catholic family that educated me in the faith, I have always been eager to learn and understand. Karol Wojtyła broadened my horizons; he helped me to understand that Christianity is a universal key to understanding reality in depth. Thus a Catholic has no reason to have any intellectual inferiority complex towards anyone.

What inspired you to co-write (with Daniele Bungaro) the book Holiness Is Always Young: St. John Paul II and the Path of World Youth Day?

Few people remember that the road to World Youth Day began in 1985 with the "Youth International Year" called by the UN. John Paul II observed it by convening in Rome an international youth meeting similar to the Youth Jubilee held in 1984, in both cases on Palm Sunday. In addition, he wrote an apostolic letter, *Dilecti amici*, drawing inspiration from the rich young man in the Gospel. As the pope explained then, "What must I do to inherit eternal life?" means nothing else that "what must I do so that my life may have full value and full meaning?"

What was the message that particularly caught your attention?

After rereading that letter, I asked myself: "Who is the young person who has never asked himself how to live a meaningful life?" But, unfortunately, the Church very often — especially in recent times, we must admit — speaks to young people about many other things, with other languages, from other perspectives, but not about what really matters. Pope Wojtyła, instead, nourished two unshakable beliefs, for his entire life; the first: there's no young man whose heart does not burn with that question; the second: even today, 2,000 years later, the Gospel is the fullest and greatest answer. That's why the history of World Youth Day deserves to be told and meditated upon. This is because these beliefs seem to me anything but obvious, judging by the way the Church approaches young people today, a stark contrast to how it was not so long ago under John Paul II.

What's the purpose of this global movement started by Wojtyła?

Wojtyła attracted about 16 million young people to his World Youth Days, from Buenos Aires in 1987 to Toronto in 2002. Did he have a precise goal in mind from the beginning? I don't know. In any case, the facts speak for themselves: secularization is not an inevitable destiny, provided the Church learns again how to awaken in young people the question mentioned above, instead of obfuscating it as many others do. And this is even more relevant today.

Is there a universal message of World Youth Day?

It is not easy to summarize it. But let me mention a song echoing very often in my head, the anthem of WYD 2000 in Rome. It begins: "From the horizon a great light travels through history and through the years overcame the darkness by becoming Memory. By illuminating our lives it clearly reveals to us that we cannot live if we do not seek the Truth...."

I have found more inspiration in that song than in the entire synod held at the Vatican four years ago on "Young people, faith, and vocational discernment," full of sociology and so poor in terms of faith. The "light" comes from "the horizon," outside of us, we cannot give it to ourselves. It "overcame the darkness." We are not condemned, as human beings, to remain without answers to the "whys" that nag and distress us. The darkness of meaninglessness and despair has been defeated. The light is not an abstract, intellectual theory, and it (or, rather, "he," Jesus) makes us understand that not seeking the truth, not taking it seriously, not desiring it, remaining indifferent to it, is like being dead in soul if not in body. I find this message extraordinarily against the current! It embodies perfectly — I think — the spirit that compelled Wojtyła to give life to WYD.

Paolo Fucili 259

How can young Christians use the treasure and beauty of Wojtyła's revolutionary movements for the young to build a dialogue with other faiths in today's secular world?

A good question! Who was St. John Paul II? What did his 27 years of pontificate mean for the Church? First of all, it is important to keep alive these memories. On this point, it is sad to see in the Church a great hurry to turn the page. You ask me how to build a dialogue with other religions, in today's secular world, starting from the legacy Pope Wojtyła left us. He placed at the center of his pontificate the question of truth, the truth about God and the truth about man. And so he gained respect and admiration even from non-Christian people, in non-Christian countries and cultures, as for example on August 19, 1985, in Casablanca, Morocco, when he addressed 80,000 young Muslims gathered for the Pan-Arab Games. It was the first time the pope spoke to such a large crowd of young non-Christians. That's why that trip to Morocco, at the end of a long journey in Africa, is one of the most famous pages of Wojtyła's pontificate. No need to say that the inter-religious and inter-cultural dialogue is even more relevant and urgent today, in our globalized world. But the John Paul II lesson is always relevant too. He believed in the need for dialogue, even between different religions, as he proved in the famous day of prayer for peace, in Assisi, on October 27, 1986, with many world religious leaders. But dialogue is built not by setting aside the "truth question," as if it were too delicate or divisive, or by asserting that "there are so many truths and everyone has his own." The aim of the dialogue is exactly to focus on the question of truth, which can only be one, while respecting the freedom of all to accept it or not.

The eighth World Youth Day took place in Denver in 1993. John Paul II came to a modern, multi-cultural, multi-racial, and not necessarily Catholic metropolis. Despite the skepticism of many, the event became a great success. How come?

The event of WYD 1993 in Denver was not a surprise. Several of John Paul II's initiatives, in fact, were greeted with skepticism when he announced them. After Buenos Aires in 1987, Santiago de Compostela in 1989, and Częstochowa in 1991—in Poland, which had just emerged from 40 years of the communist dictatorship—the Denver WYD was the first to be celebrated in a rich, modern country like the United States, at the forefront of scientific and technological progress. Surely, choosing such a place for the event seemed like a gamble, according to the theory, very popular until a few decades ago, that modernity would have decreed the disappearance — or at least the irrelevance — of religion. And the United States is the vanguard of modernity. But John Paul II thought differently. If we read once again the sermon he gave in Denver, we notice that he took the theme of Life from the modern metropolis. But then he reversed the reasoning, turned it upside down:

> Life is full of mystery.... Humanity as a whole feels the urgent need to give meaning and purpose to a world where the complexity and difficulty of being happy is increasing.... To stop asking these questions is to give up the great adventure of seeking the truth of life. Technological and economic progress alone has not satisfied man's deepest aspirations. We who live in this age know this well.

Karol Wojtyła was 73 years old in 1993. He was a son of the 20th century, the century that produced the greatest progress in human history, that's true. But it also produced immense catastrophes, such as the two world wars and totalitarianism, which the future pope suffered personally from. The man of today is no happier or less restless than the man of the past. And the evidence of it is that even in Denver an immense crowd gathered to hear such words.

During Mass at the Cherry Creek State Park in Colorado, the pope concluded his address with this dramatic challenge: "Do not be afraid to go out on the streets and into public places, like the first apostles who preached Christ and the good news of salvation in the squares of cities, towns, and villages. This is no time to be ashamed of the Gospel.... It is the time to preach it from the rooftops." In your opinion, how can we transform the pope's words into action in today's world, in particular in America?

Today, countries like the United States, but also Italy and other European countries, have become mission territory. Faith is not often present in daily life. The Church is seen as a social institution like so many others, whose faults as an institution are more conspicuous; not a living community of people who share a gift, faith.

Given that the individualistic mentality affects all ways of living and thinking today, it is inevitable that the dimension of religiosity is affected too. But even if some old "forms" and "modes" of Catholic religiosity seem already quite worn out, a "do-it-yourself" Catholicism simply cannot exist. We need to belong to a community, like a family where everyone takes care of each other. We need the prayers of the Church, the Mass, the sacraments. Even if Christianity seem to be near the end of a long history, Pope Benedict XVI was convinced that even today it can be "always fresh and new, if the question comes from the depths." As for the modalities of evangelization, certainly courage is needed, as Pope Francis reminds us tirelessly today. It's time to get rid of the mentality of "it has always been done this way," as he says of the reflexive regurgitation of the past. But that's another matter, which would take us very far away from our focus.

How much does today's Church differ from the Church of John Paul II? What was his most distinctive contribution to the Church?

There is an "if" to be stressed, in Benedict XVI's statement I quoted before. That's to say, if beforehand there is not an awakened question, in young people as in anyone else, then Christianity too will seem old and stale. From my point of view, I say without hesitation that today much has changed, undeniably, since John Paul II's time. I mention again, as an example, the 2018 Synod on Young People, where beyond the best intentions of everyone there was a dramatic lack of inspiration. It is not by chance that not only the word "truth" but also the aspiration to it do not resonate any longer at every level of the Church. The legacy of John Paul II looks like an embarrassing memory, too impermeable to the spirit of relativism and "dialogue at any cost." St. John Paul II taught entire generations of Catholics to be joyful and grateful to be Catholic, and to have no cultural subservience to any ideology or common opinion. Sometimes I suspect that this is precisely the disturbing point.

Once John Paul II said: "Nothing is impossible for God." If all is possible, what do we need to build a civilization of love today?

Everything is possible, yes, as you say, but to God, not to us! It would be an unforgivable sin of presumption to think we could build the civilization of love by ourselves. John Paul II was a great builder of the civilization of love, and not only in words. To build a civilization of love, a good starting point would be to follow the example he gave us. What struck everyone about him was his capacity for sympathy, compassion, and mercy for everyone he met, whatever his history or background. I remember many images of him smiling, as much at ease among workers having lunch in the cafeteria of a factory, as among the highest political authorities. I like to remember him above all for his firmness in not retreating before anything, even at the cost of heavy criticism and misunderstanding, in order to affirm what the truth demands and the Truth in person, Jesus. As he said at WYD 2000 in Rome: "It is Jesus in fact that you seek when you dream of happiness;... it is he who urges you to shed the masks of a false life. It is he who waits for you when nothing satisfies you from what you find...." He never hid from young people how difficult it was to live up to the moral demands of being a Christian. But there was no harshness or severity in his words. I see embodied here the Church as described by a Dominican theologian, Father Réginald Garrigou-Lagrange, in a famous paper he wrote some time ago: "The Church is intransigent in principles, because she believes, and tolerant in practice, because she loves. The enemies of the Church, on the other hand, are tolerant in principle, because they do not believe, but intransigent in practice, because they do not love."

Actually, the Lord is saying to us: "The Holy Spirit will introduce you to things that I can't tell you today!" Christianity is full of undisclosed dimensions and is always fresh and new, if the question is asked from the depths.

Pope Benedict XVI

www.ingramcontent.com/pod-product-compliance
Lightning Source LLC
Chambersburg PA
CBHW020352170426
43200CB00005B/135